Statistics
on
Social Work Education
in the United States: 1991

By

Todd M. Lennon

COUNCIL ON SOCIAL WORK EDUCATION
ALEXANDRIA, VIRGINIA

Council on Social Work Education

Julia M. Norlin, President
Donald W. Beless, Executive Director

1600 Duke Street
Alexandria, VA 22314
Phone: (703) 683-8080
Fax: (703) 683-8099

ISBN 0-87293-033-5

FOREWORD

Statistics on Social Work Education in the United States is published annually by the Council on Social Work Education. Data are provided by CSWE accredited baccalaureate and masters degree programs of social work education. Data on the number of students receiving degrees cover the academic year 1990-91. All other data are reported as of November 1, 1991.

Special appreciation is extended to Todd Lennon who compiled and analyzed the data and wrote this report. I also would like to express my appreciation to the program deans, directors, faculty and staff for their cooperation in completing the survey instruments.

Donald W. Beless
Executive Director

June 1, 1992

TABLE OF CONTENTS

LIST OF TEXT TABLES

INTRODUCTION

This report contains the results of a survey of all baccalaureate and masters degree programs in social work accredited by the Council on Social Work Education in September 1991. At the time the data were collected there were 515 social work degree programs either fully accredited or in candidacy status for accreditation. Of those programs, 156 were jointly administered masters/baccalaureate programs, 38 were masters degree programs, and 321 were baccalaureate degree programs. There were 12 masters programs and 25 baccalaureate programs in candidacy. Forty-nine doctoral programs affiliated with masters programs were also surveyed. Lists of accredited baccalaureate and graduate social work degree programs may be found in Appendices B and C.

On September 27, 1991 one survey for faculty and program data and one to three surveys for student data were sent to all accredited programs, depending upon the administration and accreditation status of the program. The surveys used were as follows:

Schedule I - Social Work Education Programs and Faculty
Schedule II - Statistics on Baccalaureate Social Work Education Programs
Schedule III - Statistics on Masters of Social Work Education Programs
Schedule IV - Statistics on Doctoral Social Work Education Programs
Schedule V - Statistics on Social Work Education Programs in Candidacy

Although deadline dates of November 1, 1991 (for Schedule I) and November 15, 1991 were requested, the number of responses received by those dates was not sufficient to begin aggregation at that time. Consequently, schedules were accepted until late February 1992.

Response rates to the schedules varied (see Table 1). Schedule I was sent to all social work programs, regardless of their accreditation status. Jointly administered baccalaureate/masters programs were sent one copy of Schedule I. Of the 438 programs sent Schedule I, 397 (90.6%) returned it. High response rates were recorded for each of the accredited programs' schedules and a majority of candidate programs responded to Schedule V. This represents the best response for this survey in recent years. However, not every program returned both faculty and student data. Despite the extended period of accepting responses and repeated appeals for returns this year, there has not been a 100% response from programs since 1982.

TABLE 1

Number of Responses to 1991 Survey Schedules I - V

Schedule Sent	Number Sent	Number Received	Percent Received
Schedule I	438	397	90.6
Schedule II	375	344	91.7
Schedule III	103	101	98.1
Schedule IV	49	49	100.0
Schedule V	37	32	86.5

Many factors have influenced the presentation of this report. Due to rounding decimals to one or two places, percent totals or sub-totals within tables may not reflect the exact sum of the numbers preceding them. Also, totals in all tables may not correspond with one another due to the variation in response rates. In many cases, programs chose not to respond to a particular item in the survey, or incorrect data were received and requests for corrections went unanswered.

SOCIAL WORK EDUCATION PROGRAMS

Geographic Distribution

      The geographic distribution of social work education programs and faculty remains virtually unchanged from last year (see Table 2). The midwestern states (Region 5) have the highest concentration of social work education programs and faculty, reporting the higher numbers at the baccalaureate and joint masters/baccalaureate levels. Stand-alone graduate programs are more spread out across the nation. The majority of programs are located in the eastern half of the nation (Regions 1-5, 69.8% of programs). Although the number of baccalaureate programs is more than two times that of graduate and joint programs, there are more than twice as many faculty in graduate and joint appointments than in baccalaureate appointments.

TABLE 2

Social Work Education Programs and Faculty, by Geographic Region and Level of Program*

Region**	Level of Program							
	Graduate Only		Joint		Baccalaureate		Total	
	Programs	Faculty	Programs	Faculty	Programs	Faculty	Programs	Faculty
1	5	228	4	79	19	101	28	408
2	6	252	6	383	30	179	42	814
3	3	103	10	297	45	187	58	587
4	5	123	10	292	51	247	66	662
5	5	179	16	476	62	341	83	996
6	4	114	8	206	28	137	40	457
7	1	50	5	150	32	127	38	327
8	2	69	3	42	9	47	14	158
9	2	112	10	276	7	36	19	424
10	1	45	2	88	6	28	9	161
Total	34	1,275	74	2,289	289	1,430	397	4,994

* Column totals may not correspond between tables within this report due to variance in response rates.

** The regional divisions in past years' statistics were identified as regions established by the U.S. Department of Health and Human Services. We could not verify these divisions with the Department this year, but in the interest of continuity they are continued this year. The states included in each region are:

Region 1 - Connecticut, Maine, Massachusetts, New Hampshire, Rhode Island, Vermont
Region 2 - New Jersey, New York, Puerto Rico, Virgin Islands
Region 3 - Delaware, District of Columbia, Maryland, Pennsylvania, Virginia, West Virginia
Region 4 - Alabama, Florida, Georgia, Kentucky, Mississippi, North Carolina, South Carolina, Tennessee
Region 5 - Illinois, Indiana, Michigan, Minnesota, Ohio, Wisconsin
Region 6 - Arkansas, Louisiana, New Mexico, Oklahoma, Texas
Region 7 - Iowa, Kansas, Missouri, Nebraska
Region 8 - Colorado, Montana, North Dakota, South Dakota, Utah, Wyoming
Region 9 - Arizona, California, Hawaii, Nevada
Region 10 - Alaska, Idaho, Oregon, Washington

Institutional Characteristics

Table 3 shows that the majority of social work education programs are located in state institutions. State institutions also employ 62.1% of all social work faculty. Only 4 programs are located in other public institutions. Church-related institutions house most of the programs located in private colleges or universities. Of all social work programs in private institutions, 117 (66.1%) are church-related baccalaureate programs. Most of these programs are very small in size; their 434 faculty are very spread out as compared with the remaining 60 private institutions' 1,335 faculty members. The institutional auspices of colleges and universities with social work degree programs have not changed significantly from year to year.

TABLE 3

Social Work Education Programs and Faculty, by Institutional Auspices and Level of Program*

Institutional Auspices	Level of Program							
	Graduate Only		Joint		Baccalaureate		Total	
	Programs	Faculty	Programs	Faculty	Programs	Faculty	Programs	Faculty
Public								
State	15	478	58	1,773	143	851	216	3,102
Other	1	104	0	0	3	19	4	123
Private								
Church-related	5	180	7	182	117	434	129	796
Other	13	513	9	334	26	126	48	973
Total	34	1,275	74	2,289	289	1,430	397	4,994

* Column totals may not correspond between tables within this report due to variance in response rates.

As noted in Table 4, graduate and joint programs are most likely to be found in institutions with more than 10,000 full-time students. Conversely, stand-alone baccalaureate programs are most likely to be found in institutions with full-time enrollments of less than 10,000. At the baccalaureate level, of those institutions with less than 2,000 students, 83.3% are located in private, church-related institutions. The other stand-alone baccalaureate programs are spread out among institutions with larger enrollments. The distribution of programs across institutions of various sizes has not changed since last year.

TABLE 4

Social Work Education Programs, by Size of College/University Enrollment and Level of Program*

Full-time Enrollment	Level of Program			
	Graduate Only	Joint	Baccalaureate	Total
Under 2,000	3	2	96	101
2,000 - 4,999	4	5	60	69
5,000 - 9,999	6	9	59	74
10,000 - 19,999	8	19	54	81
20,000 and over	13	39	20	72
Total	34	74	289	397

* Column totals may not correspond between tables within this report due to variance in response rates.

The predominant ethnic/gender identification of the colleges and universities with social work degree programs continues to be "non-ethnic, coeducational" (87.4%). Social work education programs in "black, coeducational" institutions make up 5.5% of all programs and non-ethnic, women's institutions house 4.5% of all programs. One institution was identified as "non-ethnic, men's," 2 were "black, women's," and 7 were "other ethnic, coeducational."

Number of Faculty

Baccalaureate programs typically have faculties numbering less than 10 (268 of 289 in Table 5). There are no baccalaureate programs with more than 30 faculty. Larger faculties are characteristic of joint masters/baccalaureate and stand-alone graduate programs. The mean number of faculty members in graduate and joint programs is 33.97 and the mean number of faculty members in baccalaureate programs is 4.95. These means are slightly smaller than last year with a difference of 0.33 for graduate and joint and 0.25 for baccalaureate.

TABLE 5

Social Work Education Programs, by Number of Faculty and Level of Program*

Number of Faculty	Level of Program			
	Graduate Only	Joint	Baccalaureate	Total
Less than 10	2	2	268	272
10 - 19	3	19	19	41
20 - 29	8	22	2	32
30 - 39	6	10	0	16
40 - 49	3	9	0	12
50 - 59	6	3	0	9
60 and over	5	7	0	12
Total	33	72	289	394

* Column totals may not correspond between tables within this report due to variance in response rates.

SOCIAL WORK FACULTY

Each program reported faculty data on Schedule I. Although programs reported on 4,994 faculty members, the data received on many faculty members were incomplete or inaccurate. These faulty cases were not included in the following tables, so none of the tables will show information on all of the faculty members reported by programs. Likewise, care should be taken when comparing the data in the various tables because of the various response rates.

One part of the survey asked programs to report the percentage of a full-time equivalent (FTE) each faculty member spent in social work and other institutional responsibilities. For this report, "full-time" refers to those faculty members who spend 50% or more of their time in the social work program. This distinction should be kept in mind while reviewing Tables 6 and 8 and Tables 18 through 24.

Time in Social Work Education

Of all social work faculty, 62% spend 100% of their time in the social work program. An additional 9.1% of full-time social work faculty spend 50 - 99% of their time in social work. Table 6 shows that a greater percentage of faculty in baccalaureate programs hold full-time appointments in social work than do their colleagues in graduate programs. This indicates that graduate programs are more likely to use part-time faculty than are baccalaureate programs. A very small percentage (3.8%) of faculty holding full-time college/university appointments spend less than 50% of their time in social work.

TABLE 6

Faculty, by Type of College/University Appointment, Level of Program,
and Percent of Time in Social Work Education*[1]

Percent of Time to Social Work	Type of College/University Appointment	Level of Program							
		Graduate Only		Joint		Baccalaureate		Total	
		#	%	#	%	#	%	#	%
100%	Full-time	642	57.1	1,330	63.4	901	63.7	2,873	62.0
50 - 99%	Full-time	93	8.3	168	8.0	160	11.3	421	9.1
25 - 49%	Full-time	35	3.1	17	0.8	50	3.5	102	2.2
	Part-time	127	11.3	235	11.2	180	12.7	542	11.7
Less than 25%	Full-time	24	2.1	22	1.0	26	1.8	72	1.6
	Part-time	204	18.1	326	15.5	97	6.9	627	13.5
Total		1,125	100.0	2,098	100.0	1,414	100.0	4,637	100.0

* Column totals may not correspond between tables within this report due to variance in response rates.

---

[1] Because of the definition of "full-time" used in this report, this year's Table 6 presents its data slightly differently than did previous years' versions. Previous years' reports showed that faculty who spent 50-99% of their time in social work may hold part-time college/university appointments. Since the definition of "full-time" for this report includes faculty spending 50% or more time in social work, the "part-time" line cannot be included.

Table 7 displays the distribution of time faculty members are assigned to the baccalaureate and graduate levels in jointly administered social work programs. This table indicates that joint programs devote more faculty to the graduate program than to the baccalaureate program. Over half of the faculty members in such programs spend all of their time in the graduate program. This percentage shows a decrease of 1.6% from last year. There is a corresponding increase in faculty who spend some time in the baccalaureate program. All of the changes noted, however, are negligible.

TABLE 7

Faculty in Jointly Administered Programs,
by Time Assigned to Graduate and Baccalaureate Social Work Education 1990 - 1991*

Time Assigned to Graduate and Baccalaureate Social Work Education	1990		1991		% Change
	#	%	#	%	
All to Graduate	1,112	54.7	1,093	53.1	-1.6
Most to Graduate	340	16.7	367	17.8	1.1
Equal to Both	225	11.1	218	10.6	-0.5
Most to Baccalaureate	126	6.2	142	6.9	0.7
All to Baccalaureate	231	11.4	239	11.6	0.2
Total	2,034	100.0	2,059	100.0	

* Column totals may not correspond between tables within this report due to variance in response rates.

Forty-nine of the graduate programs also offer a doctoral program. Table 8 shows how much time faculty members in those programs spend in the doctoral program. Only 7.2% of graduate faculty spend more than half of their time in the doctoral program, while 62.9% spend none. Faculty members who teach part-time in the doctoral program make up 29.8% the faculty in programs where a doctorate is offered. These proportions are comparable to those reported last year.

TABLE 8

Full-time Faculty in Programs Offering Doctoral Social Work Education,
by Percentage of Time Assigned to Doctoral Level*

Percent of Time Assigned to Doctoral Level	#	%
None	812	62.9
1 - 24%	265	20.5
25 - 49%	120	9.3
50% and over	93	7.2
Total	1,290	100.0

* Column totals may not correspond between tables within this report due to variance in response rates.

Demographic Characteristics

The following tables display various demographic characteristics of social work faculty, including age, gender, ethnicity, highest earned degree, rank, primary responsibility within the social work program, tenure, and salary. To maintain continuity with previous years' statistics, data for faculty assigned to jointly administered masters/baccalaureate programs have been aggregated with those of stand-alone masters program faculty.

Gender and Ethnicity

The distribution of male and female faculty members by age groups is displayed in Table 9. The modal age groups for males and females at each level remain the same as last year. Males are more likely to be older than females at each level. The mean ages for males are 50.2 (graduate/joint) and 47.5 (baccalaureate). The mean graduate/joint female faculty member's age is 47.3, while the mean baccalaureate female faculty member's age is 44.9. On average, baccalaureate faculty members are about three years younger than their counterparts at the graduate/joint level.

TABLE 9

Faculty, by Age, Gender, and Level of Program*

Level of Program	Age	Gender					
		Male		Female		Total	
		#	%	#	%	#	%
Graduate and Joint	Under 35	52	3.6	75	4.1	127	3.9
	35 - 44	405	28.0	697	38.6	1,102	33.9
	45 - 54	505	35.0	675	37.3	1,180	36.3
	55 and Older	482	33.4	361	20.0	843	25.9
	Total	1,444	100.0	1,808	100.0	3,252	100.0
Baccalaureate	Under 35	25	4.4	67	8.3	92	6.6
	35 - 44	185	32.3	358	44.1	543	39.2
	45 - 54	247	43.1	285	35.1	532	38.4
	55 and Older	116	20.2	102	12.6	218	15.7
	Total	573	100.0	812	100.0	1,385	100.0

* Column totals may not correspond between tables within this report due to variance in response rates.

9

Table 10 displays the ethnicity of male and female social work education faculty members. The ethnic categories used in the survey were based on previous years' surveys and the membership categories of the Council. "Foreign" faculty are those faculty who are in the United States without a resident visa. There was a slight decrease from last year in the percentage of ethnic minority faculty at the graduate/joint level. Conversely, there was a slight increase in the percentage of minorities at the baccalaureate level. African Americans continue to be the largest minority group, comprising 61.8% of all minorities at the graduate/joint level and 70.2% at the baccalaureate level. The percentage of male graduate/joint faculty members who are ethnic minorities is virtually the same as that of the women. However, 9.4 percentage points separate male and female minority faculty members at the baccalaureate level. Nearly one-third of female baccalaureate faculty members are minorities.

TABLE 10

Faculty, by Ethnicity, Gender, and Level of Program*

Level of Program	Ethnicity	Gender					
		Male		Female		Total	
		#	%	#	%	#	%
Graduate and Joint	African American	177	12.0	276	14.6	453	13.5
	Asian American	52	3.5	37	2.0	89	2.6
	Chicano/Mexican American	48	3.2	32	1.7	80	2.4
	Native American	14	0.9	12	0.6	26	0.8
	Puerto Rican	19	1.3	37	2.0	56	1.7
	Other Minority	13	0.9	16	0.8	29	0.9
	Total Minorities	323	21.8	410	21.7	733	21.8
	Foreign	6	0.4	1	0.1	7	0.2
	White	1,151	77.8	1,474	78.2	2,625	78.0
	Total	1,480	100.0	1,885	100.0	3,365	100.0
Baccalaureate	African American	88	14.8	178	21.3	266	18.6
	Asian American	11	1.8	7	0.8	18	1.3
	Chicano/Mexican American	4	0.7	9	1.1	13	0.9
	Native American	10	1.7	9	1.1	19	1.3
	Puerto Rican	9	1.5	39	4.7	48	3.4
	Other Minority	3	0.5	12	1.4	15	1.0
	Total Minorities	125	21.0	254	30.4	379	26.5
	Foreign	2	0.3	1	0.1	3	0.2
	White	469	78.7	581	69.5	1,050	73.3
	Total	596	100.0	836	100.0	1,432	100.0

* Column totals may not correspond between tables within this report due to variance in response rates.

Educational Attainment

The educational attainment of male and female social work education faculty members is displayed in Table 11. The proportions noted here are consistent with those of last year. Graduate/joint faculty are more likely to hold doctorates than are their baccalaureate-level counterparts. Comparable percentages of graduate/joint faculty hold masters or doctoral degrees in social work as their highest earned degree. Almost three times as many baccalaureate faculty members hold a masters in social work as their highest degree, than do those with a doctorate in social work. The masters degree in social work is the highest earned degree for over half of baccalaureate faculty. At both levels, men are more likely than women to hold a doctorate. Of all faculty who hold doctorates, those holding doctorates in social work are in the majority. Small proportions of social work faculty hold degrees in medicine or law or other degree categories than masters or doctorates. Likewise, very few social work faculty hold masters degrees in fields other than social work as their highest earned degree.

TABLE 11

Faculty, by Highest Earned Degree, Gender, and Level of Program*

Level of Program	Highest Earned Degree	Gender					
		Male		Female		Total	
		#	%	#	%	#	%
Graduate and Joint	Masters Social Work	429	29.5	839	45.6	1,268	38.5
	Other	33	2.3	40	2.2	73	2.2
	Doctorate Social Work	627	43.1	688	37.4	1,315	39.9
	Other	332	22.8	230	12.5	562	17.1
	Medicine or Law	24	1.6	23	1.3	47	1.4
	Other	11	0.8	18	1.0	29	0.9
	Total	1,456	100.0	1,838	100.0	3,294	100.0
Baccalaureate	Masters Social Work	293	49.5	533	64.3	826	58.1
	Other	11	1.9	24	2.9	35	2.5
	Doctorate Social Work	144	24.3	159	19.2	303	21.3
	Other	134	22.6	103	12.4	237	16.7
	Medicine or Law	8	1.4	6	0.7	14	1.0
	Other	2	0.3	4	0.5	6	0.4
	Total	592	100.0	829	100.0	1,421	100.0

* Column totals may not correspond between tables within this report due to variance in response rates.

Table 12 displays the educational attainment of social work education faculty members by ethnic categories. The most reliable percentages displayed here are under the African American and White categories--the other minority categories have relatively few cases counted and should be interpreted with caution. Keeping in mind the small numbers in most of the minority categories, there were no significant changes from last year in the proportions noted within this table. Asian Americans continue to have the highest percentage of doctorates in social work at both levels. Most of the Puerto Ricans and Native Americans teaching at the baccalaureate level have masters degrees in social work as their highest earned degree.

TABLE 12

Faculty, by Highest Earned Degree, Ethnicity, and Level of Program*

Level of Program	Highest Earned Degree	Ethnicity						
		African Am.	Asian Am.	Chicano/ Mex. Am.	Native Am.	Puerto Rican	Other & Foreign	White
Graduate and Joint	Masters Social Work Other	39.6 2.0	19.1 1.1	50.6 1.3	46.2 0.0	38.2 0.0	37.1 2.9	38.6 2.3
	Doctorate Social Work Other	37.2 18.2	51.7 27.0	32.9 15.2	34.6 11.5	49.1 12.7	34.3 22.8	40.1 16.6
	Medicine or Law Other	2.0 0.9	1.1 0.0	0.0 0.0	3.8 3.8	0.0 0.0	0.0 2.9	1.4 0.9
	Total Number	100.0 444	100.0 89	100.0 79	100.0 26	100.0 55	100.0 35	100.0 2,569
Baccalaureate	Masters Social Work Other	52.4 2.6	16.7 5.6	53.8 0.0	73.7 0.0	87.5 0.0	44.4 0.0	59.2 2.6
	Doctorate Social Work Other	25.5 18.4	55.6 22.2	30.8 15.4	15.8 10.5	6.2 2.1	22.2 33.3	20.2 16.6
	Medicine or Law Other	0.7 0.4	0.0 0.0	0.0 0.0	0.0 0.0	2.1 2.1	0.0 0.0	1.0 0.4
	Total Number	100.0 267	100.0 18	100.0 13	100.0 19	100.0 48	100.0 18	100.0 1,053

* Column totals may not correspond between tables within this report due to variance in response rates.

Almost all social work faculty hold masters degrees in social work (96.6%). Table 13 shows that those faculty members who do not have masters degrees in social work usually hold doctorates in fields other than social work.

TABLE 13

Faculty, by Highest Earned Degree,
With and Without a Masters Degree in Social Work, and Level of Program*

Level of Program	Highest Earned Degree	Degree					
		With MSW		Without MSW		Total	
		#	%	#	%	#	%
Graduate and Joint	Masters Social Work	1,264	43.1	0	0.0	1,264	41.5
	Other	17	0.6	7	5.9	24	0.8
	Doctorate Social Work	1,257	42.9	18	15.3	1,275	41.8
	Other	358	12.2	83	70.3	441	14.5
	Medicine or Law	21	0.7	7	5.9	28	0.9
	Other	14	0.5	3	2.5	17	0.6
	Total	2,931	100.0	118	100.0	3,049	100.0
Baccalaureate	Masters Social Work	824	62.4	0	0.0	824	60.9
	Other	11	0.8	7	22.6	18	1.3
	Doctorate Social Work	297	22.5	3	9.7	300	22.2
	Other	178	13.5	17	54.8	195	14.4
	Medicine or Law	10	0.8	3	9.7	13	1.0
	Other	1	0.1	1	3.2	2	0.1
	Total	1,321	100.0	31	100.0	1,352	100.0

* Column totals may not correspond between tables within this report due to variance in response rates.

Rank

Table 14 displays the distribution of rank among social work education faculty. At the graduate/joint level, faculty members are fairly evenly distributed between the three highest ranks, less so between the other ranks. However, assistant professors make up the highest percentage of females and full professors are most frequently male. Assistant professors also are the most frequent among female baccalaureate faculty members. Males at the baccalaureate level are most frequently associate professors. Although graduate/joint faculty at the ranks of full professor, associate professor, and assistant professor are evenly distributed, baccalaureate faculty become less frequent as the level of rank increases. Women are more likely to hold the rank of instructor or lecturer at both the graduate/joint and baccalaureate levels than are men.

TABLE 14

Faculty, by Rank, Gender, and Level of Program*

Level of Program	Rank	Gender					
		Male		Female		Total	
		#	%	#	%	#	%
Graduate and Joint	Professor	488	33.1	201	10.7	689	20.5
	Associate Professor	354	24.0	386	20.5	740	22.1
	Assistant Professor	244	16.6	485	25.8	729	21.7
	Instructor	93	6.3	186	9.9	279	8.3
	Lecturer	152	10.3	307	16.3	459	13.7
	Other	143	9.7	315	16.8	458	13.7
	Total	1,474	100.0	1,880	100.0	3,354	100.0
Baccalaureate	Professor	128	21.5	59	7.1	187	13.1
	Associate Professor	179	30.0	206	24.8	385	27.0
	Assistant Professor	162	27.2	312	37.6	474	33.2
	Instructor	47	7.9	108	13.0	155	10.9
	Lecturer	47	7.9	103	12.4	150	10.5
	Other	33	5.5	42	5.1	75	5.3
	Total	596	100.0	830	100.0	1,426	100.0

* Column totals may not correspond between tables within this report due to variance in response rates.

The educational attainment of faculty and their rank is displayed in Table 15. Full professors typically have doctorates. At the graduate/joint level, all three higher ranks have mostly doctorates, while the lower three categories are mostly masters degrees in social work. At the baccalaureate level, doctorates are most frequent at the full professor and associate levels. The majority of assistant professors and lower hold masters degrees in social work.

TABLE 15

Faculty, by Rank, Highest Earned Degree, and Level of Program*

Level of Program	Highest Earned Degree	Rank													
		Professor		Associate Professor		Assistant Professor		Instructor		Lecturer		Other		Total	
		#	%	#	%	#	%	#	%	#	%	#	%	#	%
Graduate and Joint	Masters Social Work	73	10.6	147	19.9	251	34.8	223	80.2	264	64.1	308	69.1	1,266	38.5
	Other	6	0.9	6	0.8	5	0.7	14	5.0	14	3.4	27	6.1	72	2.2
	Doctorate Social Work	402	58.3	401	54.3	346	47.9	20	7.2	86	20.9	56	12.6	1,311	39.9
	Other	198	28.7	174	23.6	108	15.0	14	5.0	32	7.8	34	7.6	560	17.0
	Medicine or Law	9	1.3	9	1.2	9	1.2	5	1.8	10	2.4	5	1.1	47	1.4
	Other	1	0.1	1	0.1	3	0.4	2	0.7	6	1.5	16	3.6	29	0.9
	Total	689	100.0	738	100.0	722	100.0	278	100.0	412	100.0	446	100.0	3,285	100.0
Baccalaureate	Masters Social Work	47	25.3	178	46.2	288	60.5	132	84.1	128	85.3	58	77.3	831	58.2
	Other	1	0.5	7	1.8	6	1.3	10	6.4	7	4.7	4	5.3	35	2.4
	Doctorate Social Work	60	32.3	115	29.9	110	23.1	6	3.8	7	4.7	6	8.0	304	21.3
	Other	77	41.4	81	21.0	64	13.4	5	3.2	5	3.3	7	9.3	239	16.7
	Medicine or Law	1	0.5	3	0.8	7	1.5	2	1.3	1	0.7	0	0.0	14	1.0
	Other	0	0.0	1	0.3	1	0.2	2	1.3	2	1.3	0	0.0	6	0.4
	Total	186	100.0	385	100.0	476	100.0	157	100.0	150	100.0	75	100.0	1,429	100.0

* Column totals may not correspond between tables within this report due to variance in response rates.

15

Table 16 displays the distribution of rank by ethnicity. Again, due to the small number of minority faculty members, caution should be taken in interpreting these percentages. At both levels, Asian Americans have the highest percentage of full professors among minority faculty. As noted in Table 12, Asian Americans also have the highest percentage of doctorates.

TABLE 16

Faculty, by Rank, Ethnicity and Level of Program*

Level of Program	Rank	Ethnicity						
		African Am.	Asian Am.	Chicano/ Mex. Am.	Native Am.	Puerto Rican	Other & Foreign	White
Graduate and Joint	Professor	15.0	31.5	21.3	15.4	25.0	16.7	21.1
	Assoc. Prof.	31.6	21.3	17.5	26.9	32.1	25.0	20.3
	Asst. Prof.	25.2	24.7	30.0	26.9	25.0	33.3	20.5
	Instructor	4.2	1.1	7.5	7.7	0.0	5.6	9.5
	Lecturer	10.4	9.0	12.5	11.5	10.7	8.3	14.6
	Other	13.5	12.4	11.3	11.5	7.1	11.1	14.0
	Total	100.0	100.0	100.0	100.0	100.0	100.0	100.0
	Number	452	89	80	26	56	36	2,618
Baccalaureate	Professor	11.2	27.8	23.1	0.0	0.0	5.6	14.1
	Assoc. Prof.	26.1	27.8	15.4	15.8	32.6	33.3	27.0
	Asst. Prof.	36.9	38.9	23.1	47.4	34.8	44.4	32.1
	Instructor	10.4	0.0	0.0	21.1	8.7	11.1	11.3
	Lecturer	9.7	5.6	15.4	10.5	21.7	5.6	10.2
	Other	5.6	0.0	23.1	5.3	2.2	0.0	5.2
	Total	100.0	100.0	100.0	100.0	100.0	100.0	100.0
	Number	268	18	13	19	46	18	1,058

* Column totals may not correspond between tables within this report due to variance in response rates.

Primary Responsibility

Tables 17 and 18 show the distribution of the primary responsibility of social work faculty within the social work program. Those faculty members with formal administrative titles are included under those specific titles. For those faculty without formal administrative titles, programs were asked to report the time individuals spent in classroom teaching, field instruction, field liaison responsibilities, administration, and other social work responsibilities. No definitions were given for these categories. For this report, "primary responsibility" is defined as that responsibility that receives the greatest amount of the faculty member's time. Those faculty members who spend equal amounts of time in classroom and field instruction or liaison activities were combined as were those who spend most of their time in field activities. Individuals who spend most of their time in "other" social work responsibilities or did not specify a formal administrative title but spend most of their time in administration are listed as "other."

Table 17 displays the primary responsibilities of social work faculty. This year there was a slight increase in the percent of graduate/joint faculty spending the majority of their time with teaching responsibilities. At the baccalaureate level, 70.9% of the faculty spend most of their time teaching. This reflects a slight increase as well. At both levels, most of these faculty primarily are classroom teachers. There is no significant difference between males and females in this characteristic. More males than females are primarily responsible as dean/director of graduate/joint or baccalaureate programs. On the other hand, there are more females who are classroom teachers at each level. Interestingly, although males outnumber females as dean/directors, more females are assigned administrative titles.

TABLE 17

Faculty, by Primary Responsibility, Gender, and Level of Program*

Level of Program	Primary Responsibility	Gender					
		Male		Female		Total	
		#	%	#	%	#	%
Graduate and Joint	Classroom Teaching	986	66.6	1,169	62.0	2,155	64.0
	Classroom and Field	112	7.6	158	8.4	270	8.0
	Field Instruction/Liaison	71	4.8	210	11.1	281	8.4
	Total Teaching	1,169	79.0	1,537	81.5	2,706	80.4
	Dean/Director	61	4.1	35	1.9	96	2.9
	Associate Dean/Director	32	2.2	22	1.2	54	1.6
	Assistant Dean/Director	14	0.9	24	1.3	38	1.1
	Director Undergraduate Program	20	1.4	22	1.2	42	1.2
	Director Field Instruction	21	1.4	52	2.8	73	2.2
	Asst Director Field Instruction	2	0.1	25	1.3	27	0.8
	Dir. Admissions/Minority Recruitment	9	0.6	16	0.8	25	0.7
	Dir. Continuing Education/Work Study	8	0.5	14	0.7	22	0.7
	Other Administration	68	4.6	67	3.6	135	4.0
	Total Administration	235	15.9	277	14.7	512	15.2
	Other	76	5.1	71	3.8	147	4.4
	Total	1,480	100.0	1,885	100.0	3,365	100.0
Baccalaureate	Classroom Teaching	376	63.1	511	61.1	887	61.9
	Classroom and Field	26	4.4	53	6.3	79	5.5
	Field Instruction/Liaison	9	1.5	40	4.8	49	3.4
	Total Teaching	411	69.0	604	72.2	1,015	70.9
	Dean/Director	114	19.1	97	11.6	211	14.7
	Director Field Instruction	39	6.5	96	11.5	135	9.4
	Other Administration	16	2.7	21	2.5	37	2.6
	Total Administration	169	28.4	214	25.6	383	26.7
	Other	16	2.7	18	2.2	34	2.4
	Total	596	100.0	836	100.0	1,432	100.0

* Column totals may not correspond between tables within this report due to variance in response rates.

Table 18 further breaks down the responsibilities of social work faculty. It displays the mean percentage of time spent in classroom teaching, field instruction, field liaison, administration, and other social work responsibilities. The proportion of time spent in the different responsibilities is comparable across the two levels. As would be expected, classroom teachers spend far more of their time with classroom responsibilities. However, the means indicate that, no matter what their primary responsibility, all social work faculty spend at least 10% of their time in classroom teaching. Baccalaureate faculty spend far more time in the classroom than do their graduate/joint counterparts. Considering that baccalaureate programs average under five faculty members, it is not surprising that they carry multiple responsibilities.

TABLE 18

Mean Percentage of Time Full-time Faculty Members Assigned to Responsibilities in Social Work Programs, by Primary Responsibility and Level of Program

Level of Program	Primary Responsibility	Mean Percentage Assigned				
		Classroom Teaching	Field Instruction	Field Liaison	Admini-stration	Other
Graduate and Joint	Classroom Teaching	78.04	1.05	9.29	1.15	6.15
	Classroom and Field	16.08	5.43	12.97	9.64	31.08
	Field Instruction/Liaison	10.25	19.50	54.05	1.42	2.20
	Dean/Director	15.29	0.37	2.12	77.81	4.15
	Associate Dean/Director	26.78	2.31	1.56	63.20	5.68
	Assistant Dean/Director	16.97	2.54	7.08	70.48	2.91
	Dir. Undergrad Program	41.24	1.10	7.76	45.27	4.15
	Director Field Instruction	14.99	18.36	17.60	44.42	3.25
	Asst. Dir. Field Inst.	17.07	6.15	32.52	29.18	3.07
	Dir. Admissions/ Minority Recruitment	28.00	1.20	4.92	56.28	7.48
	Dir. Continuing Ed./ Work Study	28.95	0.50	15.00	43.40	8.20
	Other Administration	37.14	2.08	7.36	37.30	11.76
	Other	36.27	0.45	3.48	14.68	45.25
Baccalaureate	Classroom Teaching	80.52	3.42	5.62	2.59	2.20
	Classroom and Field	28.13	11.10	17.73	3.75	13.19
	Field Instruction/Liaison	20.82	36.62	26.25	0.00	5.15
	Dean/Director	53.08	3.40	4.14	33.37	3.91
	Director Field Instruction	50.28	18.30	17.61	9.14	2.65
	Other Administration	44.27	4.67	12.10	25.37	7.37
	Other	33.12	2.03	6.88	18.44	34.91

Table 19 displays the number of years social work faculty were reported to have been on full-time status in the social work program. The survey did not specify the definition of "full-time." Unlike previous years, this report combines the ranks reported as instructor, lecturer, and "other." They are reported in Table 19 as "Other." Full professors at the graduate/joint level have spent the most time on the social work faculty. However, when baccalaureate faculty members spend the same amount of time on the full-time faculty as their graduate/joint colleagues, they are more often associate professors. The most striking figure in this table is the number of newly hired faculty in the "Other" category. Over 77% of the graduate/joint faculty and 69% of the baccalaureate faculty hired in 1991 were in this category. This may indicate a tendency of programs to hire more temporary or adjunct faculty. It is also important to note that a disproportionate number of males were hired at the full professor rank. The same holds true for females at the lower ranks.

TABLE 19

Faculty, by Gender, Years on Full-time Faculty, Rank, and Level of Program*

Level of Program	Rank	Gender	Years on Full-time Faculty				
			0	1 - 5	6 - 10	11 & Over	Total
Graduate and Joint	Professor	Male	16	58	48	358	480
		Female	5	30	23	139	197
	Associate Prof.	Male	17	56	54	224	351
		Female	23	77	108	171	379
	Assistant Prof.	Male	52	131	11	31	225
		Female	81	265	51	43	440
	Other	Male	220	44	12	9	285
		Female	455	131	28	37	651
	Total	Male	305	289	125	622	1,341
		Female	564	503	210	390	1,667
Baccalaureate	Professor	Male	8	11	9	92	120
		Female	3	9	8	38	58
	Associate Prof.	Male	5	33	32	101	171
		Female	8	30	41	125	204
	Assistant Prof.	Male	27	66	29	36	158
		Female	42	178	42	46	308
	Other	Male	77	24	7	1	109
		Female	134	77	8	3	222
	Total	Male	117	134	77	230	558
		Female	187	294	99	212	792

* Column totals may not correspond between tables within this report due to variance in response rates.

Tenure

The proportion of full-time social work faculty members with tenure is displayed in Tables 20 and 21. Table 20 shows that, at the graduate/joint level, many more faculty holding tenure hold a doctorate than those who do not. Over half of graduate/joint faculty members hold a doctorate in social work. At the baccalaureate level, just under half of those faculty holding tenure also hold a masters degree in social work as their highest earned degree. Social work faculty holding tenure typically hold an advanced degree in social work. Table 21 shows the highest degree earned, rank, and gender of social work faculty holding tenure. The percentage of males holding tenure in graduate/joint programs has increased slightly, while the same figure at the baccalaureate level remains virtually unchanged.

TABLE 20

Full-time Faculty With Tenure, by Highest Earned Degree and Level of Program*

Highest Earned Degree	Level of Program	
	Graduate and Joint	Baccalaureate
Masters		
Social Work	17.6	47.0
Other	1.1	1.3
Doctorate		
Social Work	54.1	28.2
Other	26.1	23.0
Medicine or Law	1.0	0.4
Other	0.1	0.2
Total: Percent	100.0	100.0
Number	1,198	557

* Column totals may not correspond between tables within this report due to variance in response rates.

TABLE 21

Full-time Faculty With Tenure,
by Rank, Highest Earned Degree, Gender, and Level of Program*

Rank	Highest Earned Degree	Graduate and Joint Programs			Baccalaureate Programs		
		Male	Female	Total	Male	Female	Total
Professor	Doctorate	32.3	12.9	45.2	14.8	6.4	21.1
	Masters	4.4	0.9	5.2	4.9	2.2	7.1
Associate Professor	Doctorate	17.0	17.4	34.4	12.2	13.8	26.0
	Masters	6.1	3.9	10.0	11.7	14.9	26.6
Assistant Professor	Doctorate	1.2	1.0	2.2	2.0	2.0	4.0
	Masters	1.2	1.8	3.0	6.0	9.1	15.1
Total: Percent		62.1	37.9	100.0	51.5	48.5	100.0
Number		725	442	1,167	283	266	549

* Column totals may not correspond between tables within this report due to variance in response rates.

Salary

Data were gathered on the salaries of full-time social work faculty. Table 22 displays the median salaries and middle 50% range of salaries of non-administrative faculty by rank and region. Medians are reported here because of the wide range of salaries reported. All salaries reported in Table 22 are adjusted to reflect a nine-month academic year. Raw salary data reported for periods other than nine months were increased or decreased proportionately. Medians are shown for regions that reported at least five cases at a particular level. This section of the survey was most often reported inaccurately or not reported at all; therefore, care should be taken when examining data, especially when comparing salary data from year to year.

As would be expected, full professors receive higher salaries than associate professors do; likewise, associate professors receive higher salaries than assistant professors do. Full professors with appointments in graduate/joint programs make 21.3% more than their baccalaureate-level counterparts do. The difference is noticeably smaller at the lower two ranks, with 13.5% and 13.7% between them. The median salaries have increased from last year--4.3%, 6.9%, and 7.3% for graduate/joint full professors, associate and assistant professors, respectively. However, their baccalaureate counterparts experienced only 0.3%, 0.7%, and 1.4% increases for corresponding ranks.

The eastern regions of the country continue to pay the highest salaries. Region 2 (New Jersey, New York, and Puerto Rico) reported median salaries in the top three regions at each level except associate professors at the graduate/joint level where it was fourth-highest. On the other end of the scale, the Rocky Mountain region (Region 8) reported median salaries in the bottom two regions in four of the six categories shown in Table 22.

Table 23 shows the median salaries reported for full-time faculty members according to their primary responsibility within the social work program. One column of salaries displays the actual salaries received by faculty members regardless of the number of months it took them to earn that salary. The other column displays the same salaries adjusted to a nine-month academic year as was done in Table 22. The deans/directors and associate deans/directors at the graduate/joint level report the highest median salary. At the baccalaureate level, field instructors/liaisons reported the highest median salary, but there were only 20 cases reported. The baccalaureate deans/directors had a slightly lower median than the field educators, but reported a greater range of salaries over 176 cases. Of the non-administrative faculty, classroom teachers were highest paid at the graduate/joint level. At the baccalaureate level, field educators reported the highest median salary. At both levels, classroom teachers outnumber the other non-administrative faculty by very wide margins. The ranges need to be interpreted with caution. One of the factors influencing this table is the definition of "full-time" as those faculty members who spend at least 50% of a full-time equivalent on social work responsibilities. Therefore, a $15,000 salary likely belongs to a faculty member who only spends half the time of his/her colleague who has a full teaching load.

TABLE 22

Median Salary and Middle 50 Percent Salary Range of Full-time Non-administrative Faculty,
by Geographic Region, Level of Program, and Rank[1]

Rank	Region[2]	Graduate and Joint Programs			Baccalaureate Programs		
		Median Salary[3]	Middle 50% Range	# of Faculty	Median Salary[3]	Middle 50% Range	# of Faculty
Professor	1	$62,244	$51,938 - 72,783	18	$40,673	$38,167 - 46,347	7
	2	59,802	52,994 - 67,048	70	59,150	55,000 - 63,222	7
	3	59,163	52,205 - 65,995	56	48,766	37,247 - 57,950	12
	4	47,700	44,376 - 55,550	45	41,375	33,675 - 55,687	8
	5	57,179	50,378 - 62,683	74	43,153	36,246 - 49,955	31
	6	47,991	42,446 - 55,301	28	**	**	2
	7	50,525	45,671 - 55,990	16	**	**	4
	8	45,800	40,568 - 47,641	11	39,800	37,350 - 43,549	9
	9	54,864	54,864 - 60,960	83	54,432	46,687 - 54,864	6
	10	52,470	44,290 - 57,226	17	**	**	3
	Total	54,866	48,148 - 61,912	418	43,153	37,457 - 54,000	89
Associate Professor	1	$43,242	$35,814 - 52,462	34	37,838	$32,400 - 44,142	13
	2	48,853	41,472 - 53,220	76	38,021	11,888 - 45,124	26
	3	45,250	39,739 - 49,050	76	37,069	31,418 - 44,502	25
	4	37,298	34,618 - 40,013	62	36,700	30,000 - 39,000	31
	5	45,350	41,413 - 50,025	91	38,947	34,506 - 43,153	57
	6	37,615	35,586 - 42,714	30	33,738	32,668 - 34,422	10
	7	41,970	36,599 - 44,100	31	32,580	25,788 - 41,025	10
	8	36,897	33,100 - 41,208	16	**	**	3
	9	46,258	42,879 - 48,192	42	**	**	3
	10	42,030	38,560 - 49,329	21	**	**	2
	Total	43,100	37,230 - 48,740	479	37,277	31,662 - 42,279	180
Assistant Professor	1	$31,381	$30,000 - 37,675	40	$34,229	$27,922 - 36,778	17
	2	36,000	25,300 - 38,465	73	31,347	20,768 - 35,851	34
	3	37,010	31,954 - 39,434	66	29,285	25,208 - 31,970	26
	4	31,000	28,800 - 34,928	44	29,007	25,000 - 33,748	53
	5	34,771	30,692 - 38,127	97	29,473	27,045 - 32,425	76
	6	31,459	29,000 - 33,570	52	27,790	23,000 - 29,314	25
	7	36,500	34,900 - 38,980	23	29,608	27,808 - 31,500	29
	8	34,500	32,686 - 35,592	24	29,000	26,000 - 30,750	8
	9	36,260	34,387 - 38,790	39	**	**	3
	10	33,228	28,989 - 36,477	31	39,436	32,100 - 48,566	6
	Total	34,290	30,600 - 37,722	489	29,580	26,000 - 33,724	277

** Less than five cases reported.

---

[1] Column totals may not correspond between tables within this report due to variance in response rates.

[2] See Table 2 on page 3 for a list of states in each region.

[3] Salary data are adjusted for a nine-month academic year.

TABLE 23

Median Salary and Range of Full-time Faculty, by Primary Responsibility and Level of Program*

Level of Program	Primary Responsibility	Salary				#
		Adjusted for Months		Unadjusted for Months		
		Median	Range	Median	Range	
Graduate and Joint	Classroom Teaching	$41,717	$14,535-94,180	$43,228	$19,380-94,180	1,069
	Classroom and Field	36,000	17,505-80,361	40,898	12,062-107,148	87
	Field Instruction/Liaison	31,039	12,600-62,777	36,809	14,000-69,752	84
	Dean/Director	54,696	27,855-102,273	72,104	35,276-125,000	77
	Associate Dean/Director	50,136	34,018-80,996	61,528	34,018-95,600	47
	Assistant Dean/Director	41,691	24,453-63,562	49,155	32,604-84,750	35
	Dir. Undergrad Program	41,624	24,750-78,344	44,652	27,118-87,049	38
	Director Field Instruction	33,944	23,400-54,993	40,539	25,806-67,214	68
	Asst. Dir. Field Instruction	33,817	15,004-45,791	38,805	20,005-54,780	20
	Dir. Admissions/ Minority Recruitment	38,096	20,085-60,386	39,722	26,780-60,386	18
	Dir. Continuing Ed./ Work Study	35,426	16,770-60,960	45,415	22,360-64,365	15
	Other Administration	43,176	18,562-88,292	48,910	24,750-98,102	100
Baccalaureate	Classroom Teaching	32,500	15,000-65,000	33,525	15,000-65,000	408
	Classroom and Field	35,250	24,000-51,146	37,000	24,000-57,000	16
	Field Instruction/Liaison	38,269	24,100-46,727	38,402	24,100-47,663	20
	Dean/Director	36,000	16,500-57,000	38,019	22,000-72,861	176

* Column totals may not correspond between tables within this report due to variance in response rates.

Table 24 compares the median salaries of full-time non-administrative faculty members, broken down into categories representing ethnicity, gender, highest earned degree, and rank. Past years' statistics have reported only classroom faculty in this table, citing "disparity between the sexes in higher and lower-paying job responsibilities." However, the number of faculty in the other non-administrative categories is so small that they were included this year. In general, female faculty members receive a lower salary than do their male counterparts. Half of the cells displaying median salaries for minority faculty members show medians lower than their white counterparts. Faculty holding masters degrees as their highest earned degree usually have a lower salary than do their colleagues holding the same rank and ethnicity. Comparisons within this table are difficult, given the number of cases reported in each cell.

23

TABLE 24

Median Salary of Full-time Non-administrative Faculty, by Ethnicity, Gender, Rank, Highest Earned Degree, and Level of Program*

Level of Program	Rank	Ethnicity	Highest Earned Degree							
			Doctorate				Masters			
			Male		Female		Male		Female	
			Salary***	#	Salary***	#	Salary***	#	Salary***	#
Graduate and Joint	Professor	White	$56,409	207	$54,864	90	$54,864	30	$57,383	6
		Minority	54,864	49	54,339	25	56,551	6	**	3
	Associate Professor	White	43,184	134	43,176	158	45,894	33	39,257	20
		Minority	45,134	46	41,639	48	42,188	17	35,437	14
	Assistant Professor	White	34,577	88	33,995	175	33,350	17	29,550	60
		Minority	36,000	37	36,488	54	30,675	19	30,675	28
Baccalaureate	Professor	White	42,996	34	42,466	14	37,750	10	42,420	8
		Minority	55,000	9	44,943	10	**	1	**	2
	Associate Professor	White	40,586	22	38,633	33	37,069	35	36,948	37
		Minority	38,015	18	37,996	14	**	4	27,900	15
	Assistant Professor	White	31,315	36	31,500	39	28,720	36	28,000	76
		Minority	33,625	10	33,622	20	29,400	11	25,963	42

* Column totals may not correspond between tables within this report due to variance in response rates.
** Less than five cases reported.
*** Salary data are adjusted for a nine-month academic year.

Table 25 shows that the main source of faculty salaries remains the university itself. Classroom teachers receive the highest percentage of their salary from inside university sources. Faculty who are involved somewhat with field education receive more of their salary from outside sources, whether at the graduate/joint or baccalaureate level. As noted before, the classroom teachers make up the vast majority of non-administrative faculty, so the means displayed in Table 25 for classroom teachers are a more accurate reflection of this characteristic than the others. With this in mind, the trend from previous years' statistics showing an increase of external funding of university faculty salaries has continued this year.

TABLE 25

Mean Percentage of Non-administrative Faculty Salary from Internal University Sources,
by Primary Level of Responsibility, Type of Appointment, and Level of Program

Level of Program	Primary Responsibility	Type of Appointment		Total
		Full-time	Part-time	
Graduate and Joint	Classroom Teaching	98.2	92.5	89.6
	Classroom and Field	77.6	77.4	
	Field Instruction/Liaison	87.8	83.6	
	Other	87.0	56.4	
Baccalaureate	Classroom Teaching	98.0	94.8	95.1
	Classroom and Field	93.8	100.0	
	Field Instruction/Liaison	90.4	88.9	
	Other	93.9	100.0	

Number of Publications

Programs were asked to report on the number of publications that actually appeared in print during the preceding academic or calendar year, whichever year conforms to their record-keeping system. The five categories of publications were defined as refereed articles, books published by formal publishing companies, published book chapters and conference proceedings, monographs, and book reviews. To adjust for multiple authorship, respondents were asked to enter the fraction of authorship undertaken by the faculty member. For example, a faculty member who wrote an article with another colleague would be reported as having written .5 of an article. Blank spaces in this section of the form were interpreted as being equal to zero, although many of these cases simply may be missing data. The ability of the programs to report every faculty member's publication is questionable; therefore, the reliability of this section of the report is not good.

Taken as a whole, on average, faculty members published .30 articles, .04 books, .12 book chapters, .17 monographs, and .08 book reviews. Incomplete data were received on many faculty, so these numbers may be somewhat misleading. Among the group of faculty members who published a total of at least one item ($n=1,139$), an average of 1.22 articles, .18 books, .51 book chapters, .69 monographs, and .32 book reviews were published. It is clear that refereed articles are the publishing medium of choice among social work faculty. Females appear to publish less frequently than do their male counterparts.

BACCALAUREATE STUDENTS

Baccalaureate social work education programs reported on various aspects of their student body on Schedule II. As noted in Table 1, 344 of 375 programs (91.7%) returned data on Schedule II. The tables in this section report data only on juniors and seniors because some programs do not allow students to choose majors until the junior year. Also, due to the November 1 deadline for statistics, many programs do not have access to data showing the major declaration of incoming freshmen. Program data are listed individually in Appendix A in Tables 100 and 101. Again, the Schedules requested different data on the same population. Responses varied within the schedules, so comparison between tables may be unreliable. For instance, one table reporting the number of juniors and seniors enrolled (one section of Schedule II) may not agree with another table reporting that same population's ethnicity (another section of the form).

Table 26 reports junior and senior enrollment in baccalaureate programs. Baccalaureate programs typically have small student bodies. Almost two-thirds of the programs have fewer than 75 juniors and seniors enrolled. Just over half have fewer than 50 juniors and seniors. Distribution across the categories is the similar to last year's statistics, except for the 75-99 and 100-149 categories. There has been a moderate shift from the 100-149 category having 2.9% more juniors and seniors to having 3.6% fewer juniors and seniors enrolled than the 75-99 category. Although this indicates a shift to smaller programs in general, the median junior and senior enrollment size this year was 49, up from 46 last year. As noted in last year's report, until 1984 there was a trend toward declining median junior and senior enrollment size. This trend seems to have halted with this year's data.

TABLE 26

Accredited Baccalaureate Programs, by Size of Full-time Junior and Senior Year Enrollment*

Junior and Senior Enrollment	#	%
Under 25	76	22.4
25 - 49	94	27.7
50 - 74	68	20.1
75 - 99	47	13.9
100 - 149	35	10.3
150 and over	19	5.6
Total	339	100.0

* Column totals may not correspond between tables within this report due to variance in response rates.

The total reported enrollment of full-time baccalaureate social work degree students is 32,777. This reflects an increase of 15.5% over last year. This figure should be interpreted cautiously, however, because 33 accredited programs were not included in last year's report. Freshmen and sophomores accounted for 11,598 of full-time students. Baccalaureate programs reported that 5,416 students are enrolled part-time in their program and 18,462 students are enrolled in one or more social work courses, but not working toward a social work degree. A review of past years' statistics shows that until 1984 there was a steady decline in baccalaureate student enrollment. Enrollment in each of the categories noted above has increased every year since 1984, except in 1989.

The gender breakdown of juniors and seniors and 1990-91 graduates is displayed in Table 27. Females continue represent the majority (85.0%) of baccalaureate students and graduates. This percentage is slightly higher (0.8%) than last year. Interestingly, there was a similar decrease in the percentage of females (1.0%) receiving baccalaureate degrees. Corresponding with the increased enrollments reported, the number of baccalaureate degrees awarded in 1990-91 increased from 7,250 to 8,778, a 21.1% increase.

TABLE 27

Juniors and Seniors Enrolled Full-time in Baccalaureate Programs on 11/1/91
and Students Awarded Baccalaureate Degrees in 1990-91, by Gender

Gender	Juniors and Seniors Enrolled		Students Awarded Degrees	
	#	%	#	%
Female	17,625	85.0	7,601	86.6
Male	3,102	15.0	1,177	13.4
Total	20,727	100.0	8,778	100.0

The ethnic distribution of juniors and seniors and 1990-91 baccalaureate degree recipients is shown in Table 28. The number of ethnic minorities enrolled in baccalaureate social work education and receiving baccalaureate degrees increased again this year. However, while the proportion of minorities enrolled increased by 0.8%, the proportion of minorities receiving baccalaureate degrees decreased by 1.3%. These proportions do not vary greatly from year to year and do not indicate a trend in any direction. Any changes from year to year may be due to the variation of response rates. "African American" continues to be the most frequent ethnic minority identification among those juniors and seniors enrolled in baccalaureate programs, outnumbering the other ethnic minorities by two-thirds. Chicano/Mexican Americans and Puerto Ricans are the next most frequent. Although the survey did not allow the specification of minorities in the "Other" category, many respondents chose to write in various Hispanic ethnic groups.

TABLE 28

Juniors and Seniors Enrolled Full-time in Baccalaureate Programs on 11/1/91
and Students Awarded Baccalaureate Degrees in 1990-91, by Ethnicity*

Ethnicity	Juniors and Seniors Enrolled		Students Awarded Degrees	
	#	%	#	%
African American	3,075	14.8	1,176	13.4
Asian American	318	1.5	109	1.2
Chicano/Mexican American	680	3.3	230	2.6
Native American	296	1.4	89	1.0
Puerto Rican	514	2.5	283	3.2
Other Minority	222	1.1	118	1.3
Total Minorities	5,105	24.6	2,005	22.8
Foreign	89	0.4	56	0.6
White	15,533	74.9	6,717	76.5
Total	20,727	100.0	8,778	100.0

* Column totals may not correspond between tables within this report due to variance in response rates.

GRADUATE STUDENTS

Data on masters and doctoral students were gathered with Schedules III and IV, respectively. Similar data were collected on each form, but only selected sections of Schedule IV were used for this report. Although the Council does not accredit doctoral education, the past practice of collecting data from doctoral programs at the same time masters program data were collected was continued this year. As is true throughout this report, some tables may not correspond with others due to the varying responses to different parts of the survey instrument.

Enrollment

Full-time enrollments in masters programs increased steadily from the mid-1950s to 1978. Table 29 shows that in 1979 full-time enrollments began to fall, bottoming out in 1986 at a 15-year low. Since 1986 programs reported an increasing number of full-time students. This year's record 19,468 full-time masters degree students continues a trend of rapidly increasing enrollment. Part-time enrollment was not affected by the decrease in full-time enrollment in the early 1980s. It has increased steadily and also has hit an all-time high of 10,232. These increases in enrollment are particularly striking in light of the fact that there has not been a 100% response to the annual statistics survey since 1985. This year's enrollments represent an 11.4% increase in full-time enrollment and 2.9% in part-time enrollment from last year's. Part-time students make up 34.5% of all masters programs' enrollments. Further, part-time students outnumber full-time students in 20 of the 101 programs responding to the survey. Forty programs reported that at least 40% of their students are enrolled part-time. It should be noted that the number of accredited masters programs has increased slowly over the years.

Enrollment in doctoral programs increased until 1980 and vacillated somewhat during the next decade. It did, however, mirror the steady decline in masters programs' enrollment in the early 1980s. This year shows a record 1,133 full-time students enrolled in doctoral education. While part-time doctoral students often outnumbered full-time students in the 1980s (and last year), they make up 46.3% of all doctoral students this year. This shows an increase in the number of part-time students over last year, although it does not represent the most part-time doctoral students enrolled in any given year.

TABLE 29

Students Enrolled in Masters and Doctoral Programs 1966 - 1991

Year	Masters Programs Full-time	Doctoral Programs Full-time	Year	Masters Programs		Doctoral Programs	
				Full-time	Part-time	Full-time	Part-time
1966	9,335	232	1979	17,397	4,942	954	535
1967	10,178	258	1980	17,122	5,274	825	710
1968	10,847	307	1981	16,552	5,761	868	794
1969	11,711	450	1982	15,131	6,174	922	798
1970	12,821	443	1983	14,265	7,225	855	954
1971	13,386	502	1984	14,275	7,294	798*	1,027*
1972	15,031	565	1985	14,055*	7,944*	702*	728*
1973	16,099	617	1986	13,981*	8,269*	601*	841*
1974	16,590	648	1987	15,241*	8,044*	703*	820*
1975	16,676	712	1988	16,239*	9,024*	1,003	911
1976	16,869	769	1989	15,777*	9,420*	857*	989*
1977	17,533	866	1990	17,475*	9,945*	838*	956*
1978	17,672	821	1991	19,468*	10,232*	1,133	978

* Response rate of less than 100 percent.

Applications and Admissions to Masters Degree Programs

Applications to masters degree programs in 1991 increased by 19.6% over 1990. Of those, applications to full-time programs rose by 22.7% and applications to part-time programs rose by 12.4%. Programs were more selective this year, accepting 3.4% fewer students for admission than last year. A higher percentage of applicants to part-time programs were accepted and registered than were applicants to full-time programs. Applicants to part-time programs also are more likely to register after they have been accepted by a program.

TABLE 30

Applications for Admission to First-year Status in Masters Degree Programs
in 1990 and 1991, by Action Taken

Year	Program	Action							
		Total Received		Considered for Admission		Accepted		Registered	
		#	%	#	%	#	%	#	%
1991	Full-time	23,839	100.0	21,463	90.0	13,915	58.4	8,472	35.5
	Part-time	9,622	100.0	8,361	86.9	5,814	60.4	4,454	46.3
	Total	33,461	100.0	29,824	89.1	19,729	59.0	12,926	38.6
1990	Full-time	19,427	100.0	17,206	88.6	12,025	61.9	7,414	38.2
	Part-time	8,561	100.0	7,516	87.8	5,452	63.7	4,458	52.1
	Total	27,988	100.0	24,722	88.3	17,477	62.4	11,872	42.4

Table 31 displays data concerning action taken on applications for advanced standing status in masters degree programs. The majority of applications (74.5%) for advanced standing came from individuals who held a baccalaureate degree in social work from an institution other than the one to which the application was made. An additional 20.0% of applications were received from graduates of baccalaureate programs under the same auspices as the prospective masters programs. The applicants who choose to stay in the same university from which they received their baccalaureate degree are more likely to be accepted and enroll than are their colleagues who apply to a masters program in a university different from the one which awarded their baccalaureate degree.

TABLE 31

Applications for Advanced Standing Status in Masters Degree Programs in 1991,
by Source/Basis and Action

Action	Source or Basis							
	Baccalaureate Social Work Program				Other Education		Total	
	Own School		Other School					
	#	%	#	%	#	%	#	%
Received	769	100.0	2,870	100.0	214	100.0	3,853	100.0
Accepted	576	74.9	1,870	65.2	150	70.1	2,596	67.4
Enrolled	537	69.8	1,333	46.4	106	49.5	1,976	51.3

Degrees Awarded

As would be expected, the number of degrees awarded to students completing masters and doctoral degrees is proportionate to the number of students enrolled at the same time. Therefore, as Table 32 shows, the number of masters degrees awarded until the 1978-79 academic year was increased from year to year. In the 1980s, the number of masters degrees awarded fluctuated up and down, with a general downward trend until the 1986-87 year. This year a record 10,969 masters degrees were awarded, a 9.0% increase over 1990. Since the 1977-78 academic year, every other year has shown an increase in the number of doctoral degrees conferred. Doctoral programs conferred 2 fewer degrees than last year, a figure that has added importance in light of the fact that 100% of the doctoral programs responded this year compared to last year's 93.8% response.

TABLE 32

Graduate Students Awarded Masters and Doctoral Degrees,
Academic Year 1965-66 through 1990-91

Academic Year	Masters Degree	Doctoral Degree	Academic Year	Masters Degree	Doctoral Degree
1965-66	3,693	56	1978-79	10,080*	174*
1966-67	4,279	54	1979-80	9,820	213*
1967-68	4,614	67	1980-81	9,750	226
1968-69	5,060	89	1981-82	9,556	284
1969-70	5,638	84	1982-83	9,034*	227*
1970-71	6,284	129	1983-84	8,053*	245*
1971-72	6,909	114	1984-85	8,798*	181*
1972-73	7,387	112	1985-86	8,134*	297*
1973-74	8,005	159	1986-87	8,811*	195*
1974-75	8,824	155	1987-88	9,891*	332
1975-76	9,080	179	1988-89	9,509*	189*
1976-77	9,254	179	1989-90	10,063*	247*
1977-78	9,476	178	1990-91	10,969*	245

* Response rate of less than 100%

Demographic Characteristics of Graduate Students

Table 33 displays the gender breakdown of graduate students. Females continue to make up the vast majority of masters degree students (82.4%). The proportion of females to males has increased slightly among full-time students and decreased slightly among part-time students. More males are enrolled in doctoral programs, however, making up one-third of all full-time students. This also represents a slight decrease in the number of males enrolled in full-time doctoral study. Gender distribution is similar for recipients of degrees at the two levels as for those enrolled. Overall, these proportions have not changed much in recent years.

TABLE 33

Full and Part-time Masters and Full-time Doctoral Students
Enrolled on 11/1/91 and Graduate Students Awarded Degrees 1990-91, by Gender*

Gender	Masters Students				Doctoral Students	
	Enrolled			Awarded Masters Degrees	Enrolled Full-time	Awarded Doctoral Degrees
	Full-time	Part-time	Total			
Male	17.2	18.5	17.6	17.8	33.2	32.2
Female	82.8	81.5	82.4	82.2	66.8	67.8
Total	100.0	100.0	100.0	100.0	100.0	100.0
Number	19,288	10,131	29,419	10,969	1,133	245

* Column totals may not correspond between tables within this report due to variance in response rates.

Table 34 displays the age of graduate students enrolled full-time and part-time in graduate social work education. Females aged 25 and under are the largest group among full-time masters students. Part-time masters students are more frequently females aged 31-40. In both full and part-time males are more likely to be in the 31-40 age group. These characteristics are consistent with last year's statistics. At the doctoral level, females are typically aged 41 and over while males are more likely to be in the 31-40 category. Last year female full-time doctoral students were younger, but in general the proportions displayed here are comparable to those of last year.

TABLE 34

Full and Part-time Masters and Doctoral Students Enrolled on 11/1/91, by Gender and Age*

Age	Gender	Masters Students		Doctoral Students	
		Full-time	Part-time	Full-time	Part-time
25 & under	Male	3.5	1.9	1.0	0.0
	Female	28.3	12.5	2.9	0.3
26 - 30	Male	4.3	3.8	3.8	2.3
	Female	17.8	18.6	7.1	5.1
31 - 40	Male	6.0	7.5	14.9	15.2
	Female	19.6	27.5	26.9	27.3
41 & over	Male	3.5	5.3	13.7	14.6
	Female	17.1	22.9	29.8	35.3
Total	Male	17.2	18.5	33.2	32.0
	Female	82.8	81.5	66.8	68.0
Total	Percent	100.0	100.0	100.0	100.0
	Number	19,152	10,097	1,133	978

* Column totals may not correspond between tables within this report due to variance in response rates.

32

Ethnic minorities made up 17.7% of full-time and 19.5% of part-time masters degree students (Table 35). There was a slightly higher percentage of minorities enrolled full-time in doctoral programs (21.8%) than last year, but part-time minority doctoral students are less frequent (17.8%) than last year. At both the masters and doctoral levels the proportion of minorities enrolled part-time decreased from last year. There was a slight increase in minority full-time masters students, but a 3.2% decrease was seen at the doctoral level. Persons in the United States on a student visa ("foreign") make up a very small percentage of masters degree students. However, foreign students received 10.2% of the doctoral degrees awarded in 1990-91.

TABLE 35

Full and Part-time Masters and Doctoral Students Enrolled on 11/1/91
and Students Awarded Degrees 1990-91, by Ethnicity*

Ethnicity	Masters Students			Doctoral Students		
	Enrolled		Awarded Masters Degrees	Enrolled		Awarded Doctoral Degrees
	Full-time	Part-time		Full-time	Part-time	
African American	9.1	10.8	8.9	12.1	11.3	8.2
Asian American	2.1	1.7	1.5	3.0	1.1	3.3
Chicano/Mexican American	2.5	3.4	2.1	1.9	1.5	0.8
Native American	0.8	0.4	0.5	1.1	0.3	0.0
Puerto Rican	2.0	1.8	2.7	2.2	1.7	1.6
Other Minority	1.3	1.3	0.9	1.4	1.7	1.2
Total Minorities	17.7	19.5	16.7	21.8	17.8	15.1
Foreign	1.1	0.4	1.1	9.4	6.1	10.2
White	81.3	80.1	82.2	68.8	76.1	74.7
Total	100.0	100.0	100.0	100.0	100.0	100.0
Number	19,288	10,131	10,969	1,133	978	245

* Column totals may not correspond between tables within this report due to variance in response rates.

Concentration of Study

Data were gathered on the primary methods concentration of every masters degree student enrolled in schools of social work. Schedule III did not define any of the "methods of practice categories" or "fields of practice or social problem categories". Programs were asked to place student information in cells that represented "methods" and "social problems". Tables 36 and 37 display that information in two different ways.

Table 36 shows that most masters degree students have or will have declared a methods concentration. Of those, 31.1% have chosen to concentrate only on that particular method of practice. Most students (68.9%), however, study a method of practice in conjunction with a primary field of practice or social problem concentration. "Direct practice" is the most popular method and "generic" practice runs a distant second. The proportions displayed in Table 36 are generally consistent with those reported last year.

TABLE 36

Masters Degree Students Enrolled on 11/1/91, by Primary Methods Concentration*

Methods	Concentration Framework							
	Methods Only		Methods Combined with Field of Practice or Social Prob.		Field of Practice or Social Problem Only (No Methods)		Total	
	#	%	#	%	#	%	#	%
Direct Practice	4,780	54.6	10,449	53.8	---	---	15,229	52.9
Community Organization and Planning	123	1.4	605	3.1	---	---	728	2.5
Administration or Management	516	5.9	618	3.2	---	---	1,134	3.9
Combination of Direct Practice with C.O. and Planning or Administration or Management	440	5.0	1,905	9.8	---	---	2,345	8.1
Combination of C.O. and Planning with Administration or Management	79	0.9	128	0.7	---	---	207	0.7
Generic	1,716	19.6	1,908	9.8	---	---	3,624	12.6
Other	279	3.2	421	2.2	---	---	700	2.4
Not Yet Determined	818	9.3	3,382	17.4	---	---	4,200	14.6
None (Field of Practice or Social Problem Only)	---	---	---	---	627	100.0	627	2.2
Total	8,751	100.0	19,416	100.0	627	100.0	28,794	100.0

* Column totals may not correspond between tables within this report due to variance in response rates.

Table 37 displays the distribution of students who are studying a particular field of practice or social problem concentration. Mental health continues to be the concentration taken by the most masters degree students (11.2%). Family services, health, and child welfare (in that order) are runners-up. Very few students choose other concentrations. Overall, there was no noticeable change between the concentrations from 1990. Over half of masters degree students were reported as either having not yet determined their social problem concentration or only concentrating on a method. A 4.4% increase in the percent of students with their concentration not yet determined is shown this year.

TABLE 37

Masters Degree Students Enrolled on 11/1/91, by Primary Field of Practice or Social Problem Concentration*

Type of Concentration	#	%
Aging/Gerontological Social Work	713	2.4
Alcohol, Drug or Substance Abuse	299	1.0
Child Welfare	1,875	6.4
Community Planning	247	0.8
Corrections/Criminal Justice	223	0.8
Family Services	2,108	7.2
Group Services	168	0.6
Health	1,946	6.6
Occupational/Industrial Social Work	211	0.7
Mental Health or Community Mental Health	3,299	11.2
Mental Retardation	122	0.4
Public Assistance/Public Welfare	120	0.4
Rehabilitation	80	0.3
School Social Work	609	2.1
Other	1,122	3.8
Combinations	465	1.6
Not Yet Determined	6,436	21.9
None (Methods Concentration Only)	9,325	31.8
Total	29,368	100.0

* Column totals may not correspond between tables within this report due to variance in response rates.

Concentration of Field Instruction

Although students may choose to study a particular field of practice or social problem, the location of their field instruction may not correspond with their study concentration. Table 38 shows the primary field of practice in which masters students were placed on November 1, 1991. The most frequent concentrations in this table are the same as in Table 37, but many students who may study in one social problem area may work in another field of practice in their practicum. Mental health claims 16.2% of field placements. Following mental health, health, family service, and child welfare lead all the other fields of practice. Over one-third of masters students either were not yet assigned field instruction on November 1, 1991 or were not to be in field instruction this year.

TABLE 38

Masters Degree Students Enrolled on 11/1/91, by Primary Field of Practice in Field Instruction*

Type of Concentration	#	%
Aging/Gerontological Social Work	899	3.1
Alcohol, Drug or Substance Abuse	799	2.7
Child Welfare	2,114	7.2
Community Planning	460	1.6
Corrections/Criminal Justice	447	1.5
Family Service	2,598	8.8
Group Services	341	1.2
Health	2,833	9.6
Occupational/Industrial Social Work	273	0.9
Mental Health or Community Mental Health	4,763	16.2
Mental Retardation	272	0.9
Public Assistance/Public Welfare	296	1.0
Rehabilitation	242	0.8
School Social Work	1,331	4.5
Other	1,390	4.7
Not Yet Assigned Field Instruction	3,986	13.6
Not in Field Instruction This Academic Year	6,324	21.5
Total	29,368	100.0

* Column totals may not correspond between tables within this report due to variance in response rates.

Financial Aid

As noted in Table 39, one-quarter of full-time graduate students receiving financial aid in 1991 were members of an ethnic minority group. A slightly higher percentage of doctoral students who are minorities received financial aid. Of those minorities receiving financial aid, over half were African American. An additional column to last year's table is included this year. It shows the proportion of those full-time students receiving financial aid to the number of students enrolled full-time. As throughout this report, comparisons between tables should be made with caution. Among masters students, 83.2% of Puerto Ricans and 80.8% of African Americans received financial aid. Almost three-quarters of all ethnic minority graduate students received financial aid as of November 1, 1991. At the doctoral level, small numbers of minorities enrolled full-time make it difficult to interpret accurately the percentage of students receiving financial aid within any ethnic minority category. However, it is clear that the African American category has a very high proportion of students within that category receiving financial aid. Because of the small numbers at the doctoral level, a year to year comparison of these percentages is not very reliable. At the masters level it can be noted that the proportion of full-time students receiving financial aid to those who do not has dropped slightly for minorities (from 79.2 to 72.4) and for all students (from 52.5 to 51.2) between 1990 and 1991.

TABLE 39

Full-time Masters and Doctoral Students Receiving Financial Grants on 11/1/91, by Ethnicity*

Ethnicity	Masters Students			Doctoral Students		
	#	Cum. %	% of all in category	#	Cum. %	% of all in category
African American	1,421	14.4	80.8	116	17.4	84.7
Asian American	255	2.6	63.3	15	2.2	44.1
Chicano/Mexican American	268	2.7	56.1	20	3.0	90.9
Native American	96	1.0	66.2	11	1.6	84.6
Puerto Rican	316	3.2	83.2	11	1.6	44.0
Other Minority	113	1.1	45.7	9	1.3	56.3
Total Minorities	2,469	25.0	72.4	182	27.3	73.7
Foreign	91	0.9	44.6	85	12.7	80.2
White	7,307	74.0	46.6	400	60.0	51.3
Total	9,867	100.0	51.2	667	100.0	58.9

* Column totals may not correspond between tables within this report due to variance in response rates.

Table 40 shows the different sources of the financial aid received by full-time masters and doctoral students on November 1, 1991. This represents all awards made, regardless of number of sources. Therefore, if one student represented in Table 39 received an award from three different sources, that student would be counted as three in this table. Schedule III contained a typographical error that allowed data entry on a line under the general heading "Federal Government." Data entered under this line were included in Table 40 under "Public Funds, Other."

Students receiving financial aid from sources other than their field placement received it most often from formal loan programs, followed by their school or university. Other sources were infrequent in comparison. Among those awards given by a student's field instruction agency, social welfare agencies and state or local governments were the most frequent. Federal work study programs, other work study programs and private foundations each gave at least 10% of financial aids awarded to field students. As would be expected, more doctoral awards were given by a student's school or university (45.3%) and by research or graduate assistantships (29.3%) than all the other sources combined. The sources of financial aid for graduate social work education have not greatly varied from year to year.

TABLE 40

Financial Grants Awarded to Full-time Masters and Doctoral Students on 11/1/91, by Source of Funds

Source of Funds	To Masters Students						To Doctoral Students	
	Funds Not Tied to Current Field Instruction		Funds Paid by Field Instruction Agency		Total Masters			
	#	%	#	%	#	%	#	%
Public Funds								
Federal Government								
Child Welfare	220	1.5	64	2.8	284	1.7	4	0.5
Office of Aging	14	0.1	1	0.0	15	0.1	3	0.4
NIAAA	1	0.0	2	0.1	3	0.0	3	0.4
NIDA	1	0.0	1	0.0	2	0.0	1	0.1
NIMH	55	0.4	18	0.8	73	0.4	28	3.4
VA	12	0.1	166	7.2	178	1.1	2	0.2
FCWSP (Work Study)	814	5.6	292	12.7	1,106	6.6	7	0.8
State or Local Government	921	6.3	473	20.6	1,394	8.3	14	1.7
Veterans Benefits	58	0.4	11	0.5	69	0.4	2	0.2
Other	529	3.6	115	5.0	644	3.8	21	2.5
Voluntary Funds								
Social Welfare Agencies	122	0.8	514	22.4	636	3.8	6	0.7
Foundations/Other Sources	306	2.1	229	10.0	535	3.2	27	3.3
School or University	4,242	29.2	70	3.1	4,312	25.7	375	45.3
Foreign Governments	11	0.1	22	1.0	33	0.2	13	1.6
Formal Loan Programs	6,279	43.3	14	0.6	6,293	37.5	65	7.9
Work Study (not federal)	87	0.6	282	12.3	369	2.2	1	0.1
Research or Graduate Assistantships	603	4.2	1	0.0	604	3.6	242	29.3
Other	234	1.6	16	0.7	250	1.5	13	1.6
Total	14,509	100.0	2,291	100.0	16,800	100.0	827	100.0

Student-Faculty Ratio

Table 41 displays the student-faculty ratios for masters and doctoral programs. For the purpose of calculating ratios, full-time students were counted as one and part-time students were counted as one-half. Faculty were counted according to the amount of time they spent at the masters and doctoral level. For instance, faculty members who spend 100% of their time in social work, but split their time between the masters program and the doctoral program, 50% would be counted toward the masters ratio and 50% to the doctoral ratio. Likewise, part-time faculty members who spend 30% of their time in social work and split it between the two programs, 15% would go to masters and 15% to doctoral. Masters programs reported a larger student-faculty ratio with a median of 13.1:1. The modal ratio group (12:1-14:1) for masters programs in Table 41 corresponds with the median. Doctoral programs have a smaller median student-faculty ratio at 10.8:1. However, the modal ratio group (15:1 and over) is well above that of the median. At both levels the median student-faculty ratio is up about one point from last year.

TABLE 41

Student-Faculty Ratio in Masters and Doctoral Programs on 11/1/91*

Student-Faculty Ratio	Masters Programs		Doctoral Programs	
	#	%	#	%
Less than 6:1	1	1.1	3	6.7
6:1 - 8:1	12	13.2	13	28.9
9:1 - 11:1	24	26.4	9	20.0
12:1 - 14:1	28	30.8	5	11.1
15:1 and over	26	28.6	15	33.3
Total	91	100.0	45	100.0
Median	13.1:1		10.8:1	

* Column totals may not correspond between tables within this report due to variance in response rates.

PROGRAMS IN CANDIDACY FOR ACCREDITATION

The characteristics of programs in candidacy status for accreditation have not changed greatly since last year. Thirty-seven programs were polled to determine the ethnic and gender identification of their graduates. Of those 37 programs, there were 2 stand-alone graduate programs, 24 stand-alone baccalaureate programs, 10 graduate programs jointly administered with baccalaureate programs, and 1 baccalaureate program jointly administered with an accredited masters program. As noted in Table 1, 32 programs responded to Schedule V. Table 42 shows that baccalaureate programs reported 353 graduates and masters programs reported 223 graduates. Because of the small numbers reported, it is difficult to state trends with reliability. However, it is clear that African American females greatly outnumber members of other ethnic minority categories graduating from baccalaureate programs in candidacy. The proportion of minorities graduating from baccalaureate candidacy programs is similar to that of fully accredited programs (20.3%). Masters programs in candidacy status graduated only 10.8% minorities, compared to nearly double that for fully accredited programs.

TABLE 42

Students Awarded Degrees in Programs in Candidacy 1990-91, by Ethnicity and Gender

Ethnicity	Baccalaureate Programs			Masters Programs		
	Male	Female	Total	Male	Female	Total
African American	5	55	60	1	7	8
Asian American	1	1	2	0	0	0
Chicano/Mexican American	2	1	3	2	8	10
Native American	0	6	6	1	5	6
Puerto Rican	0	0	0	0	0	0
Other Minority	0	0	0	0	0	0
Total Minorities	8	63	71	4	20	24
Foreign	0	0	0	1	3	4
White	35	247	282	28	167	195
Total	43	310	353	33	190	223

RECENT TRENDS IN SOCIAL WORK EDUCATION

Tables 43 and 44 display selected characteristics of social work education over the last five years. General trends may be seen in these displays, but they must be interpreted with caution. During the last eight years, the response rate has not been 100% on any schedule except for the doctoral surveys, which were 100% in 1988 and this year. As noted earlier, response rates to specific items also vary within schedules.

Table 43 shows trends in baccalaureate programs. The total number of programs, faculty, enrollments, and graduates all show a steady increase. The proportion of women and doctorates on baccalaureate faculties is increasing slightly. The decline in the proportion of minority faculty noted in last year's report seems to have stopped this year. The proportion of women enrolled in baccalaureate programs appears to be creeping up while the proportion of ethnic minorities enrolled is steady.

An analysis of trends in graduate social work education (Table 44) is not as simple or reliable as that of baccalaureate education primarily because there are more than three times as many baccalaureate programs. The most obvious trends compare with those of the baccalaureate programs. The total number of programs, faculty, full and part-time students, and graduates have steadily increased. The proportion of the different professorial ranks varies from year to year, but has not changed a great deal. The proportion of females and minorities on faculties has increased recently, as has that of female associate professors. There has been a large drop in the proportion of minorities who are assistant professors and a smaller decrease among associate professors. Salaries have increased between 18 and 20 percent over the past 5 years. All statistics for masters students have shown an increase recently. The only decrease shown is in the percent of applications accepted for first-year status in masters degree programs. Doctoral programs have shown an increase in enrollment and graduation, but the proportions of women and minorities vary too much to establish a pattern.

TABLE 43

Highlights of Recent Trends in Baccalaureate Social Work Education

	1987	1988	1989	1990	1991
Accredited Baccalaureate Programs*					
Baccalaureate Only	295	297	304	297	297
Joint	59	57	58	69	78
Institutional Auspices (Baccalaureate Only)					
Percent Public	52.0	51.3	51.9	51.8	50.5
Percent Private	48.0	48.7	48.1	48.2	49.5
Faculty (Baccalaureate Only)					
Total Number	1,195	1,122	1,197	1,241	1,432
Percent Women	54.0	55.2	56.3	55.3	58.4
Percent Ethnic Minority	25.0	23.9	23.2	23.9	26.5
Percent Holding Doctorates	36.3	34.4	36.5	37.2	38.0
Students					
Full-time Degree Students	25,920	27,906	26,154	28,154	32,777
Percent Juniors or Seniors	63.8	59.1	63.2	63.5	63.2
Percent Women	82.6	84.7	84.1	84.2	85.0
Percent Ethnic Minority	24.3	24.4	23.3	23.8	24.6
Part-time Degree Students	4,039	4,396	4,762	4,945	5,416
Others Taking Social Work Courses	14,152	15,884	16,646	17,223	18,462
Degrees Awarded					
Total Number	7,209	6,916	7,230	7,250	8,778
Percent Women	84.8	85.8	85.2	87.6	86.6
Percent Ethnic Minority	21.2	22.2	22.4	24.1	22.8

* Represents all accredited programs, not the number of programs responding to this survey.

TABLE 44

Highlights of Recent Trends in Graduate Social Work Education*

	1987	1988	1989	1990	1991
Programs					
Accredited Masters Programs**	97	96	97	99	103
Doctoral Programs	47	47	47	48	49
Faculty					
Total Number	2,638	2,898	3,165	3,357	3,365
Percent Women	50.5	52.6	54.0	54.6	56.0
Percent Ethnic Minority	22.4	22.2	22.1	22.2	21.8
Percent Doctorates	56.6	57.1	56.4	56.4	57.0
Full-time Professors	605	651	672	605	689
Percent Women	27.4	29.0	29.3	29.4	29.2
Percent Ethnic Minority	19.4	18.4	19.4	19.9	20.5
Full-time Associate Professors	703	717	750	744	740
Percent Women	44.7	46.0	48.0	47.8	52.2
Percent Ethnic Minority	26.5	22.2	26.6	27.9	22.1
Full-time Assistant Professors	636	710	730	659	729
Percent Women	66.5	66.8	65.8	64.6	66.5
Percent Ethnic Minority	30.6	22.8	26.7	28.4	21.7
Median Salary for Full-time Faculty					
Professor	$45,488	$47,293	$51,662	$52,500	$54,866
Associate Professor	36,405	37,644	40,707	40,117	43,100
Assistant Professor	29,005	30,833	32,908	31,780	34,290
Students: Masters Programs					
Full-time Students	15,241	16,239	15,777	17,475	19,468
Percent Women	80.9	81.7	81.1	82.3	82.8
Percent Ethnic Minority	15.0	16.6	16.5	16.9	17.7
Part-time Students	8,044	9,024	9,420	9,838	10,232
Applications for First Year Status	21,581	24,920	25,168	27,988	33,461
Percent Accepted	65.6	61.4	61.3	61.3	59.0
Applications for Advanced Standing	2,616	2,595	2,759	3,802	3,853
Masters Degrees Awarded	8,811	9,891	9,509	10,063	10,969
Percent Women	81.7	81.6	81.6	82.6	82.2
Percent Ethnic Minority	13.9	18.5	15.2	15.9	16.7
Students: Doctoral Programs					
Full-time Students	703	1,003	857	838	1,133
Percent Women	70.1	74.1	68.5	64.9	66.8
Percent Ethnic Minority	17.8	21.4	21.2	25.0	21.8
Part-time Students	820*	911	989	954	978
Doctoral Degrees Awarded	195	332	189	247	245
Percent Women	60.3	60.3	65.1	67.2	67.8
Percent Ethnic Minority	17.8	19.6	14.8	25.5	15.1

* None of the statistics in this table represent a 100% response rate.
** Represents all accredited programs, not the number of programs responding to this survey.

APPENDIX A

Reference Tables

List of Reference Tables

Other Tables

TABLE 100

Number of Juniors and Seniors, by Gender and Ethnicity, and Number of Freshman and Sophomore Full-time Degree Students Enrolled in Baccalaureate Programs on 11/1/91

Program		Juniors and Seniors																		Frosh and Soph	Total
	Men									**Women**									**Total**	**Total**	**Total**
	African Amer	Asian Amer	Chicano	Native Amer	Puerto Rican	White	Other	Foreign	Total	African Amer	Asian Amer	Chicano	Native Amer	Puerto Rican	White	Other	Foreign	Total			
TOTAL: Number	598	71	139	61	83	2,093	38	19	3,102	2,477	247	541	235	431	13,440	184	70	17,625	20,727	11,598	32,325
Percent	2.9%	0.3%	0.7%	0.3%	0.4%	10.1%	0.2%	0.1%	15.0%	12.0%	1.2%	2.6%	1.1%	2.1%	64.8%	0.9%	0.3%	85.0%	100.0%		
ABILENE CHRISTIAN	3	0	0	0	0	5	0	0	8	3	1	1	0	0	19	0	0	24	32	14	46
ADELPHI UNIVERSITY	0	0	0	0	0	2	0	0	2	6	0	0	2	0	55	2	0	65	67	0	67
ALABAMA A&M UNIV	6	0	0	0	0	0	0	0	6	35	0	0	0	0	2	0	1	38	44	29	73
ALABAMA STATE UNIV	2	0	0	0	0	2	0	0	4	15	0	0	0	0	0	0	0	15	19	25	44
ALBRIGHT COLLEGE	0	0	0	0	0	1	0	0	1	0	0	0	0	0	10	0	0	10	11	8	19
ALDERSON-BROADDUS	0	0	0	0	0	0	0	0	0	0	0	0	0	0	2	0	0	2	2	0	2
ANDERSON UNIVERSIT	0	0	0	0	0	2	0	0	2	1	0	0	0	0	28	0	0	29	31	8	39
ANNA MARIA COLLEGE	0	0	0	0	0	0	0	0	0	0	0	0	0	0	13	0	0	13	13	16	29
APPALACHIAN STATE	2	0	0	0	0	3	0	0	5	1	0	0	0	0	54	0	0	55	60	21	81
ARIZONA STATE UNIV	8	0	3	0	0	28	0	0	39	3	3	13	13	0	128	0	1	161	200	41	241
ARKANSAS COLLEGE	0	0	0	0	0	3	0	0	3	0	0	1	1	0	13	0	0	15	18	3	21
ARKANSAS STATE UNI	0	0	0	0	0	6	0	0	6	8	0	0	0	0	31	1	0	40	46	22	68
ASHLAND UNIVERSITY	1	0	0	0	0	1	0	0	2	1	0	0	0	0	16	0	0	17	19	0	19
ATLANTIC UNION COLL	0	0	0	0	0	0	1	0	1	8	0	0	0	0	1	5	0	14	15	27	42
AUBURN UNIVERSITY	1	0	0	1	0	3	0	0	5	6	0	1	0	0	72	0	0	79	84	42	126
AUGUSTANA COLL/IL	2	0	0	0	0	2	0	0	4	1	0	0	0	0	17	0	0	18	22	12	34
AUGUSTANA COLL/SD	1	0	0	0	0	4	0	0	5	0	0	0	0	0	23	0	0	23	28	13	41
AURORA UNIVERSITY	0	0	0	1	1	5	0	0	7	3	0	1	0	0	51	0	0	55	62	14	76
AUSTIN PEAY STATE	0	0	0	0	0	4	0	0	4	6	1	0	0	0	23	0	0	30	34	40	74
AVILA COLLEGE	0	0	0	0	0	1	0	0	1	1	0	1	0	0	15	0	0	17	18	8	26
AZUSA PACIFIC UNIV	0	0	0	0	0	2	0	0	2	0	0	1	1	0	20	0	0	22	24	10	34
BALL STATE UNIV	3	0	0	0	0	15	0	0	18	27	0	0	0	0	87	0	0	114	132	128	260
BAYLOR UNIVERSITY	0	0	0	0	0	3	0	0	3	4	2	5	0	0	54	0	0	65	68	0	68
BEMIDJI STATE UNIV	0	0	0	1	0	13	0	1	15	0	0	2	3	0	56	0	0	61	76	53	129
BENEDICT COLLEGE	4	0	0	0	0	0	0	0	4	41	0	0	0	0	1	0	2	44	48	72	120
BENNETT COLLEGE	0	0	0	0	0	0	0	0	0	11	0	0	0	0	0	0	0	11	11	19	30
BETHANY COLLEGE/KS	2	0	0	0	0	1	0	0	3	0	0	1	0	0	11	0	0	12	15	7	22
BETHANY COLLEGE/W	0	0	0	0	0	1	0	0	1	0	0	0	0	0	9	0	0	9	10	11	21
BETHEL COLLEGE/KS	1	0	0	0	0	2	0	0	3	1	0	0	0	0	24	0	0	25	28	22	50
BETHEL COLLEGE/MN	0	0	0	0	0	4	0	0	4	1	1	0	0	0	35	0	0	37	41	25	66
BLOOMSBURG UNIV	0	0	0	0	0	7	0	0	7	2	0	0	1	0	46	0	0	49	56	30	86
BLUFFTON COLLEGE	0	0	0	0	0	0	0	0	0	2	0	0	0	0	12	0	0	14	14	10	24
BOISE STATE UNIV	2	0	2	0	0	17	0	0	21	0	0	2	1	0	83	0	0	86	107	114	221
BOSTON UNIVERSITY	1	1	0	0	0	2	0	0	4	2	1	2	0	0	12	0	2	19	23	1	24
BOWIE STATE UNIV	5	0	0	0	0	2	0	0	7	28	0	0	0	0	9	3	0	40	47	51	98
BOWLING GREEN STAT	3	0	0	0	0	13	0	0	16	8	0	0	0	0	86	0	0	94	110	97	207
BRIAR CLIFF COLLEGE	2	0	0	0	0	5	0	0	7	0	0	0	0	0	30	0	0	30	37	28	65
BRIDGEWATER STATE	0	0	0	1	0	5	0	0	6	1	0	0	0	0	77	0	0	78	84	66	150
BRIGHAM YOUNG/HI	0	1	0	1	0	4	0	4	10	0	4	0	0	0	10	0	11	25	35	50	85
BRIGHAM YOUNG/UT	0	0	0	0	0	17	0	0	17	0	0	3	2	0	128	2	1	136	153	3	156

TABLE 100 (Continued)

Number of Juniors and Seniors, by Gender and Ethnicity, and Number of Freshman and Sophomore Full-time Degree Students Enrolled in Baccalaureate Programs on 11/1/91

Program	Men									Women									Juniors and Seniors Total	Frosh and Soph	Total
	African Amer	Asian Amer	Chicano	Native Amer	Puerto Rican	White	Other	Foreign	Total	African Amer	Asian Amer	Chicano	Native Amer	Puerto Rican	White	Other	Foreign	Total			
BUENA VISTA COLLEG	0	0	0	0	0	2	0	0	2	0	0	0	0	0	16	0	0	16	18	9	27
BUFFALO STATE COLL	8	0	0	0	0	19	0	0	27	17	1	0	1	3	147	0	0	169	196	38	234
CAL STATE POLY	2	2	3	0	0	5	0	0	12	23	6	27	4	1	35	2	0	98	110	40	150
CAL STATE UNIV/CHIC	3	3	2	1	0	8	0	0	17	4	0	5	1	0	53	0	0	63	80	29	109
CAL STATE UNIV/FRES	7	10	18	0	0	35	0	0	70	18	4	37	0	0	75	0	0	134	204	39	243
CAL STATE UNIV/LB	3	4	4	0	0	18	0	0	29	8	9	9	0	0	51	0	0	77	106	45	151
CAL STATE UNIV/SAC	8	10	4	3	0	36	3	0	64	36	24	28	5	0	185	17	0	295	359	40	399
CALIFORNIA UNIV/PA	1	0	0	0	0	5	0	0	6	4	0	0	0	0	45	0	0	49	55	70	125
CAPITAL UNIVERSITY	1	0	0	0	0	5	0	0	6	18	0	0	0	4	25	0	0	47	53	15	68
CARROLL COLLEGE/MT	*	*	*	*	*	*	*	*	*	*	*	*	*	*	*	*	*	*	*	0	*
CARTHAGE COLLEGE	0	0	0	0	0	4	0	0	4	2	1	0	0	0	19	0	0	22	26	18	44
CASTLETON STATE UN	0	0	0	0	0	3	0	0	3	0	1	0	0	0	24	0	0	25	28	19	47
CATHOLIC UNIV/DC	1	0	0	0	0	4	0	0	5	1	0	0	0	1	19	0	1	22	27	11	38
CATHOLIC UNIV/PR	0	0	0	0	5	0	0	0	5	0	0	0	0	56	0	0	0	56	61	29	90
CEDAR CREST COLLE	0	0	0	0	0	0	0	0	0	0	0	0	0	2	14	0	1	17	17	5	22
CENTRAL MISSOURI	2	2	0	0	0	9	0	0	13	11	1	3	0	0	113	0	0	127	140	89	229
CHRISTOPHER NEWPO	1	0	0	0	0	1	0	0	2	16	0	0	0	1	26	0	1	44	46	32	78
CLARK ATLANTA UNIV	2	0	0	0	0	0	0	0	2	13	0	0	0	0	0	0	0	13	15	14	29
CLARKE COLLEGE	0	0	0	0	0	1	0	0	1	0	0	0	0	0	8	0	0	8	9	8	17
CLEVELAND STATE	5	0	0	0	0	19	1	0	25	42	4	4	1	0	53	10	0	109	134	21	155
COLL MISERICORDIA	0	0	0	0	0	4	0	0	4	0	0	0	0	0	26	0	0	26	30	11	41
COLL OF NEW ROCHEL	0	0	0	0	0	0	0	0	0	1	0	0	0	1	7	1	1	11	11	6	17
COLL OF ST BENEDICT	1	0	0	0	0	9	0	0	10	0	0	0	0	0	36	0	0	36	46	20	66
COLL OF ST CATHERIN	0	0	0	0	0	0	0	0	0	1	0	0	1	0	79	0	0	84	84	0	84
COLL OF ST SCHOL	0	0	0	0	0	3	0	0	3	0	0	4	1	0	20	0	0	21	24	46	70
COLORADO STATE UNI	0	0	0	0	0	14	0	0	14	4	1	4	2	0	94	0	0	105	119	74	193
COLUMBIA COLLEGE/S	0	0	0	0	0	0	0	0	0	7	0	0	0	0	23	0	0	30	30	18	48
CONCORD COLLEGE	3	0	0	0	0	6	0	0	9	5	0	0	0	0	25	0	0	30	39	52	91
CONCORDIA COLL/MN	1	0	0	0	0	5	0	4	10	0	1	0	0	0	41	0	0	42	52	0	52
CONCORDIA COLL/NY	0	0	1	0	0	1	0	0	2	1	0	0	0	0	7	0	0	8	10	17	27
COPPIN STATE COLL	3	0	0	0	0	0	1	0	4	43	0	0	0	0	0	0	0	43	47	5	52
D'YOUVILLE COLLEGE	1	0	0	0	0	0	1	0	1	1	1	0	0	0	17	0	0	20	20	10	30
DAEMEN COLLEGE	3	0	0	0	0	0	0	0	3	2	0	0	0	0	16	0	0	18	21	17	38
DANA COLLEGE	2	0	0	0	0	1	0	0	3	0	0	0	0	0	13	0	0	13	16	13	29
DEFIANCE COLLEGE	0	0	0	0	0	1	0	0	2	1	0	0	0	0	15	0	0	16	18	22	40
DELTA STATE UNIV	4	0	0	0	0	4	0	0	8	21	0	0	0	0	14	0	0	35	43	21	64
DOMINICAN COLLEGE	1	0	0	0	0	2	1	0	3	1	3	0	0	2	17	0	0	23	26	20	46
DORDT COLLEGE	1	0	0	0	0	1	0	0	2	0	1	0	0	0	22	0	2	25	27	26	53
EAST CAROLINA UNIV	1	0	0	0	0	1	0	0	2	7	0	0	0	0	30	0	0	37	39	3	42
EAST CENTRAL OKLA	0	0	0	2	0	7	0	0	9	2	0	0	4	0	18	0	0	24	33	47	80
EAST TENNESSEE STA	2	0	0	0	0	16	0	0	18	4	0	0	0	0	62	0	0	66	84	61	145
EAST TEXAS STATE	3	0	0	0	0	9	0	0	12	8	0	1	0	0	28	0	0	37	49	19	68
EASTERN COLLEGE	0	0	1	0	0	1	0	0	2	1	0	0	0	0	18	0	1	20	22	21	43
EASTERN MENNONITE	0	0	0	0	0	11	0	0	11	1	0	0	0	1	28	0	2	32	43	21	64

TABLE 100 (Continued)

Number of Juniors and Seniors, by Gender and Ethnicity, and Number of Freshman and Sophomore Full-time Degree Students Enrolled in Baccalaureate Programs on 11/1/91

| Program | Juniors and Seniors | | | | | | | | | | | | | | | | | | | Frosh and Soph | Total |
| | Men | | | | | | | | | Women | | | | | | | | | Total | Total | |
	African Amer	Asian Amer	Chicano	Native Amer	Puerto Rican	White	Other	Foreign	Total	African Amer	Asian Amer	Chicano	Native Amer	Puerto Rican	White	Other	Foreign	Total			
EASTERN MICHIGAN	7	1	1	1	0	25	0	0	35	23	1	3	1	1	140	0	2	171	206	46	252
EASTERN NAZARENE	0	0	0	0	0	0	1	0	1	0	0	0	0	0	15	1	0	16	17	14	31
EASTERN WASHINGTO	1	1	1	2	0	14	0	0	19	1	3	4	6	0	61	0	0	75	94	0	94
EDINBORO UNIVERSITY	1	0	1	0	0	9	0	0	11	3	0	0	1	0	47	0	0	51	62	78	140
ELIZABETHTOWN COLL	0	0	0	0	0	2	0	0	2	0	0	0	0	0	21	0	0	21	23	18	41
ELMS COLLEGE	1	0	0	0	0	3	0	0	4	1	0	0	0	2	31	0	0	34	38	5	43
FERRIS STATE UNIV	3	0	0	0	0	8	0	0	11	16	0	0	2	0	80	0	0	98	109	95	204
FERRUM COLLEGE	3	0	1	0	0	4	0	0	8	1	0	0	0	0	23	0	0	24	32	25	57
FLORIDA A&M UNIV	3	0	0	0	0	0	0	0	3	42	0	0	0	0	3	0	0	45	48	4	52
FLORIDA ATLANTIC	2	0	0	0	0	7	0	0	9	2	1	0	0	0	33	3	0	39	48	9	57
FLORIDA INTERNATL	*	*	*	*	*	*	*	*	*	*	*	*	*	*	*	*	*	*	*	5	*
FLORIDA STATE UNIV	7	0	0	0	0	22	1	0	30	20	1	0	1	0	135	4	0	160	190	10	200
FREED-HARDEMAN UNI	2	0	0	0	0	3	0	0	5	2	1	0	0	0	24	0	0	27	32	17	49
GALLAUDET UNIVERSIT	0	0	0	0	0	1	0	0	1	1	0	0	0	0	13	0	1	15	16	0	16
GANNON UNIVERSITY	1	0	0	0	0	1	0	0	2	2	0	0	0	0	11	0	0	13	15	15	30
GEORGE MASON UNIV	4	0	0	0	0	2	0	0	6	6	2	0	0	0	76	2	0	86	92	92	184
GEORGIA STATE UNIV	3	0	0	0	1	4	0	0	8	29	0	1	0	0	44	0	0	74	82	11	93
GORDON COLLEGE	0	0	0	0	0	6	0	0	6	1	1	0	0	0	30	0	0	32	38	18	56
GOSHEN COLLEGE	0	0	1	0	0	3	0	0	4	1	0	0	1	0	21	0	0	24	28	22	50
GRAMBLING STATE	8	0	0	0	0	0	0	0	8	54	0	0	0	0	0	0	0	54	62	90	152
GRAND VALLEY STATE	1	0	1	0	0	11	0	0	13	3	0	1	0	0	68	1	0	73	86	42	128
HAMPTON UNIVERSITY	2	0	0	0	0	0	0	0	2	7	0	0	0	0	0	0	0	7	9	7	16
HARDIN-SIMMONS UNI	0	0	1	0	0	4	0	0	5	2	0	4	0	0	18	0	0	24	29	26	55
HARDING UNIVERSITY	1	0	0	0	0	3	1	0	5	1	0	0	0	0	23	0	3	27	32	17	49
HERBERT H. LEHMAN	12	0	0	0	8	2	0	0	22	58	0	0	1	40	18	2	0	119	141	7	148
HOOD COLLEGE	0	0	0	0	0	0	0	0	0	2	0	0	0	0	16	0	0	18	18	0	18
HOWARD UNIVERSITY	2	0	0	0	0	0	0	1	3	14	0	0	0	0	0	0	3	17	20	0	20
IDAHO STATE UNIV	5	0	0	4	0	20	0	0	29	2	2	0	2	0	82	0	0	88	117	61	178
ILLINOIS STATE UNIV	1	0	0	0	0	16	0	0	17	4	2	2	0	0	123	0	0	131	148	88	236
INDIANA UNIVERSITY	0	0	0	0	0	11	0	0	11	12	1	3	0	0	96	1	0	113	124	22	146
INDIANA WESLEYAN	0	0	0	0	0	1	0	0	1	1	0	0	0	0	13	0	0	14	15	24	39
INTER AMERICAN UNIV	*	*	*	*	*	*	*	*	*	*	*	*	*	*	*	*	*	*	*	126	*
IONA COLLEGE	2	0	0	0	0	3	0	0	5	8	0	0	0	3	16	0	0	27	32	12	44
IOWA STATE UNIV	1	0	0	0	0	2	0	0	3	0	0	0	0	0	53	0	0	53	56	47	103
JACKSON STATE UNIV	13	0	0	0	0	1	0	0	14	65	0	0	0	0	0	0	0	65	79	50	129
JAMES MADISON UNIV	1	0	0	0	0	3	0	0	4	3	0	0	0	0	55	0	0	58	62	18	80
JUNIATA COLLEGE	0	0	0	0	0	1	0	0	1	0	0	0	0	0	8	0	0	8	9	11	20
KANSAS STATE UNIV	2	0	0	0	0	6	0	0	8	4	0	0	0	0	73	0	0	77	85	61	146
KEAN COLLEGE	1	0	0	0	0	5	1	0	7	14	0	8	0	1	37	9	0	69	76	39	115
KEUKA COLLEGE	0	0	0	0	0	1	0	1	2	1	0	0	0	0	18	0	0	19	21	7	28
LA SIERRA UNIVERSITY	4	0	0	0	0	5	0	0	9	5	1	11	0	0	17	0	0	34	43	9	52
LAMAR UNIVERSITY	0	1	0	0	0	6	0	0	7	15	0	0	0	0	30	0	0	45	52	53	105
LIVINGSTONE COLLEG	6	0	0	0	0	0	0	1	7	4	0	0	0	0	1	0	0	5	12	35	47

TABLE 100 (Continued)

Number of Juniors and Seniors, by Gender and Ethnicity, and Number of Freshman and Sophomore Full-time Degree Students Enrolled in Baccalaureate Programs on 11/1/91

| | Juniors and Seniors | | | | | | | | | | | | | | | | | | | Frosh and Soph | |
| | Men | | | | | | | | | Women | | | | | | | | | Total | Total | Total |
Program	African Amer	Asian Amer	Chicano	Native Amer	Puerto Rican	White	Other	Foreign	Total	African Amer	Asian Amer	Chicano	Native Amer	Puerto Rican	White	Other	Foreign	Total			
LORAS COLLEGE	0	0	0	0	0	1	0	0	1	1	1	0	0	0	22	0	0	24	25	13	38
LOYOLA UNIVERSITY	0	0	0	0	0	1	0	0	1	6	1	0	1	0	23	4	0	35	36	32	68
LUBBOCK CHRISTIAN	1	0	0	0	0	2	0	0	3	2	0	3	0	0	18	0	0	23	26	25	51
LUTHER COLLEGE	0	0	0	0	0	4	0	1	5	0	0	0	0	0	35	0	0	35	40	14	54
MADONNA UNIVERSITY	2	1	0	0	0	3	0	0	6	5	1	0	0	0	35	0	0	41	47	19	66
MALONE COLLEGE	0	0	0	0	0	1	0	0	1	0	0	0	0	0	17	0	0	17	18	40	58
MANCHESTER COLLEG	0	1	0	0	0	10	0	0	11	2	0	0	0	0	20	0	0	22	33	0	33
MANKATO STATE UNIV	0	0	1	0	0	9	0	0	10	0	2	0	0	0	81	0	0	85	95	89	184
MANSFIELD UNIVERSIT	0	0	0	0	0	2	0	0	2	2	0	0	0	0	27	0	0	29	31	33	64
MARIAN COLLEGE	0	0	0	0	0	0	0	0	0	1	0	0	0	0	6	0	0	7	7	25	32
MARIST COLLEGE	2	0	0	0	1	5	0	0	8	3	0	0	0	3	37	1	0	44	52	28	80
MARQUETTE UNIVERSI	2	0	0	0	0	0	0	0	2	2	1	0	1	0	24	0	0	28	30	0	30
MARS HILL COLLEGE	3	0	0	0	0	5	0	0	8	2	0	0	0	0	18	0	0	20	28	20	48
MARSHALL UNIVERSITY	1	0	0	0	0	2	0	0	3	0	0	0	0	0	14	0	0	14	17	29	46
MARYGROVE COLLEGE	3	0	0	0	0	1	0	0	4	54	0	0	0	0	10	0	0	64	68	27	95
MARYMOUNT COLLEGE	0	0	0	0	0	0	0	0	0	2	0	0	0	2	3	1	0	8	8	0	8
MARYWOOD COLLEGE	0	0	0	0	0	4	0	0	4	0	0	0	0	0	27	0	1	28	32	28	60
MEMPHIS STATE UNIV	6	0	0	0	0	11	0	0	17	29	0	0	0	0	37	0	0	66	83	36	119
MERCY COLLEGE	4	0	0	0	2	4	0	2	12	15	0	0	0	5	10	6	2	38	50	56	106
MERCYHURST COLLEG	1	0	0	0	0	1	0	0	1	0	0	0	0	0	16	0	0	16	17	8	25
MEREDITH COLLEGE	0	0	0	0	0	0	0	0	0	1	0	0	0	0	46	0	0	47	47	5	52
MESSIAH COLLEGE	1	0	0	0	0	0	0	0	1	0	0	0	0	0	11	0	0	11	12	12	24
MICHIGAN STATE UNIV	0	0	0	0	0	7	0	0	7	5	1	0	0	0	72	0	0	78	85	61	146
MIDDLE TENNESSE ST	5	0	0	0	0	10	0	0	15	14	0	0	0	0	53	0	0	67	82	32	114
MILLERSVILLE UNIV	1	0	0	0	0	3	0	0	4	4	2	0	0	0	55	0	0	61	65	28	93
MINOT STATE UNIV	0	0	0	5	0	14	0	0	19	2	0	0	14	0	57	0	0	73	92	77	169
MISSISSIPPI VALLEY	0	0	0	0	0	3	0	0	3	0	0	0	0	0	51	0	0	51	54	72	126
MISSOURI WESTERN	0	0	0	0	0	11	0	0	11	1	0	1	0	0	43	0	0	45	56	22	78
MONMOUTH COLLEGE	0	0	0	0	0	5	0	0	5	3	0	0	0	2	25	0	0	30	35	18	53
MOORHEAD STATE UNI	1	0	0	0	0	21	0	0	22	0	0	0	6	0	160	0	1	167	189	104	293
MOREHEAD STATE UNI	3	0	0	0	0	14	0	0	17	4	0	0	0	0	69	0	0	73	90	86	176
MORGAN STATE UNIV	7	0	0	0	0	1	1	0	9	38	0	0	0	0	6	0	0	44	53	31	84
MOUNT MARY COLLEG	0	0	0	0	0	0	0	0	0	5	0	0	0	0	13	0	0	18	18	19	37
MOUNT MERCY COLLE	0	0	0	0	0	3	0	0	3	0	0	0	0	0	25	0	0	25	28	20	48
MURRAY STATE UNIV	0	0	0	0	0	9	0	0	9	2	0	0	0	0	72	0	0	74	83	42	125
NAZARETH COLLEGE	2	1	0	0	1	5	1	0	10	11	1	0	0	0	46	0	0	58	68	11	79
NEW MEXICO HIGHLAN	1	0	15	0	0	5	0	0	21	0	0	30	4	0	9	0	0	43	64	83	147
NEW MEXICO STATE	0	0	12	1	0	12	0	0	25	6	1	51	7	0	47	0	0	112	137	60	197
NEW YORK UNIVERSITY	1	1	0	0	0	1	0	0	3	5	3	0	0	8	16	0	0	32	35	11	46
NIAGARA UNIVERSITY	1	0	0	0	0	11	1	0	13	3	0	0	0	0	20	0	0	23	36	12	48
NORFOLK STATE UNIV	6	0	0	0	0	3	0	0	9	50	0	0	0	0	12	0	0	62	71	115	186
NORTH CAROLINA A&T	5	0	0	0	0	0	0	0	5	28	0	0	0	0	0	0	0	28	33	27	60
NORTH CAROLINA STA	3	0	0	1	0	7	0	0	10	18	1	1	0	0	51	0	0	71	81	51	132

TABLE 100 (Continued)

Number of Juniors and Seniors, by Gender and Ethnicity, and Number of Freshman and Sophomore Full-time Degree Students Enrolled in Baccalaureate Programs on 11/1/91

Program	Men African Amer	Asian Amer	Chicano	Native Amer	Puerto Rican	White	Other	Foreign	Total	Women African Amer	Asian Amer	Chicano	Native Amer	Puerto Rican	White	Other	Foreign	Total	Juniors and Seniors Total	Frosh and Soph Total	Total
NORTHEAST LOUISIAN	6	0	0	0	0	5	0	0	11	18	0	0	0	0	31	0	0	49	60	88	148
NORTHEASTERN ILL	5	0	2	0	1	5	0	0	13	12	4	5	0	5	27	0	0	53	66	29	95
NORTHERN ARIZONA	1	0	1	1	0	8	0	0	11	1	1	9	17	0	45	0	0	73	84	60	144
NORTHERN KENTUCKY	1	0	0	0	0	4	0	0	5	1	0	0	0	0	37	0	1	39	44	38	82
NORTHERN MICHIGAN	1	0	0	1	0	12	0	0	14	3	0	0	4	0	37	0	0	44	58	104	162
NORTHWEST NAZARE	0	0	0	0	0	9	0	0	9	0	0	0	0	0	30	0	0	30	39	23	62
NORTHWESTERN COLL	0	0	0	0	0	2	0	0	2	0	0	0	0	0	8	0	1	9	11	11	22
NORTHWESTERN STAT	5	0	1	0	0	6	2	0	14	13	1	3	2	0	41	0	0	60	74	63	137
OAKWOOD COLLEGE	9	0	0	0	0	0	0	0	9	20	0	0	0	0	0	0	0	20	29	36	65
OHIO STATE UNIV	4	0	0	0	0	18	0	0	22	9	0	1	0	0	151	0	0	161	183	73	256
OHIO UNIVERSITY	0	0	0	0	0	2	0	0	2	6	1	0	0	0	59	0	0	66	68	30	98
ORAL ROBERTS UNIV	2	0	0	0	0	4	0	0	6	15	1	3	0	1	27	3	0	50	56	20	76
OUR LADY OF THE LAK	1	0	5	0	0	1	0	0	7	0	0	15	0	0	9	0	0	24	31	33	64
PACIFIC LUTHERAN	0	0	0	0	0	1	0	0	1	4	2	1	0	0	44	1	1	53	54	8	62
PACIFIC UNION COLL	0	0	1	0	0	0	0	0	1	1	0	2	0	0	9	1	0	13	14	27	41
PAUL QUINN COLLEGE	4	0	0	0	0	0	0	0	4	12	0	0	0	0	0	0	4	16	20	25	45
PEMBROKE STATE UNI	1	0	0	2	0	1	0	0	4	7	0	0	14	0	18	0	0	39	43	25	68
PENN STATE UNIV	2	0	0	0	0	5	0	0	7	4	1	0	0	0	35	0	0	40	47	11	58
PHIL COLL OF BIBLE	0	1	0	0	0	8	0	0	9	0	1	0	0	1	17	0	0	19	28	40	68
PITTSBURG STATE UNI	2	0	0	0	0	10	0	0	12	1	1	0	0	0	58	0	0	60	72	33	105
PRAIRIE VIEW A&M	13	0	0	0	0	0	0	0	13	35	0	0	0	0	2	0	2	39	52	58	110
PROVIDENCE COLLEG	0	0	0	0	0	1	0	0	1	0	0	0	0	0	16	0	0	16	17	14	31
PURDUE UNIVERSITY	0	0	0	0	0	5	0	0	5	2	0	0	0	0	34	1	0	37	42	35	77
RADFORD UNIVERSITY	1	0	0	0	0	1	0	0	2	6	0	0	0	0	69	0	1	76	78	46	124
RAMAPO COLLEGE	2	0	0	0	1	7	0	0	10	6	1	0	0	1	52	0	1	61	71	50	121
REGIS COLLEGE	0	0	0	0	0	0	0	0	0	1	0	0	0	0	16	0	0	17	17	8	25
RHODE ISLAND COLLE	0	0	0	0	0	5	0	0	5	5	0	0	0	0	81	7	0	93	98	78	176
ROBERTS WESLEYAN	0	0	0	0	0	4	0	0	4	4	0	0	0	0	21	0	1	26	30	38	68
ROCHESTER INST TEC	0	0	0	2	0	6	1	0	9	7	1	0	0	1	49	0	1	59	68	36	104
RUTGERS UNIV/NEWAR	6	0	0	0	0	1	0	0	7	8	5	0	0	3	9	3	0	28	35	10	45
SACRED HEART UNIV	0	0	0	0	0	5	0	0	5	0	0	0	0	3	13	0	0	16	21	17	38
SAGINAW VALLEY STA	1	1	1	0	0	10	0	0	13	12	0	4	1	0	56	0	0	73	86	59	145
SALISBURY STATE	2	0	0	0	0	4	0	0	6	5	0	0	0	0	38	0	0	43	49	19	68
SALVE REGINA COLLE	0	0	0	0	0	0	0	0	0	0	0	0	0	0	15	0	0	15	15	16	31
SAN DIEGO STATE	4	2	6	1	0	9	0	0	22	9	5	22	1	0	69	0	0	106	128	45	173
SAN FRANCISCO STAT	7	3	4	1	1	7	2	0	25	33	45	12	0	4	37	9	0	140	165	0	165
SAN JOSE STATE	0	3	3	0	0	5	0	0	11	4	17	12	1	1	34	0	1	70	81	36	117
SAVANNAH STATE COL	3	0	0	0	0	1	0	0	4	29	0	0	0	0	2	0	1	32	36	62	98
SHEPHERD COLLEGE	0	0	0	0	0	3	0	0	3	2	0	0	0	0	23	0	0	25	28	55	83
SHIPPENSBURG UNIV	3	0	0	0	0	8	0	0	11	4	0	1	0	0	63	0	1	69	80	35	115
SIENA COLLEGE	0	0	0	0	0	8	0	0	8	0	0	0	0	1	29	0	0	30	38	17	55
SIOUX FALLS COLL	2	0	0	0	0	5	0	0	7	0	0	2	0	0	12	0	0	14	21	11	32
SKIDMORE COLLEGE	0	0	0	0	0	1	0	0	1	2	0	0	0	0	9	1	0	12	13	6	19
SLIPPERY ROCK UNIV	1	0	0	0	0	8	0	0	9	5	0	0	0	0	52	0	0	57	66	28	94

TABLE 100 (Continued)

Number of Juniors and Seniors, by Gender and Ethnicity, and Number of Freshman and Sophomore Full-time Degree Students Enrolled in Baccalaureate Programs on 11/1/91

Program	Men									Women									Total	Frosh and Soph	Total
	African Amer	Asian Amer	Chicano	Native Amer	Puerto Rican	White	Other	Foreign	Total	African Amer	Asian Amer	Chicano	Native Amer	Puerto Rican	White	Other	Foreign	Total			
SOUTHERN CONNECTI	1	0	0	0	2	10	0	0	13	10	2	0	0	4	83	0	0	99	112	0	112
SOUTHERN ILL/CARB	4	0	1	0	0	22	0	0	27	14	0	0	0	0	120	0	0	134	161	44	205
SOUTHERN ILL/EDW	1	0	0	1	0	11	0	0	13	15	0	0	0	0	49	0	0	64	77	11	88
SOUTHERN UNIVERSIT	*	*	*	*	*	*	*	*	*	*	*	*	*	*	*	*	*	*	*	83	*
SOUTHWEST MISSOUR	0	0	0	0	0	6	0	0	6	2	0	0	0	0	87	0	2	91	97	69	166
SOUTHWEST TEXAS	2	0	7	0	0	20	0	0	29	3	0	34	0	0	112	0	0	149	178	88	266
SOUTHWESTERN COLL	2	0	0	0	0	4	0	0	6	1	0	1	0	0	12	0	0	14	20	4	24
SPALDING UNIVERSITY	0	0	0	0	0	4	0	0	4	1	0	0	0	0	10	0	0	11	15	12	27
ST CLOUD STATE	4	2	0	1	0	31	0	0	38	2	1	0	1	0	65	0	0	69	107	147	254
ST EDWARD'S UNIV	0	0	3	0	0	2	0	0	5	1	0	5	0	0	15	0	0	21	26	17	43
ST FRANCIS COLL/IN	0	0	0	0	0	1	0	0	1	1	0	0	0	0	15	0	0	16	17	39	56
ST FRANCIS COLL/PA	0	0	0	0	0	1	0	0	1	0	0	0	0	0	12	0	0	12	13	15	28
ST JOSEPH COLLEGE	0	0	0	0	0	0	0	0	0	8	0	0	0	3	25	0	0	36	36	0	36
ST LEO COLLEGE	0	0	0	0	0	3	0	0	3	1	0	0	0	0	11	0	0	12	15	5	20
ST LOUIS UNIVERSITY	0	0	0	0	0	4	0	0	4	3	0	1	0	0	21	0	0	25	29	29	58
ST MARY OF PLAINS	1	0	0	0	0	5	0	0	6	0	0	2	0	0	11	0	0	13	19	1	20
ST OLAF COLLEGE	0	0	0	0	0	5	0	0	5	0	0	0	0	0	10	0	0	10	15	11	26
STATE UNIV COLL	2	0	0	0	1	14	0	0	17	7	0	0	1	2	98	0	0	108	125	21	146
STEPHEN F AUSTIN	0	0	0	0	0	18	0	0	18	11	1	5	1	0	103	0	0	121	139	76	215
SUNY/ALBANY	3	0	0	0	0	6	0	0	9	5	0	1	0	0	28	11	0	45	54	0	54
SUNY/STONY BROOK	1	0	0	0	0	6	0	0	7	8	0	0	0	3	33	1	0	45	52	0	52
SYRACUSE UNIVERSIT	5	0	1	0	0	6	0	0	12	10	0	1	0	0	44	0	0	55	67	98	165
TABOR COLLEGE	0	0	0	0	0	1	0	0	1	0	0	0	0	0	2	0	0	2	3	0	3
TALLADEGA COLLEGE	6	0	0	0	0	0	0	0	6	8	0	0	0	0	0	0	0	8	14	40	54
TARLETON STATE UNIV	1	0	1	0	0	8	0	0	10	3	0	0	0	0	32	1	0	36	46	28	74
TAYLOR UNIVERSITY	0	0	0	0	0	4	0	0	4	2	0	0	0	0	35	0	0	37	41	24	65
TEIKYO MARYCREST	1	0	0	0	0	3	0	0	4	3	0	0	0	0	21	0	0	24	28	7	35
TEMPLE UNIVERSITY	11	2	0	0	0	7	0	0	20	39	0	0	0	2	40	0	1	82	102	78	180
TENNESSEE STATE UN	1	0	0	0	0	2	0	0	3	29	0	0	0	0	4	0	0	33	36	54	90
TEXAS CHRISTIAN	4	0	1	0	0	4	0	0	9	7	0	0	0	0	44	0	0	53	62	44	106
TEXAS TECH UNIV	1	0	2	0	0	8	0	0	11	4	0	12	0	0	33	0	0	49	60	37	97
TEXAS WOMAN'S UNIV	0	0	0	0	0	0	0	0	0	14	0	0	0	0	43	0	0	57	57	24	81
THOMAS MORE COLLE	1	0	0	0	0	0	0	0	1	0	0	0	0	0	11	0	0	11	12	0	12
TROY STATE UNIV	2	0	0	0	0	0	0	0	2	11	0	0	0	0	31	0	0	42	44	39	83
TUSKEGEE UNIVERSIT	7	0	0	0	0	0	0	0	7	23	0	0	0	0	0	0	0	23	30	35	65
U OF AKRON	5	0	0	0	0	20	0	0	25	16	0	0	0	0	79	1	0	96	121	82	203
U OF ALABAMA/BIRM	7	0	0	0	0	8	0	0	15	17	0	0	0	0	62	0	0	79	94	36	130
U OF ALABAMA/TUSC	5	0	1	0	0	9	0	0	15	15	0	1	0	0	64	0	0	80	95	46	141
U OF ALASKA/ANCHOR	3	0	0	0	0	4	0	0	7	1	0	0	5	0	26	0	1	32	39	27	66
U OF ALASKA/FAIRB	0	0	0	3	0	2	0	0	5	1	0	1	9	0	26	0	1	38	43	24	67
U OF ARKANSAS/FAY	3	0	0	0	0	7	0	0	10	3	0	2	1	0	47	0	0	53	63	58	121
U OF ARKANSAS/PINE	2	0	0	0	0	1	0	0	3	31	0	0	0	0	2	0	0	33	36	29	65
U OF CENTRAL FLORID	0	0	0	0	0	2	1	0	3	4	0	0	0	0	26	4	0	34	37	16	53

TABLE 100 (Continued)

Number of Juniors and Seniors, by Gender and Ethnicity, and Number of Freshman and Sophomore Full-time Degree Students Enrolled in Baccalaureate Programs on 11/1/91

Program	Men African Amer	Asian Amer	Chicano	Native Amer	Puerto Rican	White	Other	Foreign	Total	Women African Amer	Asian Amer	Chicano	Native Amer	Puerto Rican	White	Other	Foreign	Total	Juniors and Seniors Total	Frosh and Soph Total	Total
U OF CINCINNATI	2	0	0	0	0	6	0	0	8	10	0	0	1	0	34	0	0	45	53	0	53
U OF DAYTON	0	0	0	0	0	0	0	0	0	2	0	0	0	0	16	0	0	18	18	0	18
U OF DC	0	0	0	0	0	1	0	0	1	13	0	0	0	0	5	0	1	19	20	23	43
U OF DETROIT MERCY	5	0	0	0	0	2	0	0	7	20	0	0	0	0	7	0	0	27	34	26	60
U OF DUBUQUE	0	0	0	0	0	1	0	0	2	0	0	0	0	0	10	0	0	10	12	8	20
U OF GEORGIA	4	0	0	0	0	14	0	0	18	14	1	0	0	0	126	0	0	141	159	70	229
U OF HAWAII	1	4	0	0	0	2	2	0	9	1	13	8	0	1	14	9	0	46	55	0	55
U OF ILLINOIS/CHI	3	0	1	0	0	7	0	0	11	6	1	5	1	2	54	0	0	69	80	0	80
U OF ILLINOIS/URB	0	2	0	0	0	9	0	0	11	1	3	2	0	0	40	0	0	46	57	14	71
U OF IOWA	1	0	0	0	0	12	0	0	13	2	0	2	0	0	50	0	1	55	68	41	109
U OF KANSAS	1	0	0	2	0	15	1	0	19	7	0	1	9	0	98	0	0	115	134	28	162
U OF KENTUCKY	13	0	0	0	0	15	0	1	29	6	0	0	0	0	98	0	1	105	134	55	189
U OF MAINE	0	0	0	0	0	10	2	0	12	0	0	0	0	0	37	5	0	42	54	16	70
U OF MARY	0	0	0	3	0	12	0	0	15	0	0	0	7	0	47	0	0	54	69	40	109
U OF MARYLAND	4	0	0	0	0	24	0	1	29	41	3	4	0	0	160	0	2	210	239	103	342
U OF MISSISSIPPI	3	0	0	0	0	10	0	0	13	10	0	0	0	0	79	0	0	89	102	30	132
U OF MISSOURI/COL	0	0	0	0	0	7	0	0	7	4	0	1	1	0	62	0	0	68	75	41	116
U OF MISSOURI/STL	1	0	0	0	0	11	0	0	12	20	0	1	0	0	45	5	0	66	78	15	93
U OF MONTANA	2	0	0	6	0	23	0	0	31	0	0	1	14	0	105	0	0	120	151	55	206
U OF MONTEVALLO	1	0	0	0	0	2	0	0	3	5	0	0	0	0	26	0	0	31	34	23	57
U OF NEBRASKA/KEAR	0	0	0	0	0	6	0	0	6	11	1	0	1	0	45	0	0	47	53	56	109
U OF NEBRASKA/OMA	1	0	1	0	0	6	0	0	8	2	0	1	0	0	63	1	0	69	77	62	139
U OF NEVADA/LV	2	0	1	0	0	11	0	0	12	10	1	2	1	0	19	1	0	33	45	30	75
U OF NEVADA/RENO	0	0	0	0	0	19	0	0	19	0	0	3	1	0	59	1	0	65	84	36	120
U OF NEW HAMPSHIRE	0	0	0	0	0	5	0	0	5	5	0	0	0	0	52	0	0	52	57	30	87
U OF NORTH ALABAMA	9	0	0	0	0	16	0	0	25	11	0	0	0	0	68	0	0	79	104	50	154
U OF NORTH CAR/GRN	2	0	0	0	0	5	0	0	7	10	1	0	0	0	32	0	0	43	50	17	67
U OF NORTH DAKOTA	1	0	0	1	0	29	3	0	34	0	1	2	7	0	87	1	0	98	132	72	204
U OF NORTH TEXAS	*	*	*	*	*	*	*	*	*	*	*	*	*	*	*	*	*	*	*	26	225
U OF NORTHERN IOWA	0	0	2	1	0	17	0	0	19	1	0	0	1	0	127	0	0	129	148	77	225
U OF OKLAHOMA	1	0	0	1	0	5	0	0	8	2	1	0	6	0	52	0	0	61	69	2	71
U OF PITTSBURGH	1	0	0	0	0	6	0	0	7	20	0	1	0	0	57	0	0	78	85	0	85
U OF PUERTO RICO/HU	0	0	0	0	34	0	0	0	34	0	0	0	0	43	0	0	0	43	77	75	152
U OF PUERTO RICO/RI	0	0	0	0	20	0	0	0	20	0	0	0	0	157	0	0	0	157	177	43	220
U OF SACRED HEART	0	0	0	0	2	0	0	0	2	0	0	0	0	33	0	0	0	33	35	28	63
U OF SOUTH DAKOTA	0	0	0	0	0	0	0	0	2	0	0	0	3	0	46	0	0	49	51	55	106
U OF SOUTH FLORIDA	0	0	1	0	0	11	0	0	12	12	0	2	0	0	61	0	0	75	87	0	87
U OF SOUTHERN IND	0	0	0	0	0	6	0	0	6	4	0	0	0	0	50	0	0	54	60	73	133
U OF SOUTHERN MAIN	0	0	0	0	0	6	3	0	9	0	1	0	1	1	41	21	0	65	74	56	130
U OF ST THOMAS	0	0	0	0	0	5	0	0	5	1	0	2	0	0	22	0	0	25	30	0	30
U OF TENNESSEE/KNO	0	0	0	0	0	4	0	0	4	7	0	0	0	0	43	0	0	50	54	36	90
U OF TENNESSEE/MAR	1	0	0	0	0	9	0	0	10	9	0	0	0	0	39	0	0	50	60	63	123
U OF TEXAS/ARLINGTO	2	0	2	0	0	9	0	0	13	9	2	6	0	0	64	0	0	81	94	42	136

TABLE 100 (Continued)

Number of Juniors and Seniors, by Gender and Ethnicity, and Number of Freshman and Sophomore Full-time Degree Students Enrolled in Baccalaureate Programs on 11/1/91

Program	Men African Amer	Asian Amer	Chicano	Native Amer	Puerto Rican	White	Other	Foreign	Total	Women African Amer	Asian Amer	Chicano	Native Amer	Puerto Rican	White	Other	Foreign	Total	Total	Frosh and Soph	Total
U OF TEXAS/AUSTIN	8	0	0	0	0	12	0	0	20	10	7	16	0	0	94	0	1	128	148	30	178
U OF TOLEDO	1	0	0	0	0	4	0	0	5	8	0	0	0	0	40	0	0	48	53	66	119
U OF VERMONT	0	0	0	0	0	1	0	0	1	0	1	1	0	0	17	0	0	19	20	39	59
U OF WASHINGTON	3	2	0	1	0	7	0	0	13	7	6	0	2	0	31	2	0	48	61	5	66
U OF WEST FLORIDA	2	0	0	0	0	11	1	0	14	10	0	0	0	0	44	0	0	54	68	2	70
U OF WISCONSIN/EAU	2	1	0	0	0	17	0	0	20	1	1	0	1	0	99	1	1	104	124	83	207
U OF WISCONSIN/GB	0	1	1	0	0	7	0	0	9	0	2	0	1	0	46	0	0	49	58	26	84
U OF WISCONSIN/LAC	2	0	0	0	0	6	0	0	8	0	4	0	1	0	78	0	0	83	91	66	157
U OF WISCONSIN/MAD	0	1	1	1	0	8	0	0	11	0	1	0	4	0	70	0	1	76	87	0	87
U OF WISCONSIN/MIL	1	0	1	2	0	22	1	0	27	6	1	1	4	0	102	1	0	115	142	98	240
U OF WISCONSIN/OSH	3	2	0	0	0	13	0	0	18	0	2	1	1	0	116	0	0	120	138	92	230
U OF WISCONSIN/SUP	0	2	0	1	0	13	0	0	16	0	0	0	2	0	26	0	0	28	44	32	76
U OF WISCONSIN/WHI	3	0	2	0	0	20	0	0	25	2	1	0	1	0	107	0	0	111	136	83	219
U OF WYOMING	2	0	4	4	0	25	0	0	35	1	0	7	5	0	80	1	0	94	129	43	172
UPSALA COLLEGE	0	0	0	0	0	0	0	0	0	6	0	0	0	0	7	0	1	14	14	5	19
UTAH STATE UNIV	1	0	0	0	0	5	0	1	7	0	1	1	0	0	66	0	0	68	75	65	140
VALPARAISO UNIV	1	0	0	0	0	2	0	0	3	1	1	0	0	0	38	0	0	40	43	31	74
VIRGINIA COMMON	3	0	2	0	0	11	0	0	16	12	1	0	1	0	65	0	0	79	95	60	155
VIRGINIA INTERMONT	3	0	0	0	0	0	0	0	3	2	0	0	0	0	22	0	0	24	27	10	37
VIRGINIA UNION UNIV	8	0	0	0	0	0	0	0	8	26	0	0	0	0	0	0	0	26	34	41	75
WARTBURG COLLEGE	0	0	0	0	0	3	0	0	3	1	0	0	0	0	24	0	0	25	28	34	62
WASHBURN UNIV	6	1	0	1	0	13	0	0	21	2	0	5	1	0	77	1	0	85	106	66	172
WAYNE STATE UNIV	6	0	1	0	0	17	0	0	24	54	1	2	2	0	101	1	0	161	185	0	185
WEBER STATE UNIV	3	1	1	0	0	36	1	0	42	1	1	4	2	0	118	1	0	127	169	128	297
WEST CHESTER UNIV	0	0	0	0	0	6	0	0	6	7	0	0	0	0	50	0	1	58	64	37	101
WEST TEXAS STATE	0	0	1	0	0	8	0	0	9	3	0	10	0	0	52	0	0	65	74	39	113
WEST VIRGINIA STATE	1	0	0	0	0	1	0	0	2	2	0	0	0	0	12	0	0	14	16	9	25
WEST VIRGINIA UNIV	3	0	0	0	0	7	0	0	10	3	0	0	0	0	70	0	0	73	83	95	178
WEST VIRGINIA WESL	0	0	0	0	0	0	0	0	0	0	0	0	0	0	4	0	1	5	5	0	5
WESTERN CAROLINA	0	1	0	1	0	16	0	0	18	2	0	0	2	0	50	0	0	54	72	20	92
WESTERN CONNECTIC	1	0	0	0	0	10	0	0	11	2	0	0	0	0	33	1	1	37	48	39	87
WESTERN KENTUCKY	3	0	0	0	0	8	0	0	11	6	0	0	0	0	57	0	0	63	74	58	132
WESTERN MARYLAND	0	0	0	0	0	2	0	0	2	0	0	0	0	0	17	0	0	17	19	20	39
WESTERN MICHIGAN	3	0	0	0	0	14	0	0	17	15	0	3	2	0	139	0	0	159	176	94	270
WESTERN NEW ENGLA	0	0	0	0	0	5	0	0	5	2	0	0	0	0	14	0	0	16	21	30	51
WHEELOCK COLLEGE	0	0	0	0	0	1	0	0	1	8	2	0	0	0	46	1	0	57	58	0	58
WICHITA STATE UNIV	4	0	2	1	0	16	0	0	23	8	1	5	0	0	74	0	1	89	112	9	121
WIDENER UNIVERSITY	0	0	0	0	0	3	0	0	3	0	0	0	0	0	21	0	0	21	24	21	45
WILLIAM WOODS COLL	0	0	0	0	0	0	0	0	0	2	0	0	0	0	12	0	0	14	14	22	36
WINONA STATE UNIV	0	0	0	0	0	10	1	1	12	1	0	0	0	0	62	0	0	63	75	70	145
WINTHROP COLLEGE	3	0	0	0	0	1	0	0	4	16	0	0	0	0	29	0	0	45	49	22	71
WRIGHT STATE UNIV	0	0	0	1	0	11	1	0	13	7	1	0	0	0	60	1	0	69	82	32	114
XAVIER UNIVERSITY	1	0	0	0	0	3	0	0	4	2	0	0	0	0	16	0	0	18	22	14	36
YORK COLLEGE	6	0	0	0	0	1	3	0	10	35	0	0	0	16	2	3	0	56	66	173	239

* Missing data

56

TABLE 101

Students Awarded Baccalaureate Degrees 1990 - 1991, by Gender and Ethnicity

Program	Men									Women									Total
	African Amer	Asian Amer	Chicano	Native Amer	Puerto Rican	White	Other	Foreign	Total	African Amer	Asian Amer	Chicano	Native Amer	Puerto Rican	White	Other	Foreign	Total	
TOTAL:																			
Number	177	26	44	13	63	819	24	11	1,177	999	83	186	76	220	5,898	94	45	7,601	8,778
Percent	2.0%	0.3%	0.5%	0.1%	0.7%	9.3%	0.3%	0.1%	13.4%	11.4%	0.9%	2.1%	0.9%	2.5%	67.2%	1.1%	0.5%	86.6%	100.0%
ABILENE CHRISTIAN	2	0	0	0	0	3	0	0	5	1	0	0	0	0	16	0	0	17	22
ADELPHI UNIVERSITY	0	0	0	0	1	3	1	0	5	4	1	0	0	1	28	1	0	34	39
ALABAMA A&M UNIV	0	0	0	0	0	0	0	0	0	4	1	0	0	0	0	0	0	5	5
ALABAMA STATE UNIV	1	0	0	0	0	0	0	0	1	6	0	0	0	0	0	0	0	6	7
ALBRIGHT COLLEGE	0	0	0	0	0	0	0	0	0	0	0	0	0	0	3	0	0	3	3
ALDERSON-BROADDUS	0	0	0	0	0	1	0	0	1	0	0	0	0	0	5	0	0	5	6
ANDERSON UNIVERSITY	0	0	0	0	0	2	0	0	2	0	0	0	0	0	17	1	0	18	20
ANNA MARIA COLLEGE	0	0	0	0	0	0	0	0	0	0	0	0	0	0	6	0	0	6	6
APPALACHIAN STATE	0	0	0	0	0	1	0	0	1	0	0	1	0	0	16	0	0	17	18
ARIZONA STATE UNIV	0	0	0	0	0	6	0	0	6	4	0	14	3	0	44	0	0	65	71
ARKANSAS COLLEGE	0	0	0	0	0	1	0	0	1	0	0	0	0	0	2	0	0	2	3
ARKANSAS STATE UNIV	0	0	0	0	0	4	0	0	4	11	0	2	0	0	31	0	0	44	48
ASHLAND UNIVERSITY	0	0	0	0	0	0	0	0	0	0	0	0	0	0	6	0	0	6	6
ATLANTIC UNION COLL	1	0	0	0	0	0	0	0	1	6	0	0	0	0	1	0	0	7	8
AUBURN UNIVERSITY	1	0	0	0	0	2	0	0	3	3	0	0	1	0	31	1	0	36	39
AUGUSTANA COLL/IL	0	0	0	0	0	1	0	1	2	0	0	0	0	0	7	0	0	7	9
AUGUSTANA COLL/SD	0	0	0	0	0	0	0	0	0	0	0	0	0	0	10	0	0	10	10
AURORA UNIVERSITY	0	0	0	0	0	0	0	0	0	5	0	0	0	0	13	0	0	18	18
AUSTIN PEAY STATE	0	0	0	0	0	1	0	0	1	2	0	0	0	0	1	0	0	3	4
AVILA COLLEGE	0	0	0	0	0	1	0	0	1	2	0	0	0	0	6	0	0	8	9
AZUSA PACIFIC UNIV	0	0	0	0	0	1	0	0	1	1	1	3	2	0	9	0	0	16	17
BALL STATE UNIV	1	1	0	0	0	5	0	0	7	8	0	0	0	0	50	0	0	58	65
BAYLOR UNIVERSITY	0	0	0	0	0	1	0	0	1	0	0	0	0	0	15	0	0	15	16
BEMIDJI STATE UNIV	0	0	0	0	0	5	0	0	5	0	0	0	0	0	14	2	0	16	21
BENEDICT COLLEGE	2	0	0	0	0	1	0	0	3	20	0	0	0	0	0	0	0	20	23
BENNETT COLLEGE	0	0	0	0	0	0	0	0	0	2	0	0	0	0	0	0	0	2	2
BETHANY COLLEGE/KS	0	0	0	0	0	2	0	0	2	0	0	0	0	0	7	0	0	7	9
BETHANY COLLEGE/WV	0	0	0	0	0	0	0	0	0	0	0	0	0	0	3	0	0	3	3
BETHEL COLLEGE/KS	0	0	0	0	0	1	0	1	2	0	0	0	0	0	7	0	0	7	9
BETHEL COLLEGE/MN	0	0	0	0	0	1	0	0	1	0	0	0	0	0	14	0	0	14	15
BLOOMSBURG UNIV	0	0	0	0	0	4	0	0	4	1	0	0	0	0	26	0	0	27	31
BLUFFTON COLLEGE	0	0	0	0	0	0	0	0	0	0	0	0	0	0	3	0	0	3	3
BOISE STATE UNIV	0	0	0	0	0	1	0	0	1	0	0	0	0	0	23	0	0	23	24
BOSTON UNIVERSITY	0	0	0	0	0	0	0	0	0	0	0	0	0	0	4	0	1	5	5
BOWIE STATE UNIV	0	0	0	0	0	0	0	0	0	8	0	0	0	0	4	0	0	12	12
BOWLING GREEN STATE	0	0	0	0	0	4	0	0	4	1	0	0	0	0	50	0	0	51	55
BRIAR CLIFF COLLEGE	0	0	0	0	0	1	0	0	1	0	0	0	0	0	16	1	0	16	17
BRIDGEWATER STATE	0	0	0	0	0	2	0	0	2	2	0	0	0	0	33	0	0	36	38
BRIGHAM YOUNG/HI	0	0	0	1	0	1	0	1	3	0	0	0	0	0	3	0	5	8	11
BRIGHAM YOUNG/UT	1	1	1	1	0	12	0	0	15	0	0	1	0	0	47	0	0	48	63

TABLE 101 (Continued)

Students Awarded Baccalaureate Degrees 1990 - 1991, by Gender and Ethnicity

Program	Men									Women									Total
	African Amer	Asian Amer	Chicano	Native Amer	Puerto Rican	White	Other	Foreign	Total	African Amer	Asian Amer	Chicano	Native Amer	Puerto Rican	White	Other	Foreign	Total	
BUENA VISTA COLLEGE	0	0	0	0	0	0	0	0	0	0	0	0	0	0	10	0	0	10	10
BUFFALO STATE COLL	2	0	0	0	0	13	0	0	15	14	1	0	1	6	68	0	0	90	105
CAL STATE POLY	0	1	2	0	0	2	0	0	5	3	2	8	0	0	11	0	0	24	29
CAL STATE UNIV/CHICO	0	0	2	0	0	3	0	0	5	0	0	2	0	0	18	0	0	20	25
CAL STATE UNIV/FRES	1	3	1	0	0	2	0	0	7	8	1	8	0	0	17	4	0	38	45
CAL STATE UNIV/LB	1	1	2	0	0	4	0	0	8	5	7	9	0	0	39	0	0	60	68
CAL STATE UNIV/SAC	1	2	2	0	0	4	1	0	10	3	3	4	2	0	47	1	0	60	70
CALIFORNIA UNIV/PA	1	0	0	0	0	2	0	0	3	1	0	0	0	0	16	0	0	17	20
CAPITAL UNIVERSITY	0	0	0	0	0	1	0	0	1	0	0	0	0	0	16	0	0	16	17
CARROLL COLLEGE/MT	0	0	0	0	0	3	0	0	3	0	0	0	0	0	20	0	0	20	23
CARTHAGE COLLEGE	0	0	0	0	0	0	0	0	0	0	0	0	1	0	6	0	0	7	7
CASTLETON STATE UNIV	0	0	0	0	0	1	0	0	1	0	0	0	0	0	4	0	0	4	5
CATHOLIC UNIV/DC	0	0	0	0	0	2	0	0	2	0	0	0	0	0	9	0	0	9	11
CATHOLIC UNIV/PR	0	0	0	0	7	0	0	0	7	0	0	0	0	29	0	0	0	29	36
CEDAR CREST COLLEGE	0	0	0	0	0	0	0	0	0	0	0	0	0	0	3	0	0	3	3
CENTRAL MISSOURI	0	0	0	0	0	2	0	0	2	1	0	0	0	0	25	0	0	26	28
CHRISTOPHER NEWPORT	0	0	0	0	0	0	0	0	0	4	0	0	0	0	5	0	0	9	9
CLARK ATLANTA UNIV	0	0	0	0	0	0	0	0	0	8	0	0	0	0	0	0	0	8	8
CLARKE COLLEGE	0	0	0	0	0	0	0	0	0	1	0	0	0	0	4	0	0	5	5
CLEVELAND STATE	1	0	0	0	0	15	0	0	16	15	0	0	0	0	46	0	0	61	77
COLL MISERICORDIA	0	0	0	0	0	2	0	0	2	0	0	0	0	0	13	0	0	13	15
COLL OF NEW ROCHELLE	0	0	0	0	0	0	0	0	0	0	0	0	0	1	4	0	0	5	5
COLL OF ST BENEDICT	1	0	0	0	0	1	0	0	2	0	0	0	0	0	13	0	0	13	15
COLL OF ST CATHERINE	0	0	0	0	0	0	0	0	0	1	0	0	0	0	38	0	0	39	39
COLL OF ST SCHOL	0	0	0	0	0	0	0	0	0	0	0	0	1	0	16	0	0	17	17
COLORADO STATE UNIV	0	1	0	0	0	2	0	0	3	3	1	2	1	0	37	0	0	44	47
COLUMBIA COLLEGE/SC	0	0	0	0	0	0	0	0	0	2	0	0	0	0	10	0	0	12	12
CONCORD COLLEGE	0	0	0	0	0	4	0	0	4	1	0	0	0	0	17	0	0	18	22
CONCORDIA COLL/MN	0	0	0	0	0	7	0	0	7	0	0	0	0	0	14	0	3	17	24
CONCORDIA COLL/NY	0	0	0	0	0	3	0	0	3	1	0	0	0	0	2	0	1	4	7
COPPIN STATE COLL	0	0	0	0	0	0	0	0	0	13	0	0	0	0	0	0	0	13	13
D'YOUVILLE COLLEGE	0	0	0	0	0	0	0	0	0	2	0	0	0	0	3	0	0	5	5
DAEMEN COLLEGE	0	0	0	0	0	1	0	0	1	0	0	0	0	0	5	0	0	5	6
DANA COLLEGE	0	0	0	0	0	0	0	0	0	0	0	0	0	0	5	0	1	6	6
DEFIANCE COLLEGE	0	0	0	0	0	0	0	0	0	1	0	0	0	0	10	0	0	11	11
DELTA STATE UNIV	0	0	0	0	0	0	0	0	0	3	0	0	0	0	7	0	0	10	10
DOMINICAN COLLEGE	0	0	0	0	0	1	0	0	1	2	0	0	0	0	10	0	0	12	13
DORDT COLLEGE	0	0	0	0	0	3	0	0	3	0	0	0	0	0	12	0	2	14	17
EAST CAROLINA UNIV	2	0	0	0	0	4	0	0	6	10	0	0	0	1	33	0	0	44	50
EAST CENTRAL OKLA	0	0	0	1	0	6	0	0	7	0	0	0	2	0	10	0	0	12	19
EAST TENNESSEE STATE	0	0	0	0	0	8	0	0	8	1	0	0	0	0	25	0	0	26	34
EAST TEXAS STATE	0	0	0	0	0	3	0	0	3	8	0	1	0	0	22	0	0	31	34
EASTERN COLLEGE	0	0	0	0	0	2	0	0	2	2	0	0	0	0	3	0	0	5	7
EASTERN MENNONITE	0	0	0	0	0	2	0	0	2	0	0	0	0	0	11	0	0	11	13

58

TABLE 101 (Continued)

Students Awarded Baccalaureate Degrees 1990 - 1991, by Gender and Ethnicity

Program	Men									Women									Total
	African Amer	Asian Amer	Chicano	Native Amer	Puerto Rican	White	Other	Foreign	Total	African Amer	Asian Amer	Chicano	Native Amer	Puerto Rican	White	Other	Foreign	Total	
EASTERN MICHIGAN	3	0	1	0	0	4	0	0	8	14	1	0	0	0	70	0	1	86	94
EASTERN NAZARENE	0	0	0	0	0	1	1	0	2	0	0	0	0	0	9	0	0	9	11
EASTERN WASHINGTON	2	0	0	0	0	3	0	0	5	0	0	1	1	0	25	0	0	27	32
EDINBORO UNIVERSITY	0	0	0	0	0	4	0	0	4	4	0	0	1	0	20	0	0	25	29
ELIZABETHTOWN COLL	0	0	0	0	0	1	0	0	1	0	0	0	0	0	9	0	0	9	10
ELMS COLLEGE	0	0	0	0	0	1	0	0	1	4	0	0	0	0	13	0	0	17	18
FERRIS STATE UNIV	3	0	0	0	0	9	0	0	12	5	0	0	1	0	47	0	0	53	65
FERRUM COLLEGE	0	0	0	0	0	0	0	0	0	1	0	0	0	0	8	0	0	9	9
FLORIDA A&M UNIV	0	0	0	0	0	1	0	0	1	17	0	0	0	0	2	0	0	19	20
FLORIDA ATLANTIC	0	1	0	0	0	2	0	0	3	2	0	0	0	0	36	1	0	39	42
FLORIDA INTERNATL	2	0	0	0	0	2	1	0	5	10	0	0	0	0	11	12	0	33	38
FLORIDA STATE UNIV	1	1	0	0	0	18	0	0	20	21	0	0	0	0	101	0	1	123	143
FREED-HARDEMAN UNIV	0	0	0	0	0	1	0	0	1	2	0	0	0	0	6	0	0	8	9
GALLAUDET UNIVERSITY	0	0	0	0	0	0	0	1	1	0	0	0	0	0	5	0	0	5	6
GANNON UNIVERSITY	1	0	0	0	0	1	0	0	2	1	0	0	0	0	4	0	0	5	7
GEORGE MASON UNIV	0	0	0	0	0	4	0	0	4	1	0	1	0	0	21	0	0	23	27
GEORGIA STATE UNIV	0	0	0	0	0	6	0	0	6	7	0	2	0	0	19	0	0	28	34
GORDON COLLEGE	0	0	0	0	0	1	0	0	1	0	0	0	0	0	12	0	0	12	13
GOSHEN COLLEGE	0	0	0	0	0	3	0	1	4	0	0	1	1	0	10	0	0	12	16
GRAMBLING STATE	6	0	0	0	0	0	0	0	6	23	0	0	0	0	2	0	0	25	31
GRAND VALLEY STATE	0	0	1	0	0	2	0	0	3	1	0	2	0	0	16	0	0	19	22
HAMPTON UNIVERSITY	2	0	0	0	0	0	0	0	2	6	0	0	0	0	0	0	0	6	8
HARDIN-SIMMONS UNIV	1	0	0	0	0	1	0	0	2	0	0	1	0	0	11	0	0	12	14
HARDING UNIVERSITY	0	0	0	0	0	2	0	0	2	0	0	1	1	0	5	0	0	7	9
HERBERT H. LEHMAN	4	0	0	0	17	1	0	0	22	26	0	0	0	2	4	0	0	32	54
HOOD COLLEGE	0	0	0	0	0	0	0	0	0	1	0	0	0	0	9	0	0	10	10
HOWARD UNIVERSITY	3	0	0	0	0	0	0	0	3	8	0	1	0	0	0	0	2	11	14
IDAHO STATE UNIV	0	0	0	0	0	7	1	0	8	0	0	0	1	0	11	0	0	12	20
ILLINOIS STATE UNIV	0	0	0	0	0	4	0	0	4	7	0	1	0	0	53	0	0	61	65
INDIANA UNIVERSITY	1	0	0	0	0	7	0	0	8	4	0	0	0	0	49	0	1	54	62
INDIANA WESLEYAN	0	0	1	0	0	0	0	0	1	2	0	0	0	0	7	0	0	9	10
INTER AMERICAN UNIV	0	0	0	0	18	0	0	0	18	0	0	0	0	57	0	0	0	57	75
IONA COLLEGE	2	0	0	0	0	0	0	0	2	2	0	0	0	3	7	0	0	12	14
IOWA STATE UNIV	0	0	0	0	0	3	0	0	3	1	0	0	0	0	29	0	0	30	33
JACKSON STATE UNIV	3	0	0	0	0	0	0	0	3	12	0	0	0	0	0	0	0	12	15
JAMES MADISON UNIV	0	0	0	0	0	2	0	0	2	3	0	0	0	0	23	0	0	26	28
JUNIATA COLLEGE	0	0	0	0	0	0	0	0	0	0	0	0	0	0	5	0	0	5	5
KANSAS STATE UNIV	0	0	0	0	0	4	0	0	4	1	0	0	0	0	32	0	0	33	37
KEAN COLLEGE	0	0	0	0	0	6	0	0	6	9	1	0	0	0	36	5	0	51	57
KEUKA COLLEGE	0	0	0	0	0	0	0	0	0	0	0	0	0	2	6	0	0	8	8
LA SIERRA UNIVERSITY	2	0	0	0	0	0	0	0	2	2	1	0	0	0	9	0	0	12	14
LAMAR UNIVERSITY	0	0	0	0	0	2	0	0	2	2	0	1	0	0	19	0	0	22	24
LIVINGSTONE COLLEGE	1	0	0	0	0	0	0	0	1	4	0	0	0	0	0	0	0	4	5

TABLE 101 (Continued)

Students Awarded Baccalaureate Degrees 1990 - 1991, by Gender and Ethnicity

Program	Men									Women									Total
	African Amer	Asian Amer	Chicano	Native Amer	Puerto Rican	White	Other	Foreign	Total	African Amer	Asian Amer	Chicano	Native Amer	Puerto Rican	White	Other	Foreign	Total	
LORAS COLLEGE	0	0	0	0	0	0	0	0	0	0	0	0	0	0	7	0	0	7	7
LOYOLA UNIVERSITY	0	0	0	0	0	1	0	0	1	4	2	0	0	0	15	0	0	21	22
LUBBOCK CHRISTIAN	0	0	0	0	0	1	0	0	1	0	0	0	0	0	3	0	0	3	4
LUTHER COLLEGE	0	1	0	0	0	2	0	0	3	0	1	0	0	0	14	0	0	15	18
MADONNA UNIVERSITY	1	0	0	0	0	2	0	0	3	2	0	1	0	0	24	0	0	27	30
MALONE COLLEGE	0	0	0	0	0	3	0	0	3	0	0	1	0	0	10	0	0	11	14
MANCHESTER COLLEGE	1	0	0	0	0	0	0	0	1	1	0	0	0	0	9	0	0	10	11
MANKATO STATE UNIV	0	2	1	0	0	4	0	0	7	1	0	0	0	0	43	0	0	44	51
MANSFIELD UNIVERSITY	0	0	0	0	0	0	0	0	0	0	0	0	0	0	12	0	0	12	12
MARIAN COLLEGE	0	0	0	0	0	0	1	0	1	0	0	0	0	0	3	0	0	3	4
MARIST COLLEGE	1	0	0	0	0	2	0	0	3	2	0	0	0	0	8	1	0	11	14
MARQUETTE UNIVERSITY	0	0	0	0	0	1	0	0	1	0	0	0	0	0	6	0	0	6	7
MARS HILL COLLEGE	1	0	0	0	0	2	0	0	3	1	0	0	0	0	4	0	0	5	8
MARSHALL UNIVERSITY	0	0	0	0	0	0	0	0	0	2	0	0	0	0	3	0	0	5	5
MARYGROVE COLLEGE	1	0	0	0	0	0	1	0	2	10	0	0	0	0	6	0	0	16	18
MARYMOUNT COLLEGE	0	0	0	0	0	0	0	0	0	0	0	0	0	1	1	0	0	2	2
MARYWOOD COLLEGE	0	0	0	0	0	1	0	0	1	0	0	0	0	0	11	0	0	11	12
MEMPHIS STATE UNIV	3	0	0	0	0	1	0	0	4	9	0	0	0	0	13	0	0	22	26
MERCY COLLEGE	2	0	0	0	0	3	0	0	5	1	0	0	0	0	4	2	0	7	12
MERCYHURST COLLEGE	0	0	0	0	0	0	0	0	0	0	0	0	0	0	6	0	0	6	6
MEREDITH COLLEGE	0	0	0	0	0	0	0	0	0	0	0	0	0	0	18	0	0	18	18
MESSIAH COLLEGE	0	0	0	0	0	1	0	0	1	0	0	0	0	0	5	0	0	5	6
MICHIGAN STATE UNIV	1	0	0	0	0	5	0	0	6	1	0	1	0	0	81	0	0	83	89
MIDDLE TENNESSE ST	0	0	0	0	0	6	0	0	6	6	0	0	0	0	14	0	0	20	26
MILLERSVILLE UNIV	0	0	0	0	0	1	0	0	1	2	0	0	0	1	25	0	0	28	29
MINOT STATE UNIV	0	0	0	0	0	4	0	0	4	0	0	0	5	0	30	0	0	35	39
MISSISSIPPI VALLEY	0	0	0	0	0	2	0	0	2	0	0	0	0	0	20	0	0	20	22
MISSOURI WESTERN	1	0	0	0	0	2	0	0	3	2	0	0	0	0	5	0	0	7	10
MONMOUTH COLLEGE	0	0	0	0	0	1	0	0	1	1	0	0	0	0	9	0	0	10	11
MOORHEAD STATE UNIV	0	0	0	0	0	7	0	0	7	0	2	0	0	0	63	0	0	65	72
MOREHEAD STATE UNIV	0	0	0	0	0	2	0	0	2	1	0	0	0	0	30	0	0	31	33
MORGAN STATE UNIV	3	0	0	0	0	0	0	0	3	25	0	0	0	0	2	0	0	27	30
MOUNT MARY COLLEGE	0	0	0	0	0	0	0	0	0	1	0	0	0	0	8	0	0	9	9
MOUNT MERCY COLLEGE	0	0	0	0	0	1	0	0	1	0	0	0	0	0	17	0	0	17	18
MURRAY STATE UNIV	0	0	0	0	0	2	0	0	2	5	0	0	0	0	20	0	0	25	27
NAZARETH COLLEGE	0	0	0	0	0	1	0	0	1	1	0	0	0	0	20	0	0	21	22
NEW MEXICO HIGHLANDS	0	0	3	0	0	0	0	0	3	0	0	9	1	0	4	0	0	14	17
NEW MEXICO STATE	1	0	2	0	0	5	0	0	8	0	1	17	3	0	23	0	0	44	52
NEW YORK UNIVERSITY	0	0	0	0	1	1	0	0	2	2	0	0	0	2	8	0	0	12	14
NIAGARA UNIVERSITY	0	0	0	0	0	1	0	0	1	1	0	0	0	0	11	0	0	12	13
NORFOLK STATE UNIV	3	0	0	0	0	0	0	0	3	19	0	0	0	0	3	0	0	22	25
NORTH CAROLINA A&T	5	0	0	0	0	0	0	0	5	10	0	0	0	0	2	0	0	12	17
NORTH CAROLINA STATE	2	0	0	0	0	4	0	0	6	9	0	1	0	0	28	0	0	38	44

TABLE 101 (Continued)

Students Awarded Baccalaureate Degrees 1990 - 1991, by Gender and Ethnicity

Program	Men									Women									Total
	African Amer	Asian Amer	Chicano	Native Amer	Puerto Rican	White	Other	Foreign	Total	African Amer	Asian Amer	Chicano	Native Amer	Puerto Rican	White	Other	Foreign	Total	
NORTHEAST LOUISIANA	0	0	0	0	0	2	0	0	2	5	0	0	0	0	13	0	1	19	21
NORTHEASTERN ILL	0	0	2	0	0	3	0	0	5	3	1	0	0	1	14	0	0	19	24
NORTHERN ARIZONA	0	0	0	0	0	1	0	0	1	0	0	4	3	0	9	0	0	16	17
NORTHERN KENTUCKY	1	0	0	0	0	2	0	0	3	0	0	0	0	0	19	0	1	20	23
NORTHERN MICHIGAN	0	0	0	0	0	7	0	0	7	1	0	0	1	0	18	0	0	20	27
NORTHWEST NAZARENE	0	0	0	0	0	0	0	1	1	0	0	0	0	0	6	0	0	6	7
NORTHWESTERN COLLEGE	0	0	0	0	0	0	0	0	0	0	0	0	0	0	9	0	1	10	10
NORTHWESTERN STATE	0	0	0	0	0	1	0	0	1	5	0	0	0	0	14	0	0	19	20
OAKWOOD COLLEGE	2	0	0	0	0	0	0	0	2	4	0	0	0	0	0	0	0	4	6
OHIO STATE UNIV	0	0	0	0	0	6	0	0	6	6	0	2	0	0	66	0	0	74	80
OHIO UNIVERSITY	1	0	0	0	0	1	0	0	2	1	0	0	0	0	18	0	0	19	21
ORAL ROBERTS UNIV	0	0	0	0	0	3	0	0	3	0	0	1	0	0	12	0	2	15	18
OUR LADY OF THE LAKE	2	0	8	0	0	2	0	0	12	3	0	12	0	0	11	0	0	26	38
PACIFIC LUTHERAN	0	0	0	0	0	5	0	0	5	2	1	0	0	0	19	0	0	22	27
PACIFIC UNION COLL	0	0	1	0	0	1	0	1	3	1	2	0	0	0	5	0	0	8	11
PAUL QUINN COLLEGE	4	0	0	0	0	0	0	0	4	3	0	0	0	0	0	0	0	3	7
PEMBROKE STATE UNIV	1	0	0	0	0	3	0	0	4	2	0	0	8	0	8	0	0	18	22
PENN STATE UNIV	0	0	1	0	0	1	0	0	2	0	0	0	0	1	10	0	0	11	13
PHIL COLL OF BIBLE	0	0	0	0	0	3	0	0	3	0	0	0	0	0	4	1	1	6	9
PITTSBURG STATE UNIV	2	0	0	0	0	5	0	0	7	2	1	0	0	0	18	0	0	21	28
PRAIRIE VIEW A&M	2	0	0	0	0	0	0	0	2	13	0	0	0	0	2	0	2	17	19
PROVIDENCE COLLEGE	0	0	0	0	0	0	0	0	0	1	0	0	0	0	4	0	0	5	5
PURDUE UNIVERSITY	0	0	0	0	0	1	0	1	2	0	1	0	0	1	11	0	0	13	15
RADFORD UNIVERSITY	0	0	0	0	0	4	0	0	4	1	0	0	0	0	23	0	0	24	28
RAMAPO COLLEGE	0	0	0	0	0	0	0	0	0	2	0	0	0	1	17	0	0	20	20
REGIS COLLEGE	0	0	0	0	0	0	0	0	0	0	0	0	0	0	9	0	0	9	9
RHODE ISLAND COLLEGE	0	0	0	0	0	2	0	0	2	0	1	0	0	0	30	4	0	35	37
ROBERTS WESLEYAN	1	0	0	0	0	0	0	0	1	0	0	0	0	0	9	1	0	10	11
ROCHESTER INST TECH	0	0	0	0	0	4	0	0	4	3	0	0	0	0	21	0	0	24	28
RUTGERS UNIV/NEWARK	1	0	0	0	0	1	0	0	2	2	0	0	0	0	3	2	0	7	9
SACRED HEART UNIV	0	0	0	0	0	1	0	0	1	0	0	0	0	0	7	0	0	7	8
SAGINAW VALLEY STATE	1	0	1	0	0	12	0	0	14	4	0	3	0	0	40	0	0	47	61
SALISBURY STATE	0	0	0	0	0	2	0	0	2	4	0	0	0	0	30	0	1	35	37
SALVE REGINA COLLEGE	0	0	0	0	0	0	0	0	0	0	0	0	0	0	9	0	0	9	9
SAN DIEGO STATE	2	1	2	0	0	5	0	0	10	3	3	6	0	0	33	0	0	45	55
SAN FRANCISCO STATE	1	2	2	0	0	3	1	0	9	4	9	0	0	0	12	4	0	29	38
SAN JOSE STATE	0	1	1	0	0	2	0	0	4	2	3	3	0	0	8	0	0	16	20
SAVANNAH STATE COLL	1	0	0	0	0	0	0	0	1	7	0	0	0	0	0	0	0	7	8
SHEPHERD COLLEGE	0	0	0	0	0	1	0	0	1	0	0	0	0	0	4	0	0	4	5
SHIPPENSBURG UNIV	2	0	0	0	0	2	0	0	4	1	0	0	0	0	23	0	0	24	28
SIENA COLLEGE	0	0	0	0	0	1	0	0	1	0	0	0	0	1	12	0	0	13	14
SIOUX FALLS COLL	0	0	0	0	0	0	0	0	0	0	0	0	0	0	4	0	0	4	4
SKIDMORE COLLEGE	0	0	0	0	0	0	0	0	0	0	0	0	0	0	2	0	0	2	2
SLIPPERY ROCK UNIV	1	0	0	0	0	2	0	0	3	0	0	0	0	0	13	0	1	14	17

TABLE 101 (Continued)

Students Awarded Baccalaureate Degrees 1990 - 1991, by Gender and Ethnicity

Program	Men									Women									Total
	African Amer	Asian Amer	Chicano	Native Amer	Puerto Rican	White	Other	Foreign	Total	African Amer	Asian Amer	Chicano	Native Amer	Puerto Rican	White	Other	Foreign	Total	
SOUTHERN CONNECTICUT	0	0	0	0	0	2	0	0	2	6	0	0	0	2	30	2	0	40	42
SOUTHERN ILL/CARB	1	0	0	0	0	17	0	0	18	3	0	0	0	0	45	0	0	48	66
SOUTHERN ILL/EDW	0	0	0	0	0	1	0	0	1	4	0	0	0	0	21	0	0	25	26
SOUTHWEST UNIVERSITY	3	0	0	0	0	2	0	0	5	20	0	0	0	0	1	0	0	21	26
SOUTHWEST MISSOURI	0	0	0	0	0	3	0	0	3	1	0	0	0	0	32	0	1	34	37
SOUTHWEST TEXAS	0	0	0	0	0	1	0	0	1	0	0	4	0	0	21	0	0	25	26
SOUTHWESTERN COLL	0	0	0	0	0	0	0	0	0	0	0	1	0	0	5	0	0	6	6
SPALDING UNIVERSITY	0	0	0	0	0	2	0	0	2	1	0	0	0	0	7	0	0	8	10
ST CLOUD STATE	0	1	0	0	0	6	0	0	7	0	0	0	0	0	54	0	0	54	61
ST EDWARD'S UNIV	0	0	0	0	0	4	0	0	4	0	0	4	0	0	4	0	0	8	12
ST FRANCIS COLL/IN	0	0	0	0	0	1	0	0	1	0	0	0	0	0	1	0	0	1	2
ST FRANCIS COLL/PA	0	0	0	0	0	2	0	0	2	0	0	0	0	0	26	0	0	26	28
ST JOSEPH COLLEGE	0	0	0	0	0	0	0	0	0	1	0	0	0	0	5	0	0	6	6
ST LEO COLLEGE	0	0	0	0	0	0	0	0	0	0	0	0	0	0	6	0	0	6	6
ST LOUIS UNIVERSITY	0	0	0	0	0	1	0	0	1	1	0	1	0	0	8	0	0	10	11
ST MARY OF PLAINS	0	0	0	0	0	1	0	0	1	0	0	0	0	0	4	0	0	4	5
ST OLAF COLLEGE	0	0	0	0	0	0	0	0	0	0	0	0	0	0	2	0	0	2	2
STATE UNIV COLL	1	0	0	0	0	7	0	0	8	4	1	0	0	1	36	0	0	42	50
STEPHEN F AUSTIN	3	0	0	0	0	2	0	0	5	3	0	0	0	0	38	0	0	41	46
SUNY/ALBANY	0	1	0	0	0	3	0	0	4	4	1	0	0	0	22	3	0	30	34
SUNY/STONY BROOK	1	0	0	0	0	0	0	0	1	7	0	0	0	2	16	1	0	26	27
SYRACUSE UNIVERSITY	0	0	0	0	0	5	0	0	5	2	0	1	0	0	16	0	0	19	24
TABOR COLLEGE	0	0	0	0	0	0	0	0	0	0	0	0	0	0	9	0	0	9	9
TALLADEGA COLLEGE	1	0	0	0	0	0	0	0	1	7	0	0	0	0	0	0	0	7	8
TARLETON STATE UNIV	1	0	0	0	0	1	0	0	2	0	0	1	0	0	12	0	0	13	15
TAYLOR UNIVERSITY	0	0	0	0	0	2	0	0	2	0	0	0	0	0	12	0	0	12	14
TEIKYO MARYCREST	0	0	0	0	0	2	0	0	2	1	0	0	0	0	7	0	0	8	10
TEMPLE UNIVERSITY	1	0	0	0	0	3	0	0	4	28	1	0	0	3	26	0	0	58	62
TENNESSEE STATE UNIV	0	0	0	0	0	0	0	0	0	13	0	1	0	0	2	0	0	16	16
TEXAS CHRISTIAN	0	0	0	0	0	0	0	0	0	2	0	1	0	0	19	0	0	22	22
TEXAS TECH UNIV	0	0	0	0	0	2	0	0	2	1	0	0	0	0	8	0	0	9	11
TEXAS WOMAN'S UNIV	0	0	0	0	0	0	0	0	0	7	0	1	0	0	21	0	0	29	29
THOMAS MORE COLLEGE	0	0	0	0	0	1	0	0	1	0	0	0	0	0	3	0	0	3	4
TROY STATE UNIV	0	0	0	0	0	0	0	0	0	0	0	0	0	0	8	0	0	8	8
TUSKEGEE UNIVERSITY	4	0	0	0	0	0	0	0	4	10	0	0	0	0	0	0	0	10	14
U OF AKRON	0	0	0	0	0	12	12	0	24	8	0	0	0	0	33	5	0	46	70
U OF ALABAMA/BIRM	0	0	0	0	0	2	0	0	2	5	0	0	0	0	15	0	0	20	22
U OF ALABAMA/TUSC	0	0	0	0	0	2	0	0	2	6	0	0	0	0	19	0	0	25	27
U OF ALASKA/ANCHOR	0	0	0	0	0	2	0	0	2	1	0	0	0	0	16	0	0	17	19
U OF ALASKA/FAIRB	0	0	0	0	0	3	0	0	3	1	0	0	2	0	14	1	0	18	21
U OF ARKANSAS/FAY	0	0	0	0	0	3	0	0	3	0	0	0	0	0	10	0	0	10	13
U OF ARKANSAS/PINE	2	0	0	0	0	0	0	0	2	9	0	0	0	0	1	0	0	10	12
U OF CENTRAL FLORIDA	0	0	0	0	0	0	0	0	0	3	1	1	0	0	19	0	0	24	24

TABLE 101 (Continued)

Students Awarded Baccalaureate Degrees 1990 - 1991, by Gender and Ethnicity

Program	Men									Women									Total
	African Amer	Asian Amer	Chicano	Native Amer	Puerto Rican	White	Other	Foreign	Total	African Amer	Asian Amer	Chicano	Native Amer	Puerto Rican	White	Other	Foreign	Total	
U OF CINCINNATI	1	0	0	0	0	1	0	0	2	5	0	0	0	0	16	0	0	21	23
U OF DAYTON	0	0	0	0	0	2	0	0	2	0	0	0	0	0	17	0	0	17	19
U OF DC	0	0	0	0	0	1	0	0	1	8	0	0	0	0	1	0	4	13	14
U OF DETROIT MERCY	7	0	0	0	0	2	0	1	10	21	0	0	0	0	9	0	0	30	40
U OF DUBUQUE	0	0	1	0	0	0	0	0	1	1	0	0	0	0	0	0	0	1	2
U OF GEORGIA	2	0	0	0	0	5	0	0	7	3	0	0	0	0	33	0	0	36	43
U OF HAWAII	0	1	0	0	0	0	0	0	1	1	11	0	0	0	5	1	0	18	19
U OF ILLINOIS/CHI	1	0	2	0	0	7	0	0	10	2	0	5	0	0	20	0	0	27	37
U OF ILLINOIS/URB	0	0	0	0	0	2	0	0	2	0	1	0	0	0	21	0	1	23	25
U OF IOWA	0	1	0	0	0	4	0	0	5	1	0	0	0	0	19	0	1	21	26
U OF KANSAS	0	0	0	1	0	6	0	0	7	5	0	3	9	0	60	0	1	78	85
U OF KENTUCKY	5	1	0	0	0	11	0	0	17	6	1	0	1	0	49	0	0	57	74
U OF MAINE	0	0	0	0	0	1	0	1	2	0	0	0	1	0	19	1	2	23	25
U OF MARY	0	0	0	2	0	10	0	0	12	0	0	0	3	0	15	0	0	18	30
U OF MARYLAND	0	0	0	0	0	6	1	0	7	11	1	1	1	0	58	0	1	73	80
U OF MISSISSIPPI	1	0	0	0	0	3	0	0	4	6	0	1	0	0	30	0	0	37	41
U OF MISSOURI/COL	0	0	0	0	0	3	0	0	3	0	0	0	0	0	26	0	0	26	29
U OF MISSOURI/STL	4	0	0	0	0	7	0	0	11	15	0	0	0	0	50	0	0	65	76
U OF MONTANA	0	0	0	1	0	5	0	0	6	1	0	0	2	0	37	0	0	40	46
U OF MONTEVALLO	1	0	0	0	0	0	0	0	1	1	0	0	0	0	7	0	0	8	9
U OF NEBRASKA/KEARN	0	0	0	0	0	1	0	0	1	1	0	0	0	0	21	0	0	22	23
U OF NEBRASKA/OMAHA	1	0	0	0	0	2	0	0	3	0	0	0	0	0	29	0	0	29	32
U OF NEVADA/LV	5	0	0	0	0	3	0	0	8	4	1	1	0	0	24	0	0	30	38
U OF NEVADA/RENO	0	0	1	0	0	8	0	0	9	0	0	0	1	0	19	0	0	20	29
U OF NEW HAMPSHIRE	0	0	0	0	0	2	0	0	2	0	0	0	0	0	19	0	0	19	21
U OF NORTH ALABAMA	2	0	0	0	0	9	0	0	11	6	0	0	0	0	27	0	0	33	44
U OF NORTH CAR/GRNB	0	0	0	0	0	2	0	0	2	1	0	0	0	0	27	0	0	28	30
U OF NORTH DAKOTA	0	0	0	1	0	6	0	0	7	0	1	0	2	0	37	1	0	41	48
U OF NORTH TEXAS	0	0	0	0	0	2	0	0	2	2	0	0	0	0	23	0	0	25	27
U OF NORTHERN IOWA	0	0	0	0	0	7	0	0	7	1	0	1	0	0	54	0	0	56	63
U OF OKLAHOMA	2	0	0	1	0	3	0	0	6	4	0	1	3	0	22	0	0	30	36
U OF PITTSBURGH	1	0	0	0	0	9	0	0	10	1	0	0	1	0	25	0	0	27	37
U OF PUERTO RICO/HUM	0	0	0	0	5	0	0	0	5	0	0	0	0	20	0	0	0	20	25
U OF PUERTO RICO/RIO	0	0	0	0	11	0	0	0	11	0	0	0	0	68	0	0	0	68	79
U OF SACRED HEART	0	0	0	0	1	0	0	0	1	0	0	0	0	8	0	0	0	8	9
U OF SOUTH DAKOTA	0	0	0	0	0	2	0	0	2	0	0	0	1	0	19	0	0	20	22
U OF SOUTH FLORIDA	0	0	0	0	0	6	0	0	6	10	0	1	0	0	49	4	0	64	70
U OF SOUTHERN IND	0	0	0	0	0	2	0	0	2	0	0	0	0	0	17	0	0	17	19
U OF SOUTHERN MAINE	0	0	0	0	0	4	1	0	5	0	0	0	1	0	20	10	0	31	36
U OF ST THOMAS	0	0	0	0	0	6	0	0	6	0	0	0	0	0	3	0	0	3	9
U OF TENNESSEE/KNOX	1	0	0	0	0	1	0	0	2	2	0	0	0	0	10	0	0	12	14
U OF TENNESSEE/MART	1	0	0	0	0	1	0	0	2	4	0	0	0	0	13	0	0	17	19
U OF TEXAS/ARLINGTON	0	0	0	0	0	6	0	0	6	7	1	2	0	0	41	0	0	51	57

63

TABLE 101 (Continued)

Students Awarded Baccalaureate Degrees 1990 - 1991, by Gender and Ethnicity

Program	Men									Women									Total
	African Amer	Asian Amer	Chicano	Native Amer	Puerto Rican	White	Other	Foreign	Total	African Amer	Asian Amer	Chicano	Native Amer	Puerto Rican	White	Other	Foreign	Total	
U OF TEXAS/AUSTIN	0	0	2	0	0	5	0	0	7	1	1	3	0	0	39	0	0	44	51
U OF TOLEDO	2	0	0	0	0	1	0	0	3	0	0	0	0	0	11	0	0	11	14
U OF VERMONT	0	0	0	0	0	0	0	0	0	0	1	0	0	0	11	0	0	12	12
U OF WASHINGTON	2	2	0	1	0	1	1	0	7	5	9	3	1	0	21	1	2	42	49
U OF WEST FLORIDA	0	0	0	0	0	4	0	0	4	2	0	2	0	0	25	0	0	29	33
U OF WISCONSIN/EAU	1	0	0	0	0	6	0	0	7	0	0	0	0	0	43	0	0	43	50
U OF WISCONSIN/GB	0	0	0	1	0	5	0	0	6	2	0	0	0	0	14	0	0	16	22
U OF WISCONSIN/LAC	0	1	0	0	0	1	0	0	2	0	0	0	0	0	35	0	0	35	37
U OF WISCONSIN/MAD	0	0	0	0	0	10	0	0	10	2	1	0	0	0	52	0	0	55	65
U OF WISCONSIN/MIL	0	0	0	0	0	12	0	0	12	8	0	0	0	0	64	0	0	72	84
U OF WISCONSIN/OSH	1	0	0	0	0	3	0	0	4	1	0	1	0	0	38	0	0	40	44
U OF WISCONSIN/SUP	0	0	0	0	0	3	0	0	3	0	0	0	2	0	13	0	0	15	18
U OF WISCONSIN/WHI	0	0	0	0	0	9	0	0	9	1	0	0	0	0	53	0	0	54	63
U OF WYOMING	1	0	0	0	0	3	0	0	4	0	0	5	0	0	38	0	0	43	47
UPSALA COLLEGE	0	0	0	0	0	1	0	0	1	2	0	0	0	0	0	0	0	2	3
UTAH STATE UNIV	0	0	0	1	0	6	0	0	7	0	0	0	0	0	10	0	0	10	17
VALPARAISO UNIV	0	0	0	0	0	4	0	0	4	1	0	0	0	0	11	0	0	12	16
VIRGINIA COMMON	0	0	1	0	0	0	0	0	1	10	0	0	0	0	36	0	0	46	47
VIRGINIA INTERMONT	0	0	0	0	0	0	0	0	0	1	0	0	0	0	5	0	0	6	6
VIRGINIA UNION UNIV	0	0	0	0	0	0	0	0	0	1	0	0	0	0	0	0	0	1	1
WARTBURG COLLEGE	0	0	0	0	0	0	0	0	0	0	0	0	0	0	14	0	0	14	14
WASHBURN UNIV	1	0	0	0	0	5	0	0	6	2	0	0	0	0	24	0	0	26	32
WAYNE STATE UNIV	3	0	0	0	0	7	0	0	10	11	1	1	0	0	36	0	0	49	59
WEBER STATE UNIV	0	0	1	1	0	11	0	0	13	0	1	1	2	0	48	1	0	53	66
WEST CHESTER UNIV	0	0	0	0	0	0	0	0	0	2	0	0	0	0	21	0	0	23	23
WEST TEXAS STATE	1	0	0	0	0	0	0	0	1	1	0	5	0	0	23	0	0	29	30
WEST VIRGINIA STATE	1	0	0	0	0	1	0	0	2	1	0	0	0	0	8	0	0	9	11
WEST VIRGINIA UNIV	0	0	0	0	0	3	1	0	4	1	0	0	0	0	18	0	0	19	23
WEST VIRGINIA WESL	1	0	0	0	0	0	0	0	1	0	0	0	0	0	2	0	0	2	3
WESTERN CAROLINA	0	0	0	0	0	3	0	0	3	1	0	0	2	0	14	1	1	19	22
WESTERN CONNECTICUT	1	0	0	0	0	1	0	0	2	1	1	0	0	0	6	0	0	8	10
WESTERN KENTUCKY	0	0	0	0	0	4	0	0	4	0	0	0	0	0	23	0	0	23	27
WESTERN MARYLAND	0	0	0	0	0	0	0	0	0	0	0	0	0	0	7	0	0	7	7
WESTERN MICHIGAN	4	0	0	0	0	4	0	0	8	5	0	0	0	0	48	0	0	53	61
WESTERN NEW ENGLAND	0	0	0	0	0	0	0	0	0	1	0	0	0	0	10	0	0	11	11
WHEELOCK COLLEGE	0	0	0	0	0	0	0	0	0	4	0	0	0	0	12	0	0	16	16
WICHITA STATE UNIV	0	0	1	0	0	6	0	0	7	5	1	2	0	0	35	0	0	43	50
WIDENER UNIVERSITY	0	0	0	0	0	0	0	0	0	1	0	0	0	0	9	0	0	10	10
WILLIAM WOODS COLL	0	0	0	0	0	0	0	0	0	0	0	0	0	0	1	0	0	1	1
WINONA STATE UNIV	0	1	0	0	0	4	0	0	5	0	0	0	0	0	50	0	2	52	57
WINTHROP COLLEGE	2	0	0	0	0	3	0	0	5	6	0	1	0	0	19	0	0	26	31
WRIGHT STATE UNIV	0	0	0	0	0	6	0	0	6	3	1	0	0	0	34	0	0	38	44
XAVIER UNIVERSITY	0	0	0	0	0	0	0	0	0	0	0	0	0	0	7	0	0	7	7
YORK COLLEGE	1	0	0	0	2	1	0	0	4	16	0	2	0	3	2	19	0	42	46

* Missing data

TABLE 200

Applications for Admission to First-year Status in Full-time Masters Degree Programs During 1991 by Action Taken

Program	Applications				Registered				Enrollment by 11/1/91			Enrollment First Year/ Full-time
	Total Received	Considered for Admission	Accepted	Accepted But Not Registered	Accepted and Registered	Accepted in Prior Years	Total Newly Enrolled in 1991	Withdrawals	Advanced Standing in First Year	Others Still in First Year	In Second Year	
TOTAL:	23,839	21,463	13,915	5,489	8,472	157	8,555	303	227	970	205	9,298
ADELPHI UNIVERSITY	311	301	283	46	237	10	245	2	0	5	0	238
ARIZONA STATE UNIV	269	244	167	64	103	0	100	3	0	0	12	100
AURORA UNIVERSITY	56	44	41	9	32	0	32	0	0	0	0	32
BARRY UNIVERSITY	90	90	87	36	51	0	51	0	0	56	0	107
BOSTON COLLEGE	404	360	235	127	108	0	107	1	0	50	0	157
BOSTON UNIVERSITY	550	513	454	289	165	9	152	22	0	0	0	152
BRIGHAM YOUNG UNIV	113	112	26	4	22	1	23	0	0	0	0	23
BRYN MAWR COLLEGE	175	158	117	56	61	6	68	0	0	22	0	90
CAL STATE UNIV/FRES	106	106	92	30	62	0	59	3	0	0	0	59
CAL STATE UNIV/LB	143	143	27	4	23	0	23	0	0	0	0	23
CAL STATE UNIV/SAC	282	226	164	49	115	0	112	3	0	0	1	111
CASE WESTERN RESERVE	205	189	174	64	110	18	163	6	41	0	0	163
CATHOLIC UNIVERSITY	172	140	138	75	63	0	65	0	2	12	0	77
CLARK ATLANTA UNIV	78	75	73	42	31	0	31	0	0	0	0	31
COLORADO STATE UNIV	78	60	36	13	23	0	23	0	0	0	0	23
COLUMBIA UNIVERSITY	974	660	575	328	247	10	252	5	0	0	26	226
EAST CAROLINA UNIV	42	42	26	0	26	0	23	3	0	0	0	23
EASTERN WASHINGTON	195	176	67	27	40	0	38	2	0	0	0	38
FLORIDA INTERNATL	227	222	115	35	80	0	80	0	0	0	0	80
FLORIDA STATE UNIV	159	136	113	17	96	0	96	0	0	0	0	96
FORDHAM UNIVERSITY	418	412	346	218	128	0	128	0	0	99	0	227
GRAMBLING STATE	63	55	45	11	34	2	34	2	0	10	1	43
GRAND VALLEY STATE	76	69	53	3	50	2	52	2	2	33	21	64
HOWARD UNIVERSITY	191	152	146	93	53	2	57	4	6	9	8	58
HUNTER COLLEGE	869	760	271	90	181	0	165	16	0	2	0	167
INDIANA UNIVERSITY	279	279	126	30	96	0	94	2	0	0	0	94
LOUISIANA STATE UNIV	187	125	87	6	81	0	80	1	0	0	0	80
LOYOLA UNIVERSITY	173	173	169	51	118	0	118	0	0	0	0	118
MARYWOOD COLLEGE	45	38	36	12	24	1	27	1	3	37	6	58
MICHIGAN STATE UNIV	187	187	70	26	44	0	43	1	0	12	0	55
NEW MEXICO HIGHLANDS	100	91	47	10	37	0	34	3	0	0	0	34
NEW YORK UNIVERSITY	717	679	515	292	223	0	216	7	0	0	28	188
NORFOLK STATE UNIV	108	88	61	10	51	5	54	2	0	9	0	63
OHIO STATE UNIV	292	215	178	65	113	0	109	4	0	0	0	109
OUR LADY OF THE LAKE	85	78	70	18	52	0	51	1	0	47	0	98
PORTLAND STATE UNIV	302	261	112	28	84	0	79	5	0	0	0	79
RHODE ISLAND COLLEGE	128	128	49	14	35	2	37	0	0	0	0	37
RUTGERS UNIVERSITY	309	217	193	62	131	11	137	8	3	0	0	137
SAN DIEGO STATE	345	345	121	40	81	0	80	1	0	0	0	80
SAN FRANCISCO STATE	379	379	62	17	45	1	46	0	0	5	0	49
SAN JOSE STATE	176	148	108	31	77	1	74	4	0	0	2	74
SIMMONS COLLEGE	357	357	245	146	99	0	99	0	0	0	0	99

TABLE 200 (Continued)

Applications for Admission to First-year Status in Full-time Masters Degree Programs During 1991 by Action Taken

Program	Applications				Registered			Withdrawals	Enrollment by 11/1/91			
	Total Received	Considered for Admission	Accepted	Accepted But Not Registered	Accepted and Registered	Accepted in Prior Years	Total Newly Enrolled in 1991		Advanced Standing in First Year	Others Still in First Year	In Second Year	Enrollment First Year/ Full-time
SMITH COLLEGE	413	411	201	99	102	7	107	2	0	0	0	107
SOUTHERN BAPTIST	56	56	38	4	34	0	33	1	0	36	0	69
SOUTHERN CONNECTICUT	193	113	55	15	40	0	38	2	0	0	0	38
SOUTHERN ILL/CARB	34	30	23	10	13	1	14	0	0	0	0	14
SOUTHERN UNIVERSITY	50	50	42	1	41	0	39	2	0	0	0	39
ST LOUIS UNIVERSITY	76	76	68	28	40	0	51	1	12	21	0	72
SUNY/ALBANY	267	267	152	56	96	0	96	0	0	34	0	130
SUNY/BUFFALO	112	83	71	26	45	0	44	1	0	9	0	53
SUNY/STONY BROOK	487	465	219	81	138	3	132	9	0	0	0	132
SYRACUSE UNIVERSITY	131	128	121	57	64	0	59	5	0	0	0	59
TEMPLE UNIVERSITY	149	149	123	70	53	0	53	1	0	0	0	53
TULANE UNIVERSITY	239	213	175	79	96	0	100	2	6	0	0	100
U OF ALABAMA	229	202	130	24	106	11	109	8	0	2	11	100
U OF ARKANSAS	102	86	66	14	52	0	50	2	0	0	0	28
U OF CALIFORNIA/BERK	485	485	129	36	93	0	91	2	0	0	0	91
U OF CALIFORNIA/LA	255	255	107	35	72	0	72	1	0	0	0	72
U OF CHICAGO	349	246	212	110	102	0	101	1	0	0	0	101
U OF CINCINNATI	150	92	77	26	51	0	50	1	0	2	12	38
U OF CONNECTICUT	321	288	153	36	117	0	114	3	0	0	0	114
U OF DENVER	352	329	272	128	144	5	148	1	0	8	24	132
U OF GEORGIA	452	337	175	54	121	2	118	5	0	0	0	118
U OF HAWAII	156	153	123	42	81	0	77	4	0	12	0	89
U OF HOUSTON	142	122	78	19	59	0	63	2	6	3	0	66
U OF ILLINOIS/CHI	360	360	296	188	108	0	108	0	0	0	0	108
U OF ILLINOIS/URB	178	157	110	38	72	0	70	2	0	49	0	119
U OF IOWA	168	157	91	24	67	0	67	0	0	0	9	58
U OF KANSAS	379	333	150	58	92	0	88	4	0	49	0	137
U OF KENTUCKY	181	145	130	23	107	6	155	1	43	5	0	160
U OF LOUISVILLE	98	82	82	21	61	4	63	2	0	38	0	101
U OF MAINE	48	35	14	1	13	1	13	1	0	0	0	13
U OF MARYLAND	524	508	366	122	244	0	237	7	0	78	4	311
U OF MICHIGAN	508	500	332	111	221	0	256	4	39	15	0	271
U OF MINNESOTA/DUL	8	8	5	1	4	4	8	0	0	3	0	11
U OF MINNESOTA/MINN	114	95	45	10	35	5	50	5	15	0	0	50
U OF MISSOURI	87	38	20	6	14	0	16	0	2	0	0	16
U OF NEBRASKA	70	54	37	10	27	1	23	5	0	0	0	23
U OF NEW ENGLAND	36	36	26	5	21	0	16	5	0	0	0	16
U OF NORTH CAROLINA	230	228	68	28	40	2	42	0	0	0	0	42
U OF OKLAHOMA	67	67	41	20	21	0	21	0	0	0	0	21
U OF PENNSYLVANIA	283	276	233	124	109	5	112	2	0	10	0	122
U OF PITTSBURGH	265	265	179	71	108	0	108	0	0	29	0	137
U OF PUERTO RICO	130	75	75	13	62	4	65	1	0	41	0	106
U OF SOUTH CAROLINA	196	161	122	39	83	6	85	4	0	15	0	100

TABLE 200 (Continued)

Applications for Admission to First-year Status in Full-time Masters Degree Programs During 1991 by Action Taken

Program	Applications			Registered				Withdrawals	Enrollment by 11/1/91			Enrollment First Year / Full-time
	Total Received	Considered for Admission	Accepted	Accepted But Not Registered	Accepted and Registered	Accepted in Prior Years	Total Newly Enrolled in 1991		Advanced Standing in First Year	Others Still in First Year	In Second Year	
U OF SOUTH FLORIDA	115	108	33	0	33	0	30	3	0	0	0	30
U OF SOUTHERN CAL	365	365	230	105	125	0	122	3	0	0	0	122
U OF SOUTHERN MISS	71	65	59	7	52	0	46	6	0	10	0	56
U OF TENNESSEE	312	255	148	57	91	0	89	2	0	5	0	94
U OF TEXAS/ARLINGTON	394	364	229	38	191	0	194	23	26	45	0	239
U OF TEXAS/AUSTIN	239	219	84	3	81	0	79	2	0	0	0	79
U OF UTAH	306	306	85	16	69	0	67	2	0	0	0	67
U OF WASHINGTON	431	424	163	65	98	0	97	1	0	0	0	97
U OF WISCONSIN/MAD	*	*	*	*	46	0	51	1	6	0	0	51
U OF WISCONSIN/MIL	249	198	147	16	131	1	143	2	13	18	0	161
VIRGINIA COMMON	340	324	225	104	121	0	119	2	0	0	0	119
WASHINGTON UNIV	364	364	332	150	182	0	174	8	0	24	11	187
WAYNE STATE UNIV	263	207	130	55	75	0	67	8	0	0	0	67
WEST VIRGINIA UNIV	107	107	97	19	78	0	73	5	0	0	29	44
WESTERN MICHIGAN	155	149	110	40	70	0	70	0	0	0	0	70
YESHIVA UNIVERSITY	583	559	491	263	228	8	215	23	2	3	0	218

* Missing data

67

TABLE 201

Applications for Admission to First-year Status in Part-time Masters Degree Programs During 1991 by Action Taken

Program	Applications Total Received	Applications Considered for Admission	Applications Accepted	Accepted But Not Registered	Registered Accepted and Registered	Registered Accepted in Prior Years	Registered Total Newly Enrolled in 1991	Withdrawals	Enrollment by 11/1/91 Advanced Standing in First Year	Enrollment by 11/1/91 Others Still in First Year	Enrollment by 11/1/91 In Second Year	Enrollment First Year/ Part-time
TOTAL:	9,622	8,361	5,814	1,360	4,454	84	4,462	159	82	1,640	41	6,100
ADELPHI UNIVERSITY	204	173	158	15	143	9	152	0	0	7	0	159
ARIZONA STATE UNIV	93	82	48	7	41	0	38	3	0	36	0	74
AURORA UNIVERSITY	81	51	46	10	36	1	33	4	0	56	0	89
BARRY UNIVERSITY	148	146	141	28	113	0	111	2	0	44	0	155
BOSTON COLLEGE	203	188	136	41	95	0	97	1	3	29	0	126
BOSTON UNIVERSITY	212	191	163	59	104	4	100	8	0	0	0	100
BRIGHAM YOUNG UNIV	0	0	0	0	0	0	0	0	0	0	0	0
BRYN MAWR COLLEGE	58	49	38	8	30	1	29	1	0	6	0	35
CAL STATE UNIV/FRES	50	50	50	0	50	0	50	0	0	0	0	50
CAL STATE UNIV/LB	150	150	102	2	100	0	96	4	0	0	0	96
CAL STATE UNIV/SAC	260	144	80	5	75	0	73	2	0	0	0	73
CASE WESTERN RESERVE	15	15	15	4	11	4	15	1	1	0	0	15
CATHOLIC UNIVERSITY	99	81	78	30	48	0	48	0	0	48	0	96
CLARK ATLANTA UNIV	6	6	6	0	6	0	6	0	0	1	0	7
COLORADO STATE UNIV	2	2	1	0	1	0	1	0	0	3	0	4
COLUMBIA UNIVERSITY	242	162	111	41	70	8	74	4	0	20	0	94
EAST CAROLINA UNIV	13	13	10	0	10	0	10	0	0	17	0	27
EASTERN WASHINGTON	15	13	12	0	12	0	12	0	0	22	0	34
FLORIDA INTERNATL	*	*	12	*	*	*	*	*	*	*	*	39
FLORIDA STATE UNIV	167	150	135	18	117	0	117	0	0	55	2	170
FORDHAM UNIVERSITY	407	376	343	104	239	0	238	1	0	0	0	238
GRAMBLING STATE	0	0	0	0	0	0	0	0	0	0	0	0
GRAND VALLEY STATE	35	30	21	3	18	0	15	3	0	49	28	36
HOWARD UNIVERSITY	67	62	62	14	48	5	45	8	0	5	0	50
HUNTER COLLEGE	453	381	115	5	110	0	110	0	0	6	0	116
INDIANA UNIVERSITY	91	91	39	11	28	0	28	0	0	0	0	28
LOUISIANA STATE UNIV	72	54	26	0	26	0	26	0	0	0	0	26
LOYOLA UNIVERSITY	222	222	216	129	87	0	87	0	0	0	0	87
MARYWOOD COLLEGE	67	62	55	6	49	3	65	0	13	4	0	69
MICHIGAN STATE UNIV	59	59	28	4	24	0	24	0	0	6	0	30
NEW MEXICO HIGHLANDS	95	88	40	7	33	0	33	0	0	0	0	33
NEW YORK UNIVERSITY	88	80	68	10	58	0	57	1	0	30	0	87
NORFOLK STATE UNIV	68	58	46	12	34	0	33	1	0	2	0	35
OHIO STATE UNIV	166	130	103	19	84	0	80	4	0	49	0	129
OUR LADY OF THE LAKE	58	57	56	8	48	0	43	5	0	13	0	56
PORTLAND STATE UNIV	125	108	56	8	48	0	43	5	0	0	0	43
RHODE ISLAND COLLEGE	132	132	30	2	28	1	29	0	0	31	0	60
RUTGERS UNIVERSITY	521	352	259	125	134	4	139	4	5	5	0	139
SAN DIEGO STATE	127	127	67	9	58	0	54	4	0	5	0	59
SAN FRANCISCO STATE	65	65	34	2	32	1	33	0	0	0	0	33
SAN JOSE STATE	74	59	49	7	42	0	42	0	0	40	0	82
SIMMONS COLLEGE	67	67	27	12	15	0	15	0	0	0	0	15

TABLE 201 (Continued)

Applications for Admission to First-year Status in Part-time Masters Degree Programs During 1991 by Action Taken

Program	Applications			Registered				Withdrawals	Enrollment by 11/1/91			Enrollment First Year/ Part-time
	Total Received	Considered for Admission	Accepted	Accepted But Not Registered	Accepted and Registered	Accepted in Prior Years	Total Newly Enrolled in 1991		Advanced Standing in First Year	Others Still in First Year	In Second Year	
SMITH COLLEGE	0	0	0	0	0	0	0	0	0	0	0	0
SOUTHERN BAPTIST	0	0	0	0	0	0	0	0	0	0	0	0
SOUTHERN CONNECTICUT	37	23	18	1	17	0	14	3	0	0	0	14
SOUTHERN ILL/CARB	15	12	7	3	4	0	4	0	0	1	0	5
SOUTHERN UNIVERSITY	55	55	43	1	42	0	40	2	0	0	0	40
ST LOUIS UNIVERSITY	85	85	77	34	43	0	53	4	14	27	0	80
SUNY/ALBANY	109	109	56	22	34	0	34	0	0	27	0	61
SUNY/BUFFALO	100	71	69	28	41	0	41	0	0	0	0	41
SUNY/STONY BROOK	0	0	0	0	0	0	0	0	0	0	0	0
SYRACUSE UNIVERSITY	104	104	97	17	80	0	80	0	0	43	0	123
TEMPLE UNIVERSITY	101	101	88	26	62	0	62	0	0	0	0	62
TULANE UNIVERSITY	62	53	47	8	39	0	36	3	0	5	0	41
U OF ALABAMA	1	1	1	0	1	0	1	0	0	0	0	1
U OF ARKANSAS	78	71	64	0	64	0	85	1	0	14	0	99
U OF CALIFORNIA/BERK	0	0	0	0	0	0	0	0	0	0	0	0
U OF CALIFORNIA/LA	0	0	0	0	0	0	0	0	0	0	0	0
U OF CHICAGO	74	47	37	13	24	0	24	0	0	4	0	28
U OF CINCINNATI	32	22	18	7	11	0	11	0	0	0	0	11
U OF CONNECTICUT	128	118	66	15	51	0	51	1	1	46	0	97
U OF DENVER	32	29	24	19	5	3	7	1	0	10	0	17
U OF GEORGIA	108	108	64	4	60	0	58	2	0	0	0	58
U OF HAWAII	49	48	46	11	35	0	35	0	0	35	0	70
U OF HOUSTON	137	101	54	5	49	0	49	4	4	58	2	105
U OF ILLINOIS/CHI	208	208	158	37	121	0	121	0	0	0	0	121
U OF ILLINOIS/URB	87	78	66	10	56	0	55	1	0	25	0	80
U OF IOWA	91	79	57	4	53	0	53	0	0	17	7	63
U OF KANSAS	176	152	66	23	43	0	39	4	0	16	0	55
U OF KENTUCKY	0	0	0	0	0	0	0	0	0	0	0	0
U OF LOUISVILLE	37	23	23	3	20	0	20	0	0	35	0	55
U OF MAINE	13	11	4	0	4	0	4	0	0	14	0	18
U OF MARYLAND	270	265	168	42	126	0	116	10	0	47	0	163
U OF MICHIGAN	53	53	28	7	21	0	24	0	3	12	0	36
U OF MINNESOTA/DUL	2	2	2	0	2	0	2	0	0	6	0	8
U OF MINNESOTA/MINN	67	60	18	6	12	3	22	3	10	0	0	22
U OF MISSOURI	10	6	6	0	6	0	6	0	0	18	0	24
U OF NEBRASKA	29	28	20	3	17	0	16	1	0	0	0	16
U OF NEW ENGLAND	50	50	30	2	28	0	26	2	0	0	0	26
U OF NORTH CAROLINA	151	149	71	2	69	2	67	4	0	39	0	108
U OF OKLAHOMA	64	64	49	0	49	0	49	0	0	41	0	90
U OF PENNSYLVANIA	29	29	29	8	21	0	21	0	0	5	0	26
U OF PITTSBURGH	70	70	51	10	41	0	41	0	0	73	0	114
U OF PUERTO RICO	0	0	0	0	0	0	0	0	0	0	0	0
U OF SOUTH CAROLINA	204	114	91	5	86	12	95	3	0	30	0	125

TABLE 201 (Continued)

Applications for Admission to First-year Status in Part-time Masters Degree Programs During 1991 by Action Taken

Program	Applications				Registered			Withdrawals	Enrollment by 11/1/91			
	Total Received	Considered for Admission	Accepted	Accepted But Not Registered	Accepted and Registered	Accepted in Prior Years	Total Newly Enrolled in 1991		Advanced Standing in First Year	Others Still in First Year	In Second Year	Enrollment First Year/ Part-time
U OF SOUTH FLORIDA	0	0	0	0	0	0	0	0	0	0	0	0
U OF SOUTHERN CAL	110	110	87	23	64	0	62	2	0	65	0	127
U OF SOUTHERN MISS	19	12	11	5	6	0	5	1	0	16	0	21
U OF TENNESSEE	219	126	79	17	62	0	62	0	0	34	0	96
U OF TEXAS/ARLINGTON	291	273	157	16	141	0	144	21	24	34	0	178
U OF TEXAS/AUSTIN	114	102	57	0	57	0	48	9	0	0	0	48
U OF UTAH	50	50	21	4	17	0	16	1	0	0	0	18
U OF WASHINGTON	63	62	29	4	25	0	25	0	0	28	0	53
U OF WISCONSIN/MAD	0	0	0	0	0	0	0	0	0	0	0	0
U OF WISCONSIN/MIL	85	71	55	1	54	0	57	0	3	0	0	57
VIRGINIA COMMON	270	264	206	65	141	0	136	5	0	128	0	264
WASHINGTON UNIV	113	113	103	56	47	0	45	2	0	31	2	74
WAYNE STATE UNIV	145	110	36	6	30	0	29	1	0	22	0	51
WEST VIRGINIA UNIV	10	10	10	0	10	0	10	0	0	0	0	10
WESTERN MICHIGAN	99	97	48	9	39	0	39	0	0	48	0	87
YESHIVA UNIVERSITY	41	36	32	13	19	3	21	2	1	2	0	23

---
* Missing data

TABLE 202 **

Applications for Admission to Advanced Standing Status in Masters Degree Programs During 1991, by Action Taken

Program	From Baccalaureate Program Under School Auspice			From Other Baccalaureate Social Work Program			On Basis of Other Education			Total Admitted Directly to Adv Standing Enrolled 11/1/91
	Applications Received	Accepted for Admission	Enrolled as of 11/1/91	Applications Received	Accepted for Admission	Enrolled as of 11/1/91	Applications Received	Accepted for Admission	Enrolled as of 11/1/91	
TOTAL:	769	576	537	2,870	1,870	1,333	214	150	106	1,976
ADELPHI UNIVERSITY	51	38	35	69	54	40	0	0	0	75
ARIZONA STATE UNIV	0	0	0	0	0	0	5	2	2	2
AURORA UNIVERSITY	9	7	7	24	18	15	0	0	0	22
BARRY UNIVERSITY	0	0	0	44	42	34	0	0	0	34
BOSTON COLLEGE	0	0	0	39	7	2	2	2	2	4
BOSTON UNIVERSITY	0	0	0	58	39	22	0	0	0	22
BRIGHAM YOUNG UNIV	0	0	0	0	0	0	0	0	0	0
BRYN MAWR COLLEGE	0	0	0	0	0	0	0	0	0	0
CAL STATE UNIV/FRES	0	0	0	0	0	0	0	0	0	0
CAL STATE UNIV/LB	0	0	0	0	0	0	0	0	0	0
CAL STATE UNIV/SAC	0	0	0	0	0	0	0	0	0	0
CASE WESTERN RESERVE	0	0	0	52	52	42	0	0	0	42
CATHOLIC UNIVERSITY	3	3	1	21	20	13	7	7	5	19
CLARK ATLANTA UNIV	0	0	0	0	0	0	0	0	0	0
COLORADO STATE UNIV	0	0	0	0	0	0	0	0	0	0
COLUMBIA UNIVERSITY	0	0	0	109	30	26	0	0	0	26
EAST CAROLINA UNIV	17	14	14	13	8	8	0	0	0	22
EASTERN WASHINGTON	0	0	0	0	0	0	0	0	0	0
FLORIDA INTERNATL	*	*	*	*	*	*	*	*	*	0
FLORIDA STATE UNIV	56	40	36	81	59	37	0	0	0	73
FORDHAM UNIVERSITY	0	0	0	151	128	88	9	6	0	88
GRAMBLING STATE	5	3	3	5	4	4	0	0	0	7
GRAND VALLEY STATE	0	0	0	4	4	4	0	0	0	4
HOWARD UNIVERSITY	1	1	0	8	8	0	0	0	0	0
HUNTER COLLEGE	0	0	0	0	0	0	4	3	3	3
INDIANA UNIVERSITY	13	17	16	31	13	13	0	0	0	29
LOUISIANA STATE UNIV	0	0	0	26	15	0	0	0	0	0
LOYOLA UNIVERSITY	0	0	0	0	0	0	0	0	0	0
MARYWOOD COLLEGE	0	0	0	28	27	6	4	3	2	8
MICHIGAN STATE UNIV	16	12	10	19	12	4	0	0	0	14
NEW MEXICO HIGHLANDS	4	4	4	90	75	63	0	0	0	67
NEW YORK UNIVERSITY	12	12	12	61	42	28	6	3	3	43
NORFOLK STATE UNIV	1	1	1	5	3	1	0	0	0	2
OHIO STATE UNIV	33	26	24	49	35	32	0	0	0	56
OUR LADY OF THE LAKE	22	8	7	41	36	23	0	0	0	30
PORTLAND STATE UNIV	0	0	0	0	0	0	0	0	0	0
RHODE ISLAND COLLEGE	6	1	1	18	3	3	0	0	0	4
RUTGERS UNIVERSITY	18	15	15	118	62	46	5	5	5	66
SAN DIEGO STATE	0	0	0	0	0	0	0	0	0	0
SAN FRANCISCO STATE	0	0	0	0	0	0	0	0	0	0
SAN JOSE STATE	0	0	0	0	0	0	0	0	0	0
SIMMONS COLLEGE	0	0	0	23	15	7	0	0	0	7
SMITH COLLEGE	0	0	0	13	4	4	33	16	16	20
SOUTHERN BAPTIST	0	0	0	0	0	0	0	0	0	0
SOUTHERN CONNECTICUT	16	12	10	16	6	4	0	0	0	14
SOUTHERN ILL/CARB	20	19	17	8	7	6	0	0	0	23
SOUTHERN UNIVERSITY	0	0	0	4	2	0	0	0	0	0
ST LOUIS UNIVERSITY	8	8	7	28	25	19	0	0	0	26
SUNY/ALBANY	20	13	12	47	29	22	0	0	0	34
SUNY/BUFFALO	0	0	0	35	30	17	0	0	0	17
SUNY/STONY BROOK	17	4	4	23	6	4	2	2	1	9
SYRACUSE UNIVERSITY	17	16	11	41	41	33	0	0	0	44
TEMPLE UNIVERSITY	21	20	16	55	49	31	0	0	0	47
TULANE UNIVERSITY	0	0	0	26	13	6	0	0	0	6
U OF ALABAMA	10	7	7	44	25	21	0	0	0	28

TABLE 202 (Continued)

Applications for Admission to Advanced Standing Status in Masters Degree Programs During 1991, by Action Taken

Program	From Baccalaureate Program Under School Auspice			From Other Baccalaureate Social Work Program			On Basis of Other Education			Total Admitted Directly to Adv Standing Enrolled 11/1/91
	Applications Received	Accepted for Admission	Enrolled as of 11/1/91	Applications Received	Accepted for Admission	Enrolled as of 11/1/91	Applications Received	Accepted for Admission	Enrolled as of 11/1/91	
U OF ARKANSAS	0	0	0	14	14	14	0	0	0	14
U OF CALIFORNIA/BERK	0	0	0	0	0	0	0	0	0	0
U OF CALIFORNIA/LA	0	0	0	0	0	0	0	0	0	0
U OF CHICAGO	0	0	0	0	0	0	0	0	0	0
U OF CINCINNATI	3	3	3	13	13	9	0	0	0	12
U OF CONNECTICUT	0	0	0	19	8	1	5	1	0	1
U OF DENVER	0	0	0	51	35	24	0	0	0	24
U OF GEORGIA	30	25	25	25	17	16	0	0	0	41
U OF HAWAII	0	0	0	0	0	0	0	0	0	0
U OF HOUSTON	0	0	0	20	13	1	0	0	0	1
U OF ILLINOIS/CHI	37	31	29	98	85	36	0	0	0	65
U OF ILLINOIS/URB	0	0	0	0	0	0	0	0	0	0
U OF IOWA	13	8	8	77	36	24	0	0	0	32
U OF KANSAS	25	12	10	73	33	30	0	0	0	40
U OF KENTUCKY	27	24	25	29	19	18	0	0	0	43
U OF LOUISVILLE	0	0	0	84	69	64	0	0	0	64
U OF MAINE	7	3	3	2	2	2	1	0	0	5
U OF MARYLAND	41	33	33	85	51	51	0	0	0	84
U OF MICHIGAN	0	0	0	39	39	5	35	29	11	16
U OF MINNESOTA/DUL	0	0	0	0	0	0	0	0	0	0
U OF MINNESOTA/MINN	0	0	0	64	21	15	41	25	10	25
U OF MISSOURI	17	13	10	66	20	15	0	0	0	25
U OF NEBRASKA	20	12	12	40	27	21	0	0	0	33
U OF NEW ENGLAND	0	0	0	20	6	5	0	0	0	5
U OF NORTH CAROLINA	0	0	0	46	22	22	4	1	1	23
U OF OKLAHOMA	13	8	7	8	6	3	38	38	38	48
U OF PENNSYLVANIA	0	0	0	0	0	0	0	0	0	0
U OF PITTSBURGH	*	*	*	*	*	*	*	*	*	0
U OF PUERTO RICO	0	0	0	0	0	0	0	0	0	0
U OF SOUTH CAROLINA	0	0	0	53	37	22	0	0	0	22
U OF SOUTH FLORIDA	0	0	0	0	0	0	0	0	0	0
U OF SOUTHERN CAL	0	0	0	0	0	0	0	0	0	0
U OF SOUTHERN MISS	0	0	0	0	0	0	0	0	0	0
U OF TENNESSEE	2	0	0	25	1	0	0	0	0	0
U OF TEXAS/ARLINGTON	0	0	0	115	70	56	0	0	0	56
U OF TEXAS/AUSTIN	25	17	17	32	11	11	1	0	0	28
U OF UTAH	0	0	0	0	0	0	0	0	0	0
U OF WASHINGTON	0	0	0	0	0	0	0	0	0	0
U OF WISCONSIN/MAD	*	*	25	*	*	24	0	0	0	49
U OF WISCONSIN/MIL	24	18	5	9	5	1	0	0	0	6
VIRGINIA COMMON	12	8	8	31	13	13	0	0	0	21
WASHINGTON UNIV	0	0	0	0	0	0	0	0	0	0
WAYNE STATE UNIV	69	52	47	158	102	77	0	0	0	124
WEST VIRGINIA UNIV	8	8	0	21	21	0	0	0	0	0
WESTERN MICHIGAN	0	0	0	0	0	0	0	0	0	0
YESHIVA UNIVERSITY	0	0	0	26	26	25	12	7	7	32

* Missing data

** Totals may not correspond between columns because of variation in item-specific response rates

TABLE 203 **

Full-time Masters Degree Students Enrolled on 11/1/91, by Ethnicity

Program	Total	African American	Asian American	Chicano/ Mexican Amer	Native American	Puerto Rican	White	Other Minority	Foreign
TOTAL:									
Number	19,288	1,758	402	478	145	380	15,673	247	204
Percent	100.0%	9.1%	2.1%	2.5%	0.8%	2.0%	81.3%	1.3%	1.1%
ADELPHI UNIVERSITY	415	10	1	0	1	6	396	0	1
ARIZONA STATE UNIV	174	12	1	17	15	0	127	0	2
AURORA UNIVERSITY	61	2	1	0	0	0	57	1	0
BARRY UNIVERSITY	204	20	1	0	1	1	170	11	0
BOSTON COLLEGE	296	10	9	0	0	0	266	5	6
BOSTON UNIVERSITY	290	17	8	11	0	0	254	0	0
BRIGHAM YOUNG UNIV	45	1	2	2	0	0	38	1	1
BRYN MAWR COLLEGE	187	16	0	0	0	1	162	4	4
CAL STATE UNIV/FRES	90	6	6	18	0	0	58	1	1
CAL STATE UNIV/LB	82	2	10	7	3	0	60	0	0
CAL STATE UNIV/SAC	222	17	18	16	3	1	163	4	0
CASE WESTERN RESERVE	346	60	4	0	2	0	272	3	5
CATHOLIC UNIVERSITY	156	10	2	1	1	2	140	0	0
CLARK ATLANTA UNIV	61	57	0	0	0	0	4	0	0
COLORADO STATE UNIV	47	2	0	2	1	0	42	0	0
COLUMBIA UNIVERSITY	617	65	22	43	0	0	475	0	12
EAST CAROLINA UNIV	68	6	0	0	0	0	61	1	0
EASTERN WASHINGTON	79	2	2	0	10	0	64	1	0
FLORIDA INTERNATL	107	14	1	0	0	0	67	25	0
FLORIDA STATE UNIV	206	13	0	1	1	4	186	1	0
FORDHAM UNIVERSITY	616	98	14	0	1	84	395	17	7
GRAMBLING STATE	*	*	*	*	*	*	*	*	*
GRAND VALLEY STATE	106	5	2	2	1	2	93	1	0
HOWARD UNIVERSITY	111	70	0	1	0	0	24	0	16
HUNTER COLLEGE	472	77	11	0	1	20	330	31	2
INDIANA UNIVERSITY	263	30	1	0	1	0	231	0	0
LOUISIANA STATE UNIV	165	11	0	0	1	0	150	2	0
LOYOLA UNIVERSITY	218	9	6	3	1	0	197	2	0
MARYWOOD COLLEGE	157	1	0	0	0	0	154	1	1
MICHIGAN STATE UNIV	139	11	0	4	2	0	121	0	1
NEW MEXICO HIGHLANDS	101	2	0	24	3	0	71	1	0
NEW YORK UNIVERSITY	505	30	9	0	0	19	427	16	4
NORFOLK STATE UNIV	129	35	5	0	0	0	86	1	2
OHIO STATE UNIV	221	12	1	1	0	1	200	0	6
OUR LADY OF THE LAKE	151	9	3	23	1	0	111	3	1
PORTLAND STATE UNIV	152	3	4	8	3	0	131	0	3
RHODE ISLAND COLLEGE	114	4	2	0	0	1	103	4	0
RUTGERS UNIVERSITY	319	33	6	7	0	6	267	0	0
SAN DIEGO STATE	190	7	5	15	0	0	163	0	0
SAN FRANCISCO STATE	113	19	20	9	2	0	59	4	0
SAN JOSE STATE	122	5	12	17	0	1	83	4	0
SIMMONS COLLEGE	201	6	1	0	1	7	186	0	0
SMITH COLLEGE	231	5	4	2	1	2	207	2	8
SOUTHERN BAPTIST	105	2	1	6	0	0	95	0	1
SOUTHERN CONNECTICUT	104	15	0	0	0	2	87	0	0
SOUTHERN ILL/CARB	38	2	0	0	0	0	36	0	0
SOUTHERN UNIVERSITY	*	*	*	*	*	*	*	*	*
ST LOUIS UNIVERSITY	98	5	1	4	0	0	87	0	1
SUNY/ALBANY	249	20	3	7	2	0	197	18	2
SUNY/BUFFALO	172	2	3	0	2	0	165	0	0
SUNY/STONY BROOK	287	49	4	0	0	15	210	7	2
SYRACUSE UNIVERSITY	148	12	0	2	1	2	131	0	0
TEMPLE UNIVERSITY	139	32	0	0	0	2	96	0	9
TULANE UNIVERSITY	216	14	0	0	0	0	189	13	0
U OF ALABAMA	214	31	1	0	2	0	166	0	14
U OF ARKANSAS	82	3	0	0	0	0	79	0	0
U OF CALIFORNIA/BERK	191	21	16	21	5	3	122	0	3
U OF CALIFORNIA/LA	148	13	23	16	1	0	92	2	1
U OF CHICAGO	189	22	6	7	0	0	154	0	0
U OF CINCINNATI	97	17	2	0	0	0	77	0	1

73

TABLE 203 (Continued)

Full-time Masters Degree Students Enrolled on 11/1/91, by Ethnicity

Program	Total	African American	Asian American	Chicano/ Mexican Amer	Native American	Puerto Rican	White	Other Minority	Foreign
U OF CONNECTICUT	193	22	2	0	0	12	157	0	0
U OF DENVER	267	13	4	11	2	0	235	0	2
U OF GEORGIA	180	24	2	0	0	0	153	1	0
U OF HAWAII	138	4	39	2	1	0	67	19	6
U OF HOUSTON	156	11	2	8	0	1	126	6	2
U OF ILLINOIS/CHI	380	28	6	15	1	4	322	1	3
U OF ILLINOIS/URB	194	9	2	1	0	0	180	0	2
U OF IOWA	111	6	3	0	1	0	97	0	4
U OF KANSAS	274	11	2	6	6	0	249	0	0
U OF KENTUCKY	312	17	0	0	1	0	293	1	0
U OF LOUISVILLE	142	9	1	1	0	0	130	0	1
U OF MAINE	22	0	0	1	1	0	18	2	0
U OF MARYLAND	676	82	4	12	2	0	574	0	2
U OF MICHIGAN	501	65	17	9	2	4	392	2	10
U OF MINNESOTA/DUL	18	0	0	0	1	0	16	0	1
U OF MINNESOTA/MINN	136	8	5	3	2	0	113	0	5
U OF MISSOURI	95	5	0	1	0	0	89	0	0
U OF NEBRASKA	97	5	1	0	1	0	83	7	0
U OF NEW ENGLAND	47	0	0	0	0	0	47	0	0
U OF NORTH CAROLINA	151	9	0	0	0	0	141	1	0
U OF OKLAHOMA	69	3	1	3	7	0	55	0	0
U OF PENNSYLVANIA	193	26	3	1	0	0	158	0	5
U OF PITTSBURGH	202	18	0	0	1	1	178	0	4
U OF PUERTO RICO	168	0	0	0	0	166	1	0	1
U OF SOUTH CAROLINA	228	28	3	4	0	0	192	0	1
U OF SOUTH FLORIDA	54	3	0	0	0	0	49	1	1
U OF SOUTHERN CAL	273	18	12	33	1	0	206	0	3
U OF SOUTHERN MISS	85	13	0	0	0	0	72	0	0
U OF TENNESSEE	204	21	0	1	0	0	181	1	0
U OF TEXAS/ARLINGTON	340	7	6	17	1	0	307	0	2
U OF TEXAS/AUSTIN	151	7	1	15	1	0	125	0	2
U OF UTAH	132	1	1	12	10	0	106	2	0
U OF WASHINGTON	192	13	20	6	11	0	134	8	0
U OF WISCONSIN/MAD	185	10	4	2	6	1	157	0	5
U OF WISCONSIN/MIL	183	4	0	0	0	0	178	1	0
VIRGINIA COMMON	324	36	0	8	2	0	278	0	0
WASHINGTON UNIV	297	31	1	2	7	0	233	0	23
WAYNE STATE UNIV	276	57	3	5	3	0	206	1	1
WEST VIRGINIA UNIV	117	5	0	0	3	0	108	0	1
WESTERN MICHIGAN	108	6	0	2	1	0	97	2	0
YESHIVA UNIVERSITY	391	39	3	0	0	9	336	4	0

* Missing data

** Totals between columns may not correspond because of variation in item-specific response rates

TABLE 204 **

Full-time Masters Degree Students Enrolled on 11/1/91, by Age and Gender

Program	Total	Total		25 & under		26 - 30		31 - 40		41 & over	
		Men	Women	Men	Women	Men	Women	Men	Women	Men	Women
TOTAL:											
Number	19,288	3,315	15,973	661	5,429	823	3,410	1,146	3,751	665	3,267
Percent	100.0%	17.2%	82.8%	3.4%	28.1%	4.3%	17.7%	5.9%	19.4%	3.4%	16.9%
ADELPHI UNIVERSITY	415	40	375	3	86	3	65	27	90	7	134
ARIZONA STATE UNIV	174	41	133	4	28	9	36	19	35	9	34
AURORA UNIVERSITY	61	9	52	1	17	2	3	4	14	2	18
BARRY UNIVERSITY	204	40	164	5	36	12	22	17	48	6	58
BOSTON COLLEGE	296	34	262	6	106	7	51	14	65	7	40
BOSTON UNIVERSITY	290	32	258	10	136	10	77	6	32	6	13
BRIGHAM YOUNG UNIV	45	21	24	4	10	11	3	6	7	0	4
BRYN MAWR COLLEGE	187	13	174	3	42	2	39	6	47	2	46
CAL STATE UNIV/FRES	90	22	68	4	22	8	14	4	19	6	13
CAL STATE UNIV/LB	82	15	67	1	16	3	19	8	12	3	20
CAL STATE UNIV/SAC	222	40	182	9	53	14	46	10	36	7	47
CASE WESTERN RESERVE	346	51	295	10	92	11	60	15	70	15	73
CATHOLIC UNIVERSITY	156	21	135	1	47	6	35	11	17	3	36
CLARK ATLANTA UNIV	61	9	52	3	24	1	12	3	7	2	9
COLORADO STATE UNIV	47	6	41	0	8	2	6	3	14	1	13
COLUMBIA UNIVERSITY	617	92	525	20	209	24	118	29	113	19	85
EAST CAROLINA UNIV	68	9	59	2	23	2	15	2	13	3	8
EASTERN WASHINGTON	79	11	68	1	6	2	7	1	19	7	36
FLORIDA INTERNATL	107	15	92	5	32	2	15	7	33	1	12
FLORIDA STATE UNIV	206	14	192	6	105	2	42	4	19	2	26
FORDHAM UNIVERSITY	616	130	486	8	117	40	157	56	147	26	65
GRAMBLING STATE	*	*	*	*	*	*	*	*	*	*	*
GRAND VALLEY STATE	106	24	82	4	19	13	20	5	30	2	13
HOWARD UNIVERSITY	111	13	98	1	33	6	32	4	25	2	8
HUNTER COLLEGE	472	100	372	13	80	22	79	36	106	29	107
INDIANA UNIVERSITY	263	50	213	8	52	10	38	20	62	12	61
LOUISIANA STATE UNIV	165	22	143	13	69	2	17	3	41	4	16
LOYOLA UNIVERSITY	218	37	181	12	86	11	37	8	33	6	25
MARYWOOD COLLEGE	157	29	128	2	32	4	19	14	37	9	40
MICHIGAN STATE UNIV	139	31	108	7	28	6	18	8	33	10	29
NEW MEXICO HIGHLANDS	101	30	71	2	2	4	16	12	25	12	28
NEW YORK UNIVERSITY	505	84	421	21	197	25	102	29	69	9	53
NORFOLK STATE UNIV	129	24	105	6	26	2	18	8	37	8	24
OHIO STATE UNIV	221	24	197	8	101	5	40	11	29	0	27
OUR LADY OF THE LAKE	151	33	118	3	26	5	25	13	38	12	29
PORTLAND STATE UNIV	152	33	119	2	20	8	21	14	40	9	38
RHODE ISLAND COLLEGE	114	16	98	0	13	5	25	7	23	4	37
RUTGERS UNIVERSITY	319	41	278	15	122	9	51	9	48	8	57
SAN DIEGO STATE	190	27	163	3	46	8	41	13	48	3	28
SAN FRANCISCO STATE	113	27	86	1	12	6	28	9	25	11	21
SAN JOSE STATE	122	21	101	2	28	5	24	9	27	5	22
SIMMONS COLLEGE	201	38	163	7	49	15	47	12	34	4	33
SMITH COLLEGE	231	28	203	3	44	10	66	9	42	6	51
SOUTHERN BAPTIST	105	42	63	9	32	17	20	12	10	4	1
SOUTHERN CONNECTICUT	104	15	89	1	22	5	24	8	29	1	14
SOUTHERN ILL/CARB	38	9	29	2	16	3	4	3	4	1	5
SOUTHERN UNIVERSITY	*	*	*	*	*	*	*	*	*	*	*
ST LOUIS UNIVERSITY	98	21	77	3	34	5	18	7	11	6	14
SUNY/ALBANY	249	45	204	14	79	13	40	14	51	4	34
SUNY/BUFFALO	172	27	145	7	58	6	24	12	29	2	34
SUNY/STONY BROOK	287	62	225	10	46	10	42	22	58	20	79
SYRACUSE UNIVERSITY	148	20	128	2	46	5	15	5	36	8	31
TEMPLE UNIVERSITY	139	24	115	5	58	6	23	5	15	8	19
TULANE UNIVERSITY	216	31	185	13	98	4	33	11	35	3	19
U OF ALABAMA	214	40	174	9	50	12	30	12	49	7	45
U OF ARKANSAS	82	20	62	5	27	4	5	4	16	7	14
U OF CALIFORNIA/BERK	191	37	154	8	48	7	57	17	29	5	20
U OF CALIFORNIA/LA	148	21	127	5	52	9	30	3	22	4	23
U OF CHICAGO	189	32	157	15	82	6	40	9	22	2	13
U OF CINCINNATI	97	20	77	2	9	2	17	14	44	2	7

TABLE 204 (Continued)

Full-time Masters Degree Students Enrolled on 11/1/91, by Age and Gender

Program	Total	Total		25 & under		26 - 30		31 - 40		41 & over	
		Men	Women	Men	Women	Men	Women	Men	Women	Men	Women
U OF CONNECTICUT	193	34	159	4	41	8	40	14	42	8	36
U OF DENVER	267	41	226	4	50	8	49	21	72	8	55
U OF GEORGIA	180	41	139	9	57	6	24	13	24	13	34
U OF HAWAII	138	31	107	5	31	13	23	8	30	5	23
U OF HOUSTON	156	29	127	4	34	7	21	11	41	7	31
U OF ILLINOIS/CHI	380	64	316	16	114	26	91	12	60	10	51
U OF ILLINOIS/URB	194	27	167	10	76	6	25	8	41	3	25
U OF IOWA	111	18	93	5	36	3	18	7	26	3	13
U OF KANSAS	274	52	222	5	44	14	45	24	65	9	68
U OF KENTUCKY	312	79	233	13	60	15	55	37	68	14	50
U OF LOUISVILLE	142	35	107	5	36	12	20	11	23	7	28
U OF MAINE	22	6	16	0	1	0	3	4	4	2	8
U OF MARYLAND	676	106	570	18	163	21	119	38	154	29	134
U OF MICHIGAN	501	88	413	26	186	22	69	23	75	17	83
U OF MINNESOTA/DUL	18	5	13	0	1	1	4	3	7	1	1
U OF MINNESOTA/MINN	136	20	116	*	*	*	*	*	*	*	*
U OF MISSOURI	95	19	76	4	26	4	14	8	16	3	20
U OF NEBRASKA	97	15	82	4	16	3	22	5	28	3	16
U OF NEW ENGLAND	47	10	37	1	7	1	5	4	11	4	14
U OF NORTH CAROLINA	151	15	136	1	51	5	25	7	34	2	26
U OF OKLAHOMA	69	16	53	6	17	1	9	6	16	3	11
U OF PENNSYLVANIA	193	21	172	10	128	6	21	4	15	1	8
U OF PITTSBURGH	202	47	155	15	77	10	24	11	23	11	31
U OF PUERTO RICO	168	25	143	0	36	0	55	23	50	2	2
U OF SOUTH CAROLINA	228	30	198	17	92	9	51	1	36	3	19
U OF SOUTH FLORIDA	54	7	47	2	10	3	4	1	19	1	14
U OF SOUTHERN CAL	273	22	251	6	125	5	51	8	38	3	37
U OF SOUTHERN MISS	85	14	71	3	30	4	8	3	15	4	18
U OF TENNESSEE	204	30	174	10	54	8	40	10	52	2	28
U OF TEXAS/ARLINGTON	340	62	278	10	86	18	55	22	61	12	76
U OF TEXAS/AUSTIN	151	26	125	1	65	9	20	10	26	6	14
U OF UTAH	132	41	91	6	20	11	19	10	27	14	25
U OF WASHINGTON	192	25	167	1	45	7	42	9	53	8	27
U OF WISCONSIN/MAD	185	26	159	12	57	3	34	8	35	3	33
U OF WISCONSIN/MIL	183	32	151	16	84	8	23	8	30	0	14
VIRGINIA COMMON	324	45	279	12	105	15	59	13	60	5	55
WASHINGTON UNIV	297	49	248	15	107	14	50	15	48	5	43
WAYNE STATE UNIV	276	36	240	5	74	10	35	11	48	10	83
WEST VIRGINIA UNIV	117	31	86	8	42	5	15	11	13	7	16
WESTERN MICHIGAN	108	21	87	6	26	6	15	6	22	3	24
YESHIVA UNIVERSITY	391	111	280	17	62	28	80	35	74	31	64

---

* Missing data

** Totals may not correspond between columns because of variation in item-specific response rates

TABLE 205 **

Masters Degree Students, by Primary Methods Concentration

Program	Total	Methods Only								Methods Combined with Fields of Practice or Social Problem								Fields of Practice Only (No Methods Concentration)
		Direct Practice	Community Organization & Planning	Administration or Management	Combo of Dir Pract w/ CO & Planning or Admin & Man	Combo of CO & Planning w/ Admin & Man	Generic	Other	Not Yet Determined	Direct Practice	Community Organization & Planning	Administration or Management	Combo of Dir Pract w/ CO & Planning or Admin & Man	Combo of CO & Planning w/ Admin & Man	Generic	Other	Not Yet Determined	
TOTAL:	29,368	4,780	123	516	440	79	1,716	279	818	10,449	605	618	1,905	128	1,908	421	3,382	627
ADELPHI UNIVERSITY	584	0	0	0	0	0	0	0	0	583	1	0	0	0	0	0	0	0
ARIZONA STATE UNIV	298	107	0	0	0	17	174	0	0	0	0	0	0	0	0	0	0	142
AURORA UNIVERSITY	181	0	0	0	0	0	0	0	0	0	0	0	0	0	181	0	0	0
BARRY UNIVERSITY	411	0	0	0	0	0	0	0	0	148	0	0	0	0	0	0	263	0
BOSTON COLLEGE	430	110	8	4	0	0	0	0	0	284	11	8	0	5	0	0	0	0
BOSTON UNIVERSITY	598	0	0	0	0	0	0	0	0	553	44	1	0	0	0	0	0	0
BRIGHAM YOUNG UNIV	45	0	0	0	0	0	0	0	0	45	0	0	0	0	0	0	0	0
BRYN MAWR COLLEGE	222	178	26	8	0	0	0	0	10	0	0	0	0	0	0	0	0	0
CAL STATE UNIV/FRES	184	104	0	0	0	0	0	30	0	0	0	0	0	0	0	0	50	0
CAL STATE UNIV/LB	353	0	0	0	0	0	0	0	0	0	0	0	353	0	0	0	0	0
CAL STATE UNIV/SAC	427	0	0	0	0	0	0	0	0	237	0	3	80	0	0	0	107	0
CASE WESTERN RESERV	387	0	0	0	0	0	0	0	0	294	21	28	2	0	0	0	42	0
CATHOLIC UNIVERSITY	312	0	0	0	0	0	0	0	0	102	0	0	0	0	105	5	100	0
CLARK ATLANTA UNIV	68	0	0	0	0	0	0	0	0	49	0	0	4	0	0	0	15	0
COLORADO STATE UNIV	51	0	0	0	0	0	0	0	0	0	0	0	0	0	0	51	0	0
COLUMBIA UNIVERSITY	785	0	0	0	0	0	0	0	0	271	258	18	27	0	69	1	141	0
EAST CAROLINA UNIV	117	0	0	0	0	0	0	0	0	96	0	20	0	0	0	0	1	0
EASTERN WASHINGTON	113	*	*	*	*	*	*	*	*	*	*	*	*	*	*	113	*	*
FLORIDA INTERNATL	*	*	*	*	*	*	*	*	*	*	*	*	*	*	*	*	*	*
FLORIDA STATE UNIV	415	208	0	8	18	0	181	0	0	0	0	0	0	0	0	0	0	0
FORDHAM UNIVERSITY	983	0	0	0	0	0	0	0	0	330	0	51	0	0	227	8	367	0
GRAMBLING STATE	133	0	0	0	0	0	68	0	0	42	0	0	0	0	23	0	0	0
GRAND VALLEY STATE	188	0	0	0	0	0	0	0	0	0	0	0	0	0	188	0	0	0
HOWARD UNIVERSITY	165	0	0	0	0	0	0	0	0	111	3	13	0	0	0	0	36	0
HUNTER COLLEGE	684	0	0	0	0	0	0	0	212	398	25	49	0	0	0	0	0	0
INDIANA UNIVERSITY	315	0	0	0	0	0	0	0	0	137	0	0	0	23	0	0	155	0
LOUISIANA STATE UNIV	218	0	0	0	0	0	0	0	0	0	0	0	90	0	0	0	128	0
LOYOLA UNIVERSITY	466	192	0	0	0	0	0	0	0	274	0	0	0	0	0	0	0	0
MARYWOOD COLLEGE	242	87	0	17	0	0	61	0	0	0	0	0	0	0	0	0	0	0
MICHIGAN STATE UNIV	171	75	0	8	0	0	56	0	32	0	0	0	0	0	0	0	0	0
NEW MEXICO HIGHLAND	148	0	0	0	0	0	0	0	0	141	2	5	0	0	0	0	0	0
NEW YORK UNIVERSITY	609	609	0	0	0	0	0	0	0	0	0	0	0	0	0	0	0	0
NORFOLK STATE UNIV	180	0	0	0	0	0	0	0	0	180	0	0	0	0	0	0	0	0
OHIO STATE UNIV	390	0	0	0	0	0	0	0	0	118	6	18	0	0	0	0	248	0
OUR LADY OF THE LAKE	243	243	0	0	0	0	0	0	0	0	0	0	0	0	0	0	0	0
PORTLAND STATE UNIV	275	0	0	0	0	0	0	0	0	197	16	15	0	0	47	0	0	0

TABLE 205 (Continued)

Masters Degree Students, by Primary Methods Concentration

Program	Total	Methods Only								Methods Combined with Fields of Practice or Social Problem								Fields of Practice Only (No Methods Concentration)
		Direct Practice	Community Organization & Planning	Administration or Management	Combo of Dir Pract w/ CO & Planning or Admin & Man	Combo of CO & Planning w/ Admin & Man	Generic	Other	Not Yet Determined	Direct Practice	Community Organization & Planning	Administration or Management	Combo of Dir Pract w/ CO & Planning or Admin & Man	Combo of CO & Planning w/ Admin & Man	Generic	Other	Not Yet Determined	
RHODE ISLAND COLLEGE	178	0	0	0	0	0	0	0	0	0	0	0	81	0	97	0	0	0
RUTGERS UNIVERSITY	802	213	0	83	0	0	0	16	0	357	13	68	0	0	0	52	0	0
SAN DIEGO STATE	321	102	0	20	0	0	0	0	0	0	0	0	0	0	199	0	0	0
SAN FRANCISCO STATE	218	84	23	50	1	0	52	0	8	0	0	0	0	0	0	0	0	0
SAN JOSE STATE	247	0	0	0	0	0	0	0	0	0	0	0	247	0	0	0	0	0
SIMMONS COLLEGE	274	0	0	0	0	0	0	0	0	0	0	0	0	0	0	0	0	0
SMITH COLLEGE	231	0	0	0	0	0	0	0	0	231	0	0	0	0	0	0	0	0
SOUTHERN BAPTIST	105	0	0	0	0	0	0	0	0	38	0	1	22	0	0	0	44	0
SOUTHERN CONNECTIC	154	0	0	0	0	0	0	0	0	146	0	8	0	0	0	0	0	0
SOUTHERN ILL/CARB	52	0	0	0	0	0	0	0	0	52	0	0	0	0	0	0	0	0
SOUTHERN UNIVERSITY	*	*	*	*	*	*	*	*	*	*	*	*	*	*	*	*	*	*
ST LOUIS UNIVERSITY	206	206	0	0	0	0	0	0	0	0	0	0	0	0	0	0	0	0
SUNY/ALBANY	340	280	0	51	9	0	0	0	0	0	0	0	0	0	0	0	0	0
SUNY/BUFFALO	244	0	0	0	0	0	0	0	0	116	0	0	0	0	0	0	128	0
SUNY/STONY BROOK	323	241	0	73	9	0	0	0	0	0	0	0	0	0	0	0	0	0
SYRACUSE UNIVERSITY	351	0	0	0	0	0	0	0	0	122	0	0	229	0	0	0	0	0
TEMPLE UNIVERSITY	392	324	22	46	0	0	0	0	0	0	0	0	0	0	0	0	0	0
TULANE UNIVERSITY	257	0	0	0	0	0	0	0	0	257	0	0	0	0	0	0	0	0
U OF ALABAMA	219	0	0	0	0	0	0	0	0	106	0	12	0	0	0	0	101	279
U OF ARKANSAS	181	0	0	0	0	0	0	0	62	91	0	5	0	0	0	0	23	0
U OF CALIFORNIA/BERK	191	0	0	0	0	0	0	0	0	154	0	0	0	37	0	0	0	0
U OF CALIFORNIA/LA	148	0	0	0	0	0	0	0	0	63	0	10	0	0	0	3	72	0
U OF CHICAGO	265	222	0	0	0	43	0	0	0	0	0	0	0	0	0	0	0	0
U OF CINCINNATI	144	0	0	0	0	0	0	0	0	52	0	13	0	0	0	0	79	0
U OF CONNECTICUT	346	0	0	0	0	0	0	0	0	224	86	36	0	0	0	0	0	0
U OF DENVER	300	0	0	0	0	0	114	0	0	0	0	0	116	0	0	0	70	0
U OF GEORGIA	241	0	0	0	0	0	0	0	0	84	0	0	8	0	0	0	149	0
U OF HAWAII	245	0	0	0	0	0	0	0	0	53	0	6	8	0	165	0	13	0
U OF HOUSTON	331	0	0	0	0	0	0	0	0	0	0	0	0	0	0	0	110	0
U OF ILLINOIS/CHI	580	0	0	0	0	0	0	0	0	566	0	14	0	0	0	0	0	0
U OF ILLINOIS/URB	274	0	0	0	0	0	0	0	0	214	0	60	0	0	0	0	0	0
U OF IOWA	261	140	0	0	121	0	0	0	0	0	0	0	0	0	0	0	0	0
U OF KANSAS	361	28	0	2	0	0	0	0	0	311	0	20	0	0	0	0	0	0
U OF KENTUCKY	312	0	0	0	0	0	312	0	0	0	0	0	0	0	0	0	0	0
U OF LOUISVILLE	197	0	0	0	0	0	0	0	0	124	0	14	0	0	0	0	59	0
U OF MAINE	56	0	0	0	0	0	0	0	0	56	0	0	0	0	0	0	0	0
U OF MARYLAND	912	306	1	40	43	0	312	210	0	0	0	0	0	0	0	0	0	0
U OF MICHIGAN	547	445	30	49	0	0	0	23	0	0	0	0	0	0	0	0	0	0

TABLE 205 (Continued)

Masters Degree Students, by Primary Methods Concentration

Program	Total	Methods Only — Direct Practice	Community Organization & Planning	Administration or Management	Combo of Dir Pract w/ CO & Planning or Admin & Man	Combo of CO & Planning w/ Admin & Man	Generic	Other	Not Yet Determined	Methods Combined — Direct Practice	Community Organization & Planning	Administration or Management	Combo of Dir Pract w/ CO & Planning or Admin & Man	Combo of CO & Planning w/ Admin & Man	Generic	Other	Not Yet Determined	Fields of Practice Only (No Methods Concentration)
U OF MINNESOTA/DUL	35	0	0	0	0	0	0	0	0	0	0	0	0	0	0	35	0	0
U OF MINNESOTA/MINN	170	0	0	0	0	0	0	0	0	88	0	6	1	0	0	0	75	0
U OF MISSOURI	121	0	0	0	0	0	0	0	0	66	0	13	0	0	0	0	42	0
U OF NEBRASKA	187	40	0	0	25	5	0	0	0	16	0	0	4	5	0	0	92	0
U OF NEW ENGLAND	114	0	0	0	0	0	0	0	0	42	0	4	0	0	0	0	68	0
U OF NORTH CAROLINA	264	0	0	0	0	0	0	0	0	89	0	16	13	0	0	146	0	0
U OF OKLAHOMA	159	0	0	0	0	0	0	0	0	0	0	10	59	0	0	0	90	0
U OF PENNSYLVANIA	231	9	1	0	0	0	0	0	0	67	5	0	0	4	117	0	28	0
U OF PITTSBURGH	346	0	12	0	0	0	0	0	0	285	26	34	0	0	0	1	0	0
U OF PUERTO RICO	168	0	12	31	0	0	0	0	0	80	0	0	0	0	0	0	45	206
U OF SOUTH CAROLINA	353	0	0	0	0	0	0	0	0	101	28	0	0	0	113	0	111	0
U OF SOUTH FLORIDA	54	54	0	0	0	0	0	0	0	0	0	0	0	0	0	0	0	0
U OF SOUTHERN CAL	428	0	0	0	0	0	187	0	0	216	0	0	0	25	0	0	0	0
U OF SOUTHERN MISS	122	0	0	0	0	0	0	0	0	0	0	0	0	0	122	0	0	0
U OF TENNESSEE	337	185	0	2	0	14	34	0	102	0	0	0	0	0	0	0	0	0
U OF TEXAS/ARLINGTON	598	140	0	12	0	0	54	0	392	0	0	0	0	0	0	0	0	0
U OF TEXAS/AUSTIN	279	0	0	0	0	0	0	0	0	0	0	0	0	0	0	0	0	0
U OF UTAH	182	0	0	0	0	0	0	0	0	68	0	0	0	3	89	6	16	0
U OF WASHINGTON	273	0	0	0	0	0	0	0	0	90	11	9	9	12	0	6	0	0
U OF WISCONSIN/MAD	185	0	0	0	0	0	0	0	0	47	0	0	0	0	118	0	20	0
U OF WISCONSIN/MIL	318	0	0	0	0	0	0	0	0	288	0	30	0	0	0	0	0	0
VIRGINIA COMMON	653	0	0	0	214	0	0	0	0	172	0	0	0	4	0	0	263	0
WASHINGTON UNIV	407	0	0	0	0	0	0	0	0	0	0	0	407	0	0	0	0	0
WAYNE STATE UNIV	381	0	0	0	0	0	0	0	0	371	0	0	0	10	0	0	0	0
WEST VIRGINIA UNIV	145	0	0	0	0	0	0	0	0	0	0	0	145	0	0	0	0	0
WESTERN MICHIGAN	225	54	0	12	0	0	111	0	0	0	0	0	0	0	48	0	0	0
YESHIVA UNIVERSITY	436	0	0	0	0	0	0	0	0	356	49	0	0	0	0	0	31	0

* Missing data

** Totals between columns may not correspond because of variation in item-specific response rates

TABLE 206 **

Masters Degree Students, by Primary Field of Practice or Social Problem Concentration

Program	Total	Aging/ Geron- tological Social Work	Alcohol, Drug or Sub- stance Abuse	Child Welfare	Commu- nity Planning	Correc- tions/ Criminal Justice	Family Services	Group Services	Health	Occupa- tional/ Industrial Social Work	Mental Health or Comm'ity Mental Health	Mental Retarda- tion	Public Assist/ Public Welfare	Rehabili- tation	School Social Work	Other Fields of Practice or Social Problems	Combos	Not Yet Deter- mined	None (Methods Concen- tration Only)
TOTAL:	29,368	713	299	1,875	247	223	2,108	168	1,946	211	3,299	122	120	80	609	1,122	465	6,436	9,325
ADELPHI UNIVERSITY	584	4	0	0	1	0	96	0	149	10	0	0	0	0	0	0	2	322	0
ARIZONA STATE UNIV	298	0	0	0	0	0	0	0	0	0	0	0	0	0	0	0	0	0	298
AURORA UNIVERSITY	181	0	0	0	0	0	47	0	0	0	31	0	0	0	29	0	0	74	0
BARRY UNIVERSITY	411	0	0	0	0	0	81	0	20	0	47	0	0	0	0	0	0	263	0
BOSTON COLLEGE	430	11	0	7	0	10	0	0	3	9	0	0	0	0	0	0	0	268	122
BOSTON UNIVERSITY	598	4	28	34	26	4	28	40	102	2	153	24	0	0	6	11	0	136	0
BRIGHAM YOUNG UNIV	45	0	0	0	0	0	45	0	0	0	0	0	0	0	0	0	0	0	0
BRYN MAWR COLLEGE	222	0	0	0	0	0	0	0	0	0	0	0	0	0	0	0	0	0	222
CAL STATE UNIV/FRES	184	0	0	0	0	0	0	0	0	0	0	0	0	0	0	0	0	50	134
CAL STATE UNIV/LB	353	146	0	207	0	0	0	0	0	0	0	0	0	0	0	0	0	0	0
CAL STATE UNIV/SAC	427	4	15	33	14	6	6	15	45	2	90	0	26	0	25	39	0	107	0
CASE WESTERN RESERVE	387	21	16	24	19	9	27	12	45	3	63	11	0	4	16	0	65	52	0
CATHOLIC UNIVERSITY	312	0	0	9	0	0	39	0	0	0	0	0	0	0	0	54	5	205	0
CLARK ATLANTA UNIV	68	0	1	11	3	1	5	0	10	0	12	1	0	0	9	0	0	15	0
COLORADO STATE UNIV	51	0	0	0	0	0	0	0	0	0	0	0	0	0	0	51	0	0	0
COLUMBIA UNIVERSITY	785	36	0	0	0	0	258	0	301	40	0	0	0	0	0	9	0	141	0
EAST CAROLINA UNIV	117	4	0	0	0	53	57	0	8	0	39	0	0	0	0	0	0	9	0
EASTERN WASHINGTON	113	5	0	2	0	3	12	0	6	7	8	0	0	0	8	0	0	72	0
FLORIDA INTERNATL	*	*	*	*	*	*	*	*	*	*	*	*	*	*	*	*	*	*	*
FLORIDA STATE UNIV	415	0	0	0	0	0	0	0	0	0	0	0	0	0	0	0	0	0	415
FORDHAM UNIVERSITY	983	25	62	106	3	4	94	9	58	7	194	9	5	14	26	0	0	367	0
GRAMBLING STATE	133	6	0	29	0	0	20	0	0	0	10	0	0	0	0	0	0	0	68
GRAND VALLEY STATE	188	13	16	21	7	1	21	10	8	3	13	2	8	0	14	0	5	51	0
HOWARD UNIVERSITY	165	5	2	15	3	5	18	1	22	0	13	0	9	2	5	10	0	53	2
HUNTER COLLEGE	684	46	17	58	24	9	64	7	56	24	102	8	0	12	29	7	9	0	212
INDIANA UNIVERSITY	315	6	0	0	0	0	0	0	31	0	67	0	0	0	0	0	56	155	0
LOUISIANA STATE UNIV	218	0	0	0	0	0	0	0	0	0	37	0	0	0	0	0	0	128	0
LOYOLA UNIVERSITY	466	14	3	47	0	3	54	0	46	7	39	3	0	6	52	0	0	0	192
MARYWOOD COLLEGE	242	0	0	0	0	0	0	0	0	0	0	0	0	0	0	0	0	0	242
MICHIGAN STATE UNIV	171	0	0	0	0	0	0	0	0	0	0	0	0	0	0	0	0	0	171
NEW MEXICO HIGHLANDS	148	19	7	18	2	7	11	1	17	0	27	8	2	4	11	8	0	6	0
NEW YORK UNIVERSITY	609	0	0	0	0	0	0	0	0	0	0	0	0	0	0	0	0	0	609
NORFOLK STATE UNIV	180	15	10	18	2	14	15	20	15	0	15	10	23	8	15	0	0	0	0
OHIO STATE UNIV	390	9	0	47	0	0	0	0	23	0	52	4	0	0	1	6	0	248	0
OUR LADY OF THE LAKE	243	0	0	0	0	0	0	0	0	0	0	0	0	0	0	0	0	0	243
PORTLAND STATE UNIV	275	8	11	59	0	7	23	0	22	0	84	3	0	4	9	2	0	47	0
RHODE ISLAND COLLEGE	178	0	0	77	0	0	0	0	0	0	0	0	0	0	0	0	101	0	0
RUTGERS UNIVERSITY	802	25	30	32	19	5	87	0	60	4	165	12	7	8	26	10	0	0	312
SAN DIEGO STATE	321	21	0	0	0	0	83	0	34	0	61	0	0	0	0	0	0	0	122
SAN FRANCISCO STATE	218	0	0	0	0	0	0	0	0	0	0	0	0	0	0	0	0	0	218

TABLE 206 (Continued)

Masters Degree Students, by Primary Field of Practice or Social Problem Concentration

Program	Total	Aging/ Gerontological Social Work	Alcohol, Drug or Substance Abuse	Child Welfare	Community Planning	Corrections/ Criminal Justice	Family Services	Group Services	Health	Occupational/ Industrial Social Work	Mental Health or Community Mental Health	Mental Retardation	Public Assist/ Public Welfare	Rehabilitation	School Social Work	Other Fields of Practice or Social Problems	Combos	Not Yet Determined	None (Methods Concentration Only)
SAN JOSE STATE	247	26	0	112	0	0	0	0	0	0	0	0	0	0	24	0	85	0	0
SIMMONS COLLEGE	274	0	0	0	0	0	0	0	0	0	0	0	0	0	0	0	0	0	274
SMITH COLLEGE	231	1	2	5	0	2	42	0	16	0	159	0	0	1	3	0	0	0	0
SOUTHERN BAPTIST	105	2	0	4	2	2	7	1	1	0	10	0	0	0	0	32	0	44	0
SOUTHERN CONNECTICUT	154	12	0	0	0	0	0	0	32	0	0	0	0	0	0	102	0	8	0
SOUTHERN ILL/CARB	52	0	0	6	0	0	0	0	11	0	20	0	0	0	15	0	0	0	0
SOUTHERN UNIVERSITY	*	*	*	*	*	*	*	*	*	*	*	*	*	*	*	*	*	*	*
ST LOUIS UNIVERSITY	206	0	0	0	21	0	112	0	48	0	0	0	0	0	0	0	0	25	0
SUNY/ALBANY	340	0	0	0	0	0	0	0	0	0	0	0	0	0	0	0	0	0	340
SUNY/BUFFALO	244	6	0	0	0	0	0	0	21	0	0	0	0	0	0	89	0	128	0
SUNY/STONY BROOK	323	0	0	0	0	0	0	0	0	0	0	0	0	0	0	0	0	0	323
SYRACUSE UNIVERSITY	351	20	0	0	0	0	0	0	38	28	84	0	0	0	0	2	0	179	0
TEMPLE UNIVERSITY	392	0	0	0	0	0	0	0	0	0	0	0	0	0	0	0	0	0	392
TULANE UNIVERSITY	257	8	0	0	0	0	24	0	30	0	67	0	0	0	0	0	0	128	0
U OF ALABAMA	219	2	0	37	0	0	0	0	32	0	35	0	0	0	0	12	0	101	0
U OF ARKANSAS	181	7	5	17	3	5	2	0	13	0	31	2	5	6	0	0	0	23	62
U OF CALIFORNIA/BERK	191	17	0	72	0	0	0	0	39	0	63	0	0	0	0	0	0	0	0
U OF CALIFORNIA/LA	148	4	0	16	1	0	6	0	7	0	37	1	2	0	0	2	0	72	0
U OF CHICAGO	265	0	0	0	0	0	0	0	0	0	0	0	0	0	0	0	0	0	265
U OF CINCINNATI	144	0	2	7	0	0	32	2	0	0	22	0	0	0	0	0	0	79	0
U OF CONNECTICUT	346	0	0	0	0	0	0	0	0	0	0	0	0	0	0	78	0	268	0
U OF DENVER	300	3	11	0	0	0	61	0	17	0	46	0	0	0	0	0	0	48	114
U OF GEORGIA	241	5	4	6	3	0	8	0	26	1	27	1	1	0	10	0	0	149	0
U OF HAWAII	245	9	0	9	0	0	19	0	18	0	25	0	0	0	0	0	0	165	0
U OF HOUSTON	331	0	0	0	0	0	0	0	0	0	0	0	0	0	0	0	0	110	221
U OF ILLINOIS/CHI	580	8	3	93	0	0	23	0	30	22	110	2	0	0	89	0	0	200	0
U OF ILLINOIS/URB	274	0	0	61	0	0	5	0	48	9	99	0	0	0	50	2	0	0	0
U OF IOWA	261	0	0	0	0	0	0	0	0	0	0	0	0	0	0	0	0	0	261
U OF KANSAS	361	2	0	24	0	0	17	0	13	0	57	0	0	0	0	0	0	218	30
U OF KENTUCKY	312	0	0	0	0	0	0	0	0	0	0	0	0	0	0	0	0	0	312
U OF LOUISVILLE	197	5	0	12	3	2	30	0	25	3	49	0	6	0	3	0	0	59	0
U OF MAINE	56	0	0	5	0	0	7	0	5	0	9	0	0	0	0	0	0	30	0
U OF MARYLAND	912	0	0	0	0	0	0	0	0	0	0	0	0	0	0	0	0	0	912
U OF MICHIGAN	547	0	0	0	0	0	0	0	0	0	0	0	0	0	0	0	0	0	547
U OF MINNESOTA/DUL	35	0	0	0	0	0	0	0	0	0	0	0	0	0	0	35	0	0	0
U OF MINNESOTA/MINN	170	6	2	8	4	1	20	6	10	0	18	2	0	2	16	0	0	75	0
U OF MISSOURI	121	0	0	0	0	0	23	0	13	0	30	0	0	0	0	13	0	42	0
U OF NEBRASKA	187	5	0	15	0	0	0	0	0	0	0	0	0	0	0	10	0	87	70
U OF NEW ENGLAND	114	0	0	0	0	0	0	0	0	0	0	0	0	0	0	46	0	68	0
U OF NORTH CAROLINA	264	7	0	0	0	0	45	0	14	0	36	0	0	0	0	16	0	146	0

TABLE 206 (Continued)

Masters Degree Students, by Primary Field of Practice or Social Problem Concentration

Program	Total	Aging/ Gerontological Social Work	Alcohol, Drug or Substance Abuse	Child Welfare	Community Planning	Corrections/ Criminal Justice	Family Services	Group Services	Health	Occupational/ Industrial Social Work	Mental Health or Comm'ity Mental Health	Mental Retardation	Public Assist/ Public Welfare	Rehabilitation	School Social Work	Other Fields of Practice or Social Problems	Combos	Not Yet Determined	None (Methods Concentration Only)
U OF OKLAHOMA	159	1	1	3	1	0	14	2	16	0	18	0	2	1	0	90	0	10	0
U OF PENNSYLVANIA	231	2	0	10	4	8	8	0	20	0	15	0	0	0	9	117	0	28	10
U OF PITTSBURGH	346	0	0	106	0	16	0	0	0	0	194	0	0	0	0	30	0	0	0
U OF PUERTO RICO	168	0	0	0	0	0	74	0	6	0	0	0	0	0	0	0	0	45	43
U OF SOUTH CAROLINA	353	16	17	19	9	14	12	14	35	0	55	5	10	1	7	6	0	133	0
U OF SOUTH FLORIDA	54	0	0	0	0	0	0	0	0	0	0	0	0	0	0	0	0	0	54
U OF SOUTHERN CAL	428	0	0	67	25	0	0	0	17	17	53	0	0	0	0	0	0	62	187
U OF SOUTHERN MISS	122	0	0	0	0	0	0	0	0	0	0	0	0	0	0	122	0	0	0
U OF TENNESSEE	337	0	0	0	0	0	0	0	0	0	0	0	0	0	0	0	0	0	337
U OF TEXAS/ARLINGTON	598	0	0	0	0	0	0	0	0	0	0	0	0	0	0	0	0	0	598
U OF TEXAS/AUSTIN	279	8	3	9	0	2	17	0	7	0	19	0	7	2	15	0	0	190	0
U OF UTAH	182	6	0	0	0	4	0	0	22	0	0	2	0	0	0	45	89	16	0
U OF WASHINGTON	273	6	4	13	2	4	24	1	34	0	23	2	1	0	10	6	0	142	0
U OF WISCONSIN/MAD	185	5	0	55	0	0	0	0	14	0	41	3	0	0	0	0	0	67	0
U OF WISCONSIN/MIL	318	0	0	0	0	12	138	0	62	0	68	0	0	0	38	0	0	0	0
VIRGINIA COMMON	653	0	0	47	0	9	0	0	21	0	89	0	0	0	10	0	0	263	214
WASHINGTON UNIV	407	18	0	104	0	0	0	0	34	0	128	0	0	0	0	28	53	42	0
WAYNE STATE UNIV	381	0	0	32	10	0	44	0	30	19	90	0	0	0	21	0	0	135	0
WEST VIRGINIA UNIV	145	23	0	0	0	0	61	0	0	0	58	0	0	0	0	0	0	3	0
WESTERN MICHIGAN	225	0	0	0	0	0	0	0	0	0	0	0	0	0	0	0	0	48	177
YESHIVA UNIVERSITY	436	26	27	47	36	4	42	27	40	0	92	9	8	9	6	32	0	31	0

* Missing data
** Totals between columns may not correspond because of variation in item-specific response rates

TABLE 207 **

Masters Degree Students, by Primary Field of Practice in Field Instruction

Program	Total	Aging/ Geron- tological Social Work	Alcohol, Drug or Substance Abuse	Child Welfare	Commu- nity Planning	Correc- tions/ Criminal Justice	Family Services	Group Services	Health	Occupa- tional/ Industrial Social Work	Mental Health or Comm'ity Mental Health	Mental Retarda- tion	Public Assist/ Public Welfare	Rehabili- tation	School Social Work	Other Fields of Practice or Social Problems	Not Yet Assigned	Not in Field Instruction
TOTAL:	29,368	899	799	2,114	460	447	2,598	341	2,833	273	4,763	272	296	242	1,331	1,390	3,986	6,324
ADELPHI UNIVERSITY	584	37	59	21	1	8	39	20	49	12	99	19	2	3	44	4	162	5
ARIZONA STATE UNIV	298	8	3	44	2	4	17	1	27	3	51	2	0	0	10	8	80	38
AURORA UNIVERSITY	181	4	3	12	0	3	35	0	5	0	31	1	0	0	29	8	0	50
BARRY UNIVERSITY	411	6	16	21	0	5	27	1	46	1	40	0	4	0	5	3	0	236
BOSTON COLLEGE	430	12	8	58	4	16	22	0	21	13	103	4	0	4	10	19	26	110
BOSTON UNIVERSITY	598	4	28	34	26	4	28	40	102	2	153	24	0	0	6	11	136	0
BRIGHAM YOUNG UNIV	45	0	0	1	0	4	5	0	3	0	8	0	2	0	2	0	23	1
BRYN MAWR COLLEGE	222	9	10	26	5	6	19	9	28	0	61	2	1	2	8	5	0	31
CAL STATE UNIV/FRES	184	1	2	13	2	0	8	4	3	0	15	1	0	0	10	0	72	53
CAL STATE UNIV/LB	353	16	0	22	2	6	16	6	39	0	46	2	0	0	6	4	0	188
CAL STATE UNIV/SAC	427	4	15	33	14	6	6	15	45	2	90	0	26	0	25	39	0	107
CASE WESTERN RESERV	387	21	16	24	19	9	27	0	45	3	63	11	0	4	16	0	87	42
CATHOLIC UNIVERSITY	312	6	5	21	7	5	22	0	31	0	89	1	21	4	10	0	0	90
CLARK ATLANTA UNIV	68	0	1	11	3	1	5	0	10	0	12	1	0	0	9	0	15	55
COLORADO STATE UNIV	51	0	0	0	0	0	0	0	0	0	0	0	0	0	0	24	0	27
COLUMBIA UNIVERSITY	785	36	0	0	0	0	258	0	301	40	0	0	0	0	0	9	0	141
EAST CAROLINA UNIV	117	3	0	0	0	0	48	0	3	0	29	0	0	0	0	7	0	27
EASTERN WASHINGTON	113	5	0	2	0	0	12	0	6	0	8	0	0	0	8	0	72	0
FLORIDA INTERNATL	*	*	*	*	*	*	*	*	*	*	*	*	*	*	*	*	*	*
FLORIDA STATE UNIV	415	11	25	36	0	11	15	0	35	0	28	1	8	7	17	1	110	110
FORDHAM UNIVERSITY	983	25	62	106	3	4	94	9	58	7	194	9	5	14	26	0	0	367
GRAMBLING STATE	133	3	5	15	0	1	12	2	2	0	25	3	0	0	0	0	0	65
GRAND VALLEY STATE	188	1	5	9	3	1	11	2	4	0	11	0	4	1	9	0	0	126
HOWARD UNIVERSITY	165	5	2	12	3	5	21	1	22	0	13	0	9	2	5	10	0	55
HUNTER COLLEGE	684	46	17	58	24	9	64	7	56	24	102	8	0	12	29	16	0	212
INDIANA UNIVERSITY	315	0	2	5	0	0	12	0	14	0	36	0	0	0	7	127	84	28
LOUISIANA STATE UNIV	218	6	6	26	0	12	21	0	20	1	44	2	1	2	7	9	0	61
LOYOLA UNIVERSITY	466	14	3	47	0	3	54	13	46	7	39	3	0	6	52	0	0	192
MARYWOOD COLLEGE	242	10	8	16	7	2	44	2	32	0	15	3	0	4	9	2	0	77
MICHIGAN STATE UNIV	171	7	8	6	1	4	15	2	16	1	36	1	4	4	17	17	0	32
NEW MEXICO HIGHLAND	148	19	7	18	2	7	11	1	17	0	27	8	2	4	11	8	6	0
NEW YORK UNIVERSITY	609	25	31	41	0	0	101	0	80	10	248	19	0	4	37	13	0	0
NORFOLK STATE UNIV	180	15	10	18	2	14	15	20	15	0	15	10	23	8	15	0	0	0
OHIO STATE UNIV	390	9	4	13	1	2	7	7	26	0	61	4	1	0	1	6	0	248
OUR LADY OF THE LAKE	243	0	1	8	0	0	7	0	19	0	22	3	0	1	3	4	33	142
PORTLAND STATE UNIV	275	8	11	59	0	7	23	0	22	0	84	3	0	0	9	2	0	47
RHODE ISLAND COLLEGE	178	4	11	42	0	2	12	0	13	0	43	0	2	0	11	0	0	38
RUTGERS UNIVERSITY	802	25	30	32	19	5	87	0	60	4	165	12	7	8	26	10	0	312
SAN DIEGO STATE	321	26	0	42	0	0	50	0	47	0	73	0	0	0	12	0	0	71
SAN FRANCISCO STATE	218	7	3	7	12	0	6	17	20	3	23	0	2	1	6	0	3	108

TABLE 207 (Continued)

Masters Degree Students, by Primary Field of Practice in Field Instruction

Program	Total	Aging/Geron-tological Social Work	Alcohol, Drug or Substance Abuse	Child Welfare	Commu-nity Planning	Correc-tions/Criminal Justice	Family Services	Group Services	Health	Occupa-tional/Industrial Social Work	Mental Health or Comm'ity Mental Health	Mental Retarda-tion	Public Assist/Public Welfare	Rehabili-tation	School Social Work	Other Fields of Practice or Social Problems	Not Yet Assigned	Not in Field Instruction
SAN JOSE STATE	247	22	3	46	1	0	25	6	11	0	44	3	3	2	28	8	0	45
SIMMONS COLLEGE	274	4	8	26	0	4	15	0	48	5	103	2	0	4	19	10	16	10
SMITH COLLEGE	231	1	2	5	0	2	42	0	16	0	159	0	0	1	3	0	0	0
SOUTHERN BAPTIST	105	2	0	4	2	2	7	1	1	0	10	0	0	0	0	32	44	0
SOUTHERN CONNECTIC	154	2	3	17	1	2	11	0	15	0	21	0	0	0	5	0	0	77
SOUTHERN ILL/CARB	52	0	0	3	0	0	0	0	11	0	17	0	0	0	11	0	2	8
SOUTHERN UNIVERSITY	*	*	*	*	*	*	*	*	*	*	*	*	*	*	*	*	*	*
ST LOUIS UNIVERSITY	206	0	1	4	6	3	8	5	8	1	5	9	8	1	3	6	83	72
SUNY/ALBANY	340	11	22	35	3	6	22	6	36	1	38	9	8	6	37	17	0	83
SUNY/BUFFALO	244	10	9	18	3	7	30	15	18	0	26	7	4	7	14	0	1	75
SUNY/STONY BROOK	323	15	41	24	8	11	21	0	22	1	41	4	4	0	30	52	0	49
SYRACUSE UNIVERSITY	351	26	25	36	8	3	40	0	36	15	60	8	2	1	36	1	0	54
TEMPLE UNIVERSITY	392	18	8	29	2	6	18	1	51	0	15	6	0	3	13	20	5	197
TULANE UNIVERSITY	257	8	0	0	2	0	24	0	30	0	67	0	0	0	0	0	128	0
U OF ALABAMA	219	12	8	26	10	7	16	8	21	0	40	5	0	4	4	3	19	36
U OF ARKANSAS	181	7	5	17	7	5	2	0	11	0	31	2	4	5	0	0	23	62
U OF CALIFORNIA/BERK	191	17	0	69	0	0	0	0	38	0	62	0	0	0	0	0	72	5
U OF CALIFORNIA/LA	148	4	0	16	1	0	6	0	7	0	34	1	0	0	2	2	72	3
U OF CHICAGO	265	9	5	21	6	2	17	0	43	0	62	2	3	1	16	63	13	2
U OF CINCINNATI	144	0	2	7	0	0	32	2	0	0	22	0	0	0	0	0	79	0
U OF CONNECTICUT	346	12	11	10	25	9	43	0	52	1	53	1	8	7	18	18	0	78
U OF DENVER	300	8	14	44	7	4	24	8	18	1	44	3	12	1	38	21	0	53
U OF GEORGIA	241	5	4	6	3	6	8	0	26	1	27	1	1	0	10	0	106	43
U OF HAWAII	245	16	5	10	2	11	30	3	17	0	37	1	4	1	7	0	24	77
U OF HOUSTON	331	7	0	3	11	8	26	0	42	2	39	3	0	4	10	3	113	60
U OF ILLINOIS/CHI	580	8	3	89	0	0	23	0	30	22	114	2	0	0	89	0	200	0
U OF ILLINOIS/URB	274	0	0	17	0	0	2	0	13	0	20	0	0	0	21	0	45	156
U OF IOWA	261	4	3	13	5	0	36	1	21	0	14	0	4	2	9	6	74	69
U OF KANSAS	361	8	5	39	0	7	23	1	40	0	94	1	7	2	36	11	0	88
U OF KENTUCKY	312	9	11	14	9	8	16	1	19	2	43	1	0	2	13	9	155	0
U OF LOUISVILLE	197	2	2	4	2	2	3	0	4	1	14	2	3	1	3	2	97	55
U OF MAINE	56	2	5	4	0	0	4	0	7	0	13	1	0	0	2	2	0	14
U OF MARYLAND	912	42	14	56	9	23	106	0	150	19	157	8	32	45	41	0	0	210
U OF MICHIGAN	547	16	16	23	12	29	46	7	27	3	50	0	5	2	18	14	259	20
U OF MINNESOTA/DUL	35	0	1	1	1	0	0	4	0	0	2	0	1	0	2	0	0	23
U OF MINNESOTA/MINN	170	6	2	8	4	1	20	6	10	0	18	2	0	2	16	0	41	34
U OF MISSOURI	121	0	0	0	0	0	23	0	13	0	30	0	0	0	0	13	42	0
U OF NEBRASKA	187	6	1	15	3	2	17	0	14	0	10	0	0	2	2	6	70	39
U OF NEW ENGLAND	114	1	2	5	1	1	14	0	7	2	33	0	2	5	7	1	0	33
U OF NORTH CAROLINA	264	5	0	0	0	0	38	0	13	0	32	0	2	0	0	13	146	17

TABLE 207 (Continued)

Masters Degree Students, by Primary Field of Practice in Field Instruction

Program	Total	Aging/ Geron- tological Social Work	Alcohol, Drug or Substance Abuse	Child Welfare	Commu- nity Planning	Correc- tions/ Criminal Justice	Family Services	Group Services	Health	Occupa- tional/ Industrial Social Work	Mental Health or Comm'ity Mental Health	Mental Retarda- tion	Public Assist/ Public Welfare	Rehabili- tation	School Social Work	Other Fields of Practice or Social Problems	Not Yet Assigned	Not in Field Instructi on
U OF OKLAHOMA	159	1	1	3	1	0	14	2	16	0	18	0	2	1	0	90	10	0
U OF PENNSYLVANIA	231	11	2	35	9	15	16	7	42	3	29	1	0	2	21	10	0	28
U OF PITTSBURGH	346	7	8	4	11	13	8	4	19	8	41	0	0	4	3	2	100	114
U OF PUERTO RICO	168	0	0	0	0	0	74	0	6	0	0	0	0	0	0	43	45	0
U OF SOUTH CAROLINA	353	16	17	19	9	14	12	14	35	0	55	5	10	1	7	6	22	111
U OF SOUTH FLORIDA	54	0	0	1	0	0	8	0	8	0	3	0	0	0	2	2	30	0
U OF SOUTHERN CAL	428	0	0	62	25	0	0	0	17	17	52	0	0	0	0	187	62	6
U OF SOUTHERN MISS	122	0	0	0	0	0	0	0	0	0	0	0	0	0	0	45	77	0
U OF TENNESSEE	337	10	14	23	1	4	36	0	37	4	62	1	12	6	10	15	52	50
U OF TEXAS/ARLINGTON	598	5	0	28	5	5	41	0	32	2	55	0	2	1	30	0	392	0
U OF TEXAS/AUSTIN	279	8	3	9	0	2	17	0	7	0	19	0	7	2	15	0	28	162
U OF UTAH	182	6	8	11	2	7	0	0	29	1	70	0	2	0	13	9	8	16
U OF WASHINGTON	273	6	4	13	2	4	24	1	34	1	23	2	1	0	10	6	107	35
U OF WISCONSIN/MAD	185	10	6	10	10	5	21	0	11	0	33	7	8	0	20	7	20	17
U OF WISCONSIN/MIL	318	7	12	18	4	12	46	2	35	0	53	0	2	6	38	0	0	83
VIRGINIA COMMON	653	3	7	5	4	15	27	0	22	0	75	1	4	2	14	214	45	215
WASHINGTON UNIV	407	8	6	31	11	11	18	28	42	4	30	10	2	0	12	3	164	27
WAYNE STATE UNIV	381	1	12	47	10	0	47	5	46	19	99	2	1	0	40	5	29	18
WEST VIRGINIA UNIV	145	3	7	2	2	0	7	0	1	0	11	0	4	0	0	0	29	79
WESTERN MICHIGAN	225	8	7	23	4	9	26	0	20	3	40	2	0	0	20	15	0	48
YESHIVA UNIVERSITY	436	26	27	47	36	4	42	27	40	0	92	9	8	9	6	32	0	31

* Missing data

** The totals between columns may not correspond because of variation in item-specific response rates

85

TABLE 208

Full-time Masters Students Receiving Financial Aid Not Tied to Current Field Instruction, by Source of Funds

Column groupings: **Public Funds** = Federal Government (Child Welfare, Office of Aging, NIAAA, NIDA, NIMH, VA, FCWSP, Other), State or Local Gov't, Veterans' Benefits. **Voluntary Funds** = Social Welfare Agencies, Foundations or Other.

Program	Total Full-time Students	Child Welfare	Office of Aging	NIAAA	NIDA	NIMH	VA	FCWSP	Other	State or Local Gov't	Veterans' Benefits	Social Welfare Agencies	Foundations or Other	School or University	Foreign Gov't	Formal Loan Programs	Work Study	Research or Graduate Assists	Other	Total From All Sources
TOTAL:	19,288	220	14	1	1	55	12	814	921	58	529	122	306	4,242	11	6,279	87	603	234	14,509
ADELPHI UNIVERSITY	415	0	0	0	0	0	0	0	5	0	11	0	1	58	0	0	0	23	2	100
ARIZONA STATE UNIV	174	0	0	0	0	0	0	2	0	0	21	0	7	48	0	88	0	6	0	172
AURORA UNIVERSITY	61	9	0	0	0	0	0	0	3	0	0	0	0	26	0	56	0	1	1	96
BARRY UNIVERSITY	204	0	0	0	0	0	0	0	43	0	0	0	0	5	0	0	0	0	0	48
BOSTON COLLEGE	296	8	0	0	0	0	0	27	1	0	5	1	10	24	2	364	0	22	24	488
BOSTON UNIVERSITY	290	5	0	0	0	4	0	27	0	0	139	0	4	180	0	0	0	0	0	359
BRIGHAM YOUNG UNIV	45	0	0	0	0	0	0	0	1	1	1	1	2	6	0	21	1	15	5	54
BRYN MAWR COLLEGE	187	0	0	0	0	0	0	0	1	0	18	0	2	120	0	87	0	0	0	228
CAL STATE UNIV/FRES	90	*	*	*	*	*	*	*	*	*	*	*	*	1	0	0	1	1	0	3
CAL STATE UNIV/LB	82	1	0	0	0	0	0	0	21	0	0	22	0	0	0	33	0	0	1	78
CAL STATE UNIV/SAC	222	*	*	*	*	*	*	*	*	*	*	*	*	*	*	*	*	*	*	*
CASE WESTERN RESERV	346	1	0	0	0	0	0	94	0	0	0	0	0	147	0	134	0	0	0	376
CATHOLIC UNIVERSITY	156	7	0	0	0	0	0	0	2	0	0	0	4	17	0	48	0	0	5	83
CLARK ATLANTA UNIV	61	0	0	0	0	0	0	0	0	0	0	0	0	19	0	0	0	0	0	19
COLORADO STATE UNIV	47	2	0	0	0	0	0	0	0	0	0	0	0	1	0	0	0	5	2	10
COLUMBIA UNIVERSITY	617	0	0	0	0	0	0	0	57	0	0	0	8	166	0	641	0	0	0	872
EAST CAROLINA UNIV	68	0	0	0	0	0	0	0	0	0	0	0	0	0	0	0	0	11	0	11
EASTERN WASHINGTON	79	0	0	0	0	0	0	0	3	1	1	0	0	49	0	39	8	6	1	108
FLORIDA INTERNATL	107	10	0	0	0	0	0	28	0	3	0	0	0	23	0	15	0	6	0	85
FLORIDA STATE UNIV	206	0	0	0	0	3	0	0	0	0	0	15	1	0	0	*	6	31	0	56
FORDHAM UNIVERSITY	616	8	0	0	0	0	0	0	98	0	0	8	0	191	0	353	0	0	0	658
GRAMBLING STATE	*	4	0	0	0	0	0	0	4	0	0	0	0	0	0	0	0	0	11	19
GRAND VALLEY STATE	106	0	0	0	0	0	0	2	1	0	0	0	0	4	0	45	0	8	0	60
HOWARD UNIVERSITY	111	0	0	0	0	6	0	0	4	0	0	1	20	27	0	78	0	6	0	142
HUNTER COLLEGE	472	0	0	0	0	0	0	0	0	0	0	0	105	40	0	0	0	0	0	145
INDIANA UNIVERSITY	263	0	0	0	0	0	3	7	0	2	0	0	0	39	0	52	0	3	0	106
LOUISIANA STATE UNIV	165	0	0	0	0	0	0	0	7	0	45	0	0	5	0	0	1	16	0	74
LOYOLA UNIVERSITY	218	0	0	0	0	0	0	0	35	0	0	0	0	39	0	98	0	15	3	190
MARYWOOD COLLEGE	157	0	0	0	0	0	0	0	12	0	0	0	0	23	0	98	0	2	0	135
MICHIGAN STATE UNIV	139	0	0	0	0	0	0	0	0	0	0	0	0	20	0	0	0	1	0	21
NEW MEXICO HIGHLAND	101	0	0	0	0	0	0	0	0	0	0	0	0	4	0	0	0	1	0	5
NEW YORK UNIVERSITY	505	5	0	0	0	0	0	0	0	0	0	0	0	283	0	302	6	0	0	596
NORFOLK STATE UNIV	129	0	0	0	0	0	0	0	0	0	0	0	0	5	0	129	0	0	0	134
OHIO STATE UNIV	221	5	0	0	0	1	0	3	15	0	0	0	24	4	0	0	2	2	0	56
OUR LADY OF THE LAKE	151	0	0	0	0	0	0	0	15	0	4	0	0	5	0	69	0	0	0	93
PORTLAND STATE UNIV	152	*	*	*	*	*	*	*	*	*	*	*	*	*	*	*	*	3	*	*
RHODE ISLAND COLLEGE	114	0	0	0	0	0	0	3	5	0	0	0	0	0	0	107	0	0	2	117
RUTGERS UNIVERSITY	319	6	0	0	0	6	0	0	69	0	0	0	0	5	0	141	0	3	2	232
SAN DIEGO STATE	190	8	0	0	0	6	0	0	0	0	0	0	0	8	1	0	0	2	0	25

TABLE 208 (Continued)

Full-time Masters Students Receiving Financial Aid Not Tied to Current Field Instruction, by Source of Funds

Program	Total Full-time Students	Federal Government — Child Welfare	Office of Aging	NIAAA	NIDA	NIMH	VA	FCWSP	Other	State or Local Gov't	Veterans' Benefits	Voluntary Funds — Social Welfare Agencies	Foundations or Other	School or University	Foreign Gov't	Formal Loan Programs	Work Study	Research or Graduate Assists	Other	Total From All Sources
SAN FRANCISCO STATE	113	0	0	0	0	0	0	6	0	0	44	2	0	38	0	0	0	1	0	91
SAN JOSE STATE	122	4	6	0	0	0	0	0	0	0	0	0	0	2	0	0	0	0	0	12
SIMMONS COLLEGE	201	5	0	0	0	0	1	32	0	1	124	0	0	126	0	103	0	0	0	392
SMITH COLLEGE	231	0	0	0	0	0	0	16	0	2	4	0	0	116	0	89	0	0	0	227
SOUTHERN BAPTIST	105	0	0	0	0	0	0	0	0	0	45	0	0	0	0	0	0	4	12	57
SOUTHERN CONNECTIC	104	0	0	0	0	0	0	0	0	0	0	0	0	0	0	0	0	4	0	4
SOUTHERN ILL/CARB	38	0	0	0	0	0	2	0	2	0	2	0	0	16	0	20	0	7	8	57
SOUTHERN UNIVERSITY	*	*	*	*	*	*	*	*	*	*	*	*	*	*	*	*	*	*	*	*
ST LOUIS UNIVERSITY	98	0	0	0	0	0	0	0	0	0	0	1	1	0	0	0	0	0	0	2
SUNY/ALBANY	249	4	2	0	0	0	2	0	0	0	5	4	0	0	0	0	0	41	0	58
SUNY/BUFFALO	172	0	0	0	0	0	0	4	0	0	0	0	7	0	0	70	0	0	0	81
SUNY/STONY BROOK	287	0	0	0	0	0	0	4	99	0	0	0	0	25	0	123	0	0	2	253
SYRACUSE UNIVERSITY	148	0	0	0	0	4	0	0	0	0	5	0	0	32	0	0	0	10	1	52
TEMPLE UNIVERSITY	139	0	0	0	0	0	0	6	19	0	0	0	0	44	0	*	0	7	0	76
TULANE UNIVERSITY	216	1	0	0	0	0	0	78	0	0	0	0	0	155	0	160	0	1	0	395
U OF ALABAMA	214	25	0	0	0	0	0	0	17	2	0	0	4	35	0	0	0	0	0	83
U OF ARKANSAS	82	0	0	0	0	0	0	0	0	0	0	0	0	1	0	26	0	4	0	31
U OF CALIFORNIA/BERK	191	0	0	0	0	10	0	25	1	1	2	0	9	57	2	103	1	2	0	213
U OF CALIFORNIA/LA	148	0	0	0	0	0	0	12	0	0	0	1	1	5	0	120	6	0	0	145
U OF CHICAGO	189	5	0	0	0	0	0	0	25	0	4	1	1	159	0	0	0	0	0	195
U OF CINCINNATI	97	0	0	0	0	6	0	0	0	0	0	0	0	30	0	0	0	3	3	42
U OF CONNECTICUT	193	0	0	0	0	6	0	75	0	2	0	3	2	145	0	126	0	1	0	360
U OF DENVER	267	10	0	0	0	0	0	8	18	4	1	1	7	107	0	209	0	6	1	372
U OF GEORGIA	180	4	0	0	0	0	0	1	0	1	2	0	0	0	0	0	0	38	0	46
U OF HAWAII	138	2	0	0	0	0	0	0	10	0	1	0	10	16	0	14	0	0	0	53
U OF HOUSTON	156	0	0	0	0	0	0	0	2	*	0	0	1	4	0	0	0	4	0	11
U OF ILLINOIS/CHI	380	0	0	0	0	0	0	0	0	0	0	0	0	21	0	0	0	0	0	21
U OF ILLINOIS/URB	194	0	0	0	0	0	1	0	0	0	2	0	0	8	0	44	0	35	0	90
U OF IOWA	111	1	0	0	0	0	0	5	0	0	0	0	0	3	1	32	0	26	0	68
U OF KANSAS	274	1	0	0	0	3	0	0	0	0	7	0	0	0	0	0	0	2	20	35
U OF KENTUCKY	312	0	0	0	0	0	0	0	0	0	14	0	16	0	0	0	0	8	0	38
U OF LOUISVILLE	142	0	0	0	0	0	0	0	0	0	0	0	0	50	0	0	0	0	0	50
U OF MAINE	22	0	0	0	0	0	0	0	1	0	5	0	0	2	0	11	0	1	0	20
U OF MARYLAND	676	0	0	0	0	0	0	30	86	6	0	0	1	185	0	443	0	0	0	751
U OF MICHIGAN	501	0	1	0	0	4	0	102	3	1	0	0	3	242	0	266	0	5	0	627
U OF MINNESOTA/DUL	18	0	0	0	0	0	0	0	0	0	0	0	0	3	0	7	0	0	0	10
U OF MINNESOTA/MINN	136	8	0	0	0	0	0	0	0	0	0	0	0	21	0	0	0	10	0	39
U OF MISSOURI	95	3	0	0	0	0	0	0	0	0	0	0	0	20	0	0	0	0	6	29
U OF NEBRASKA	97	0	0	0	0	0	0	0	1	0	0	0	2	1	0	45	1	13	0	63
U OF NEW ENGLAND	47	0	0	0	0	0	0	0	0	0	0	0	0	0	0	57	0	0	0	57

TABLE 208 (Continued)

Full-time Masters Students Receiving Financial Aid Not Tied to Current Field Instruction, by Source of Funds

Program	Total Full-time Students	Public Funds — Federal Government								State or Local Gov't	Veterans' Benefits	Voluntary Funds — Social Welfare Agencies	Voluntary Funds — Foundations or Other	School or University	Foreign Gov't	Formal Loan Programs	Work Study	Research or Graduate Assists	Other	Total From All Sources
		Child Welfare	Office of Aging	NIAAA	NIDA	NIMH	VA	FCWSP	Other											
U OF NORTH CAROLINA	151	0	2	0	0	0	0	1	0	0	0	0	0	28	0	76	0	0	0	107
U OF OKLAHOMA	69	0	0	0	0	0	0	0	12	3	3	0	1	9	0	26	1	6	0	61
U OF PENNSYLVANIA	193	0	0	0	0	0	0	0	0	2	0	0	12	102	0	184	26	0	0	326
U OF PITTSBURGH	202	5	3	0	0	0	0	0	0	0	0	0	0	68	0	0	0	0	0	76
U OF PUERTO RICO	168	0	0	0	0	0	0	0	26	0	0	45	3	0	0	7	0	3	0	84
U OF SOUTH CAROLINA	228	5	0	0	0	0	0	7	6	10	7	4	3	21	0	33	0	30	0	126
U OF SOUTH FLORIDA	54	0	0	0	0	1	0	0	2	0	0	2	2	14	0	12	0	12	0	45
U OF SOUTHERN CAL	273	0	0	0	0	0	0	97	0	1	2	8	4	111	0	177	0	1	0	401
U OF SOUTHERN MISS	85	5	0	0	0	0	0	0	0	0	0	0	0	2	0	0	0	11	0	18
U OF TENNESSEE	204	0	0	0	0	0	0	0	17	0	2	1	5	30	0	83	1	8	28	175
U OF TEXAS/ARLINGTON	340	25	0	0	0	0	0	28	22	1	2	0	4	35	0	0	0	4	0	121
U OF TEXAS/AUSTIN	151	0	0	0	0	0	0	0	0	0	0	0	0	24	0	*	*	23	0	47
U OF UTAH	132	0	0	0	0	0	0	0	0	0	0	0	0	15	0	8	0	0	0	23
U OF WASHINGTON	192	0	0	0	0	0	0	38	10	0	0	0	0	8	0	155	25	0	0	236
U OF WISCONSIN/MAD	185	5	0	0	0	4	0	0	0	0	0	0	1	29	0	0	0	0	0	39
U OF WISCONSIN/MIL	183	0	0	0	1	0	0	0	0	0	0	0	0	5	0	0	0	9	0	15
VIRGINIA COMMON	324	0	0	1	0	0	0	0	0	3	0	0	1	5	0	124	0	37	0	171
WASHINGTON UNIV	297	6	0	0	0	0	0	46	6	1	1	0	8	216	5	230	0	25	0	544
WAYNE STATE UNIV	276	12	0	0	0	0	0	0	0	0	0	0	0	62	0	4	0	0	0	78
WEST VIRGINIA UNIV	117	0	0	0	0	0	0	0	2	0	0	0	0	18	0	0	0	4	1	25
WESTERN MICHIGAN	108	0	0	0	0	0	0	0	0	0	0	0	1	0	0	98	1	15	3	118
YESHIVA UNIVERSITY	391	5	0	0	0	0	0	0	131	0	0	0	0	179	0	98	0	0	0	413

* Missing data

TABLE 209

Full-time Masters Students Receiving Financial Aid Paid Directly by Field Instruction Agency, by Source of Funds

Program	Total Full-time Students	Public Funds — Federal Government								State or Local Gov't	Veterans' Benefits	Voluntary Funds		School or University	Foreign Gov't	Formal Loan Programs	Work Study	Research or Graduate Assists	Other	Total From All Sources
		Child Welfare	Office of Aging	NIAAA	NIDA	NIMH	VA	FCWSP	Other			Social Welfare Agencies	Foundations or Other							
TOTAL:	19,288	64	1	2	1	18	166	292	473	11	115	514	229	70	22	14	282	1	16	2,291
ADELPHI UNIVERSITY	415	0	0	0	0	0	4	0	3	0	10	5	0	0	0	0	50	0	0	72
ARIZONA STATE UNIV	174	0	0	0	0	9	3	0	12	0	0	4	0	0	0	0	0	0	0	28
AURORA UNIVERSITY	61	0	0	0	0	0	0	0	29	0	0	0	0	0	0	0	0	0	0	29
BARRY UNIVERSITY	204	0	0	0	0	0	1	0	0	0	0	0	0	0	0	0	0	0	0	1
BOSTON COLLEGE	296	0	0	0	0	0	11	13	18	0	0	12	0	0	0	0	0	0	0	54
BOSTON UNIVERSITY	290	0	0	0	0	0	0	0	0	0	0	0	0	0	0	0	0	0	0	0
BRIGHAM YOUNG UNIV	45	0	0	0	0	0	1	0	8	0	12	0	0	0	0	0	0	0	0	21
BRYN MAWR COLLEGE	187	0	0	0	0	0	1	0	0	0	0	0	0	0	0	0	0	0	0	1
CAL STATE UNIV/FRES	90	*	*	*	*	*	0	*	*	*	*	*	*	*	*	*	*	*	*	*
CAL STATE UNIV/LB	82	21	0	0	0	6	0	0	0	0	0	12	0	0	0	0	0	0	0	39
CAL STATE UNIV/SAC	222	*	*	*	*	*	*	*	*	*	*	*	*	*	*	*	*	*	*	*
CASE WESTERN RESERV	346	0	0	0	0	0	0	0	0	0	0	0	0	0	0	0	0	0	0	0
CATHOLIC UNIVERSITY	156	0	0	0	0	0	1	0	2	0	0	0	3	0	0	0	0	0	0	6
CLARK ATLANTA UNIV	61	0	0	0	0	0	0	0	0	0	0	10	0	0	0	0	0	0	0	10
COLORADO STATE UNIV	47	0	0	0	0	0	0	0	0	0	0	0	0	0	0	0	0	0	4	4
COLUMBIA UNIVERSITY	617	0	0	0	0	0	0	230	0	0	0	15	10	0	0	0	0	0	0	255
EAST CAROLINA UNIV	68	0	0	0	0	0	0	0	3	0	0	0	0	0	0	0	0	0	0	3
EASTERN WASHINGTON	79	0	0	0	0	0	0	0	0	0	0	0	0	0	0	0	0	0	0	0
FLORIDA INTERNATL	107	0	0	0	0	0	0	0	0	0	0	0	0	0	0	0	0	0	0	0
FLORIDA STATE UNIV	206	0	0	0	0	0	0	0	1	0	0	0	0	0	0	0	0	0	0	1
FORDHAM UNIVERSITY	616	0	0	0	0	0	4	0	36	0	0	20	0	0	0	0	0	0	0	60
GRAMBLING STATE	*	3	0	0	0	0	0	0	0	0	0	0	0	0	0	0	0	0	0	3
GRAND VALLEY STATE	106	0	0	0	0	0	0	0	0	0	0	0	0	0	0	0	0	0	0	0
HOWARD UNIVERSITY	111	0	0	0	0	0	0	0	4	0	0	0	0	0	0	0	8	0	0	12
HUNTER COLLEGE	472	0	0	0	0	0	0	0	4	0	10	3	0	0	0	0	0	0	0	17
INDIANA UNIVERSITY	263	0	0	0	0	0	0	0	7	0	0	0	0	0	0	0	0	0	0	7
LOUISIANA STATE UNIV	165	0	0	0	0	0	2	0	6	0	1	3	0	0	0	0	0	0	0	12
LOYOLA UNIVERSITY	218	0	0	0	0	0	0	0	0	0	0	0	0	0	0	0	0	0	0	0
MARYWOOD COLLEGE	157	0	0	0	0	0	2	0	0	0	0	0	0	0	0	0	47	0	0	49
MICHIGAN STATE UNIV	139	0	0	0	0	0	0	0	0	0	0	0	0	0	0	0	8	0	0	8
NEW MEXICO HIGHLAND	101	6	0	0	0	0	0	0	23	0	0	0	0	0	0	0	0	0	0	29
NEW YORK UNIVERSITY	505	0	0	0	0	0	0	0	16	0	0	0	17	0	0	0	0	0	0	33
NORFOLK STATE UNIV	129	0	0	0	0	0	2	0	6	0	0	0	0	0	0	0	0	0	0	8
OHIO STATE UNIV	221	5	0	0	0	0	5	0	0	0	2	9	0	0	0	0	0	0	0	21
OUR LADY OF THE LAKE	151	0	0	0	0	0	0	0	0	0	0	0	0	0	0	0	0	0	0	0
PORTLAND STATE UNIV	152	*	*	*	*	*	*	*	*	*	*	*	*	*	*	*	*	*	*	*
RHODE ISLAND COLLEGE	114	0	0	0	0	0	0	40	0	0	0	0	0	0	0	0	0	0	0	40
RUTGERS UNIVERSITY	319	0	0	0	0	0	0	0	1	3	0	32	3	0	0	0	41	0	0	80
SAN DIEGO STATE	190	0	0	0	0	0	4	0	0	0	0	31	0	0	0	0	0	0	0	35
SAN FRANCISCO STATE	113	0	0	0	0	0	0	0	0	0	0	15	0	0	0	0	0	0	0	15

TABLE 209 (Continued)

Full-time Masters Students Receiving Financial Aid Paid Directly by Field Instruction Agency, by Source of Funds

Program	Total Full-time Students	Public Funds											Voluntary Funds		School or University	Foreign Gov't	Formal Loan Programs	Work Study	Research or Graduate Assists	Other	Total From All Sources
		Federal Government							Other	State or Local Gov't	Veterans' Benefits		Social Welfare Agencies	Foundations or Other							
		Child Welfare	Office of Aging	NIAAA	NIDA	NIMH	VA	FCWSP													
SAN JOSE STATE	122	*	*	*	*	*	*	*	*	*	*	*	*	*	*	*	*	*	*	*
SIMMONS COLLEGE	201	0	0	2	0	0	0	2	0	0	0	1	0	0	0	0	0	0	0	5
SMITH COLLEGE	231	0	0	0	0	0	0	0	0	0	0	0	48	0	0	0	0	0	0	48
SOUTHERN BAPTIST	105	0	0	0	0	0	0	0	3	0	0	2	4	0	0	0	0	0	0	9
SOUTHERN CONNECTIC	104	0	0	0	0	0	0	0	0	0	0	0	0	0	0	0	0	0	0	0
SOUTHERN ILL/CARB	38	0	0	0	0	0	0	0	2	0	0	0	0	3	0	0	0	0	0	5
SOUTHERN UNIVERSITY	*	*	*	*	*	*	*	*	*	*	*	*	*	*	*	*	*	*	*	*
ST LOUIS UNIVERSITY	98	0	0	0	0	0	0	0	0	0	0	0	0	0	0	0	0	0	0	0
SUNY/ALBANY	249	0	0	0	0	0	3	0	0	0	0	0	0	0	0	0	0	0	0	3
SUNY/BUFFALO	172	0	0	0	0	0	0	6	0	3	0	0	0	0	0	0	0	0	0	9
SUNY/STONY BROOK	287	0	0	0	0	0	0	0	2	0	0	0	0	0	0	0	0	0	0	2
SYRACUSE UNIVERSITY	148	0	0	0	0	0	0	0	0	0	0	0	0	0	0	0	0	0	0	0
TEMPLE UNIVERSITY	139	0	0	0	0	0	6	0	0	0	6	3	0	1	0	0	0	0	0	16
TULANE UNIVERSITY	216	0	0	0	0	0	2	0	0	0	2	0	0	0	0	0	0	0	0	4
U OF ALABAMA	214	0	0	0	0	0	10	0	0	0	5	2	0	0	0	0	7	0	0	24
U OF ARKANSAS	82	9	0	0	0	0	9	0	4	0	0	6	0	0	0	0	0	0	0	28
U OF CALIFORNIA/BERK	191	0	0	0	0	0	0	0	0	0	0	12	0	0	0	0	0	0	0	12
U OF CALIFORNIA/LA	148	0	0	0	0	0	6	0	2	0	0	2	0	12	0	0	0	0	3	25
U OF CHICAGO	189	0	0	0	0	0	0	0	13	0	0	0	0	0	0	0	0	0	0	13
U OF CINCINNATI	97	0	0	0	0	0	0	0	0	0	0	0	0	0	0	0	0	0	0	0
U OF CONNECTICUT	193	0	0	0	0	0	0	0	0	0	0	0	0	0	0	0	0	0	0	0
U OF DENVER	267	0	0	0	0	0	3	0	0	0	0	3	10	0	0	0	0	0	0	16
U OF GEORGIA	180	0	0	0	0	0	6	0	0	0	0	2	0	0	0	0	0	0	0	8
U OF HAWAII	138	6	0	0	0	0	2	0	31	*	1	14	2	1	0	0	0	1	9	67
U OF HOUSTON	156	0	0	0	0	0	4	0	2	*	0	20	1	1	0	0	0	0	0	28
U OF ILLINOIS/CHI	380	0	0	0	0	0	3	0	88	0	0	0	10	0	0	0	0	0	0	101
U OF ILLINOIS/URB	194	0	0	0	0	0	1	0	0	*	38	14	0	47	0	14	0	0	0	114
U OF IOWA	111	0	0	0	0	0	0	0	0	0	0	3	0	0	0	0	0	0	0	3
U OF KANSAS	274	0	0	0	0	0	0	0	0	0	0	0	0	0	0	0	0	0	0	0
U OF KENTUCKY	312	0	0	0	0	0	4	0	0	*	0	0	0	0	0	0	0	0	0	4
U OF LOUISVILLE	142	0	0	0	0	0	1	0	2	0	0	0	0	0	0	0	0	0	0	3
U OF MAINE	22	1	0	0	0	0	0	0	1	0	0	0	0	0	0	0	0	0	0	2
U OF MARYLAND	676	0	0	0	1	0	6	0	37	0	0	2	34	5	0	0	0	0	0	85
U OF MICHIGAN	501	0	0	0	0	0	1	0	0	0	0	9	0	0	0	0	0	0	0	10
U OF MINNESOTA/DUL	18	0	0	0	0	0	0	0	0	0	0	0	0	0	0	0	0	0	0	0
U OF MINNESOTA/MINN	136	0	0	0	0	0	0	0	0	0	0	15	0	0	0	0	0	0	0	15
U OF MISSOURI	95	0	0	0	0	0	0	0	0	0	0	0	0	0	0	0	0	0	0	0
U OF NEBRASKA	97	0	0	0	0	0	0	0	0	0	0	0	0	0	0	0	0	0	0	0
U OF NEW ENGLAND	47	0	0	0	0	0	0	0	0	0	0	0	0	0	0	0	0	0	0	0
U OF NORTH CAROLINA	151	0	0	0	0	0	0	0	0	0	2	0	0	0	0	0	0	0	0	2

TABLE 209 (Continued)

Full-time Masters Students Receiving Financial Aid Paid Directly by Field Instruction Agency, by Source of Funds

Program	Total Full-time Students	Public Funds								State or Local Gov't	Veterans' Benefits	Voluntary Funds		School or University	Foreign Gov't	Formal Loan Programs	Work Study	Research or Graduate Assists	Other	Total From All Sources
		Federal Government										Social Welfare Agencies	Foundations or Other							
		Child Welfare	Office of Aging	NIAAA	NIDA	NIMH	VA	FCWSP	Other											
U OF OKLAHOMA	69	3	1	0	0	3	0	0	0	0	2	0	0	0	0	0	0	0	0	9
U OF PENNSYLVANIA	193	0	0	0	0	0	2	0	6	0	0	0	0	0	0	0	0	0	0	8
U OF PITTSBURGH	202	0	0	0	0	0	7	0	0	0	9	0	0	0	0	0	0	0	0	16
U OF PUERTO RICO	168	0	0	0	0	0	0	0	0	0	0	5	0	0	0	0	0	0	0	5
U OF SOUTH CAROLINA	228	0	0	0	0	0	4	0	0	0	0	0	0	0	0	0	14	0	0	18
U OF SOUTH FLORIDA	54	0	0	0	0	0	3	0	2	0	0	0	0	0	0	0	0	0	0	5
U OF SOUTHERN CAL	273	0	0	0	0	0	2	0	0	0	0	28	0	0	0	0	15	0	0	45
U OF SOUTHERN MISS	85	0	0	0	0	0	4	0	0	0	0	0	0	0	0	0	0	0	0	4
U OF TENNESSEE	204	0	0	0	0	0	2	0	0	5	0	11	0	0	0	0	0	0	0	18
U OF TEXAS/ARLINGTON	340	4	0	0	0	0	0	0	57	0	3	0	0	0	0	0	0	0	0	64
U OF TEXAS/AUSTIN	151	1	0	0	0	0	0	0	0	0	0	2	0	0	0	0	0	0	0	3
U OF UTAH	132	0	0	0	0	0	10	0	24	0	5	60	0	0	0	0	0	0	0	99
U OF WASHINGTON	192	0	0	0	0	0	0	0	0	0	0	0	0	0	0	0	0	0	0	0
U OF WISCONSIN/MAD	185	0	0	0	0	0	9	1	3	0	0	0	0	0	0	0	0	0	0	13
U OF WISCONSIN/MIL	183	0	0	0	0	0	4	0	0	0	0	0	0	0	0	0	0	0	0	4
VIRGINIA COMMON	324	0	0	0	0	0	5	0	8	0	7	0	0	0	0	0	0	0	0	20
WASHINGTON UNIV	297	0	0	0	0	0	0	0	0	0	0	37	8	0	0	0	0	0	0	45
WAYNE STATE UNIV	276	0	0	0	0	0	3	0	0	0	0	14	5	0	0	0	0	0	0	22
WEST VIRGINIA UNIV	117	0	0	0	0	0	0	0	0	0	0	0	0	0	0	0	0	0	0	0
WESTERN MICHIGAN	108	0	0	0	0	0	3	0	0	0	0	0	0	0	0	0	0	0	0	3
YESHIVA UNIVERSITY	391	5	0	0	0	0	0	0	7	0	0	76	74	0	22	0	92	0	0	276

* Missing data

TABLE 210

Unduplicated Count of Full-time Masters Degree Students Receiving Financial Aid From All Sources and Number of Grants Awarded

Program	Total Full-time Students	Students Receiving Grants	Total Number of Grants Awarded	Programs	Total Full-time Students	Students Receiving Grants	Total Number of Grants Awarded
TOTAL:	19,288	9,867	16,785				
ADELPHI UNIVERSITY	415	172	172	U OF ARKANSAS	82	50	59
ARIZONA STATE UNIV	174	139	200	U OF CALIFORNIA/BERK	191	126	225
AURORA UNIVERSITY	61	67	125	U OF CALIFORNIA/LA	148	126	170
BARRY UNIVERSITY	204	49	49	U OF CHICAGO	189	154	208
BOSTON COLLEGE	296	223	542	U OF CINCINNATI	97	42	42
BOSTON UNIVERSITY	290	179	359	U OF CONNECTICUT	193	174	360
BRIGHAM YOUNG UNIV	45	24	75	U OF DENVER	267	160	388
BRYN MAWR COLLEGE	187	145	229	U OF GEORGIA	180	52	54
CAL STATE UNIV/FRES	90	3	*	U OF HAWAII	138	90	120
CAL STATE UNIV/LB	82	33	117	U OF HOUSTON	156	38	39
CAL STATE UNIV/SAC	222	*	*	U OF ILLINOIS/CHI	380	122	122
CASE WESTERN RESERVE	346	276	376	U OF ILLINOIS/URB	194	116	204
CATHOLIC UNIVERSITY	156	71	89	U OF IOWA	111	71	71
CLARK ATLANTA UNIV	61	19	29	U OF KANSAS	274	35	35
COLORADO STATE UNIV	47	14	14	U OF KENTUCKY	312	40	42
COLUMBIA UNIVERSITY	617	345	1,127	U OF LOUISVILLE	142	50	53
EAST CAROLINA UNIV	68	14	14	U OF MAINE	22	15	22
EASTERN WASHINGTON	79	63	108	U OF MARYLAND	676	419	836
FLORIDA INTERNATL	107	58	85	U OF MICHIGAN	501	332	637
FLORIDA STATE UNIV	206	*	57	U OF MINNESOTA/DUL	18	10	10
FORDHAM UNIVERSITY	616	535	718	U OF MINNESOTA/MINN	136	44	54
GRAMBLING STATE	*	*	22	U OF MISSOURI	95	29	29
GRAND VALLEY STATE	106	46	60	U OF NEBRASKA	97	36	63
HOWARD UNIVERSITY	111	74	154	U OF NEW ENGLAND	47	*	57
HUNTER COLLEGE	472	162	162	U OF NORTH CAROLINA	151	95	109
INDIANA UNIVERSITY	263	117	113	U OF OKLAHOMA	69	52	70
LOUISIANA STATE UNIV	165	86	86	U OF PENNSYLVANIA	193	102	334
LOYOLA UNIVERSITY	218	49	190	U OF PITTSBURGH	202	62	92
MARYWOOD COLLEGE	157	98	184	U OF PUERTO RICO	168	89	89
MICHIGAN STATE UNIV	139	25	29	U OF SOUTH CAROLINA	228	144	144
NEW MEXICO HIGHLANDS	101	34	34	U OF SOUTH FLORIDA	54	26	50
NEW YORK UNIVERSITY	505	264	629	U OF SOUTHERN CAL	273	197	446
NORFOLK STATE UNIV	129	142	142	U OF SOUTHERN MISS	85	16	22
OHIO STATE UNIV	221	72	77	U OF TENNESSEE	204	150	193
OUR LADY OF THE LAKE	151	71	93	U OF TEXAS/ARLINGTON	340	127	185
PORTLAND STATE UNIV	152	*	*	U OF TEXAS/AUSTIN	151	45	50
RHODE ISLAND COLLEGE	114	157	157	U OF UTAH	132	*	122
RUTGERS UNIVERSITY	319	98	312	U OF WASHINGTON	192	161	236
SAN DIEGO STATE	190	54	60	U OF WISCONSIN/MAD	185	50	52
SAN FRANCISCO STATE	113	55	106	U OF WISCONSIN/MIL	183	19	19
SAN JOSE STATE	122	28	*	VIRGINIA COMMON	324	168	191
SIMMONS COLLEGE	201	185	397	WASHINGTON UNIV	297	286	589
SMITH COLLEGE	231	171	275	WAYNE STATE UNIV	276	100	100
SOUTHERN BAPTIST	105	100	66	WEST VIRGINIA UNIV	117	25	25
SOUTHERN CONNECTICUT	104	4	4	WESTERN MICHIGAN	108	117	121
SOUTHERN ILL/CARB	38	38	62	YESHIVA UNIVERSITY	391	283	689
SOUTHERN UNIVERSITY	*	*	*				
ST LOUIS UNIVERSITY	98	46	2				
SUNY/ALBANY	249	38	61				
SUNY/BUFFALO	172	55	90				
SUNY/STONY BROOK	287	113	255				
SYRACUSE UNIVERSITY	148	52	52				
TEMPLE UNIVERSITY	139	76	92				
TULANE UNIVERSITY	216	183	399				
U OF ALABAMA	214	100	107				

* Missing data

TABLE 300

Number of Faculty Assigned 50 Percent or More Time to Social Work Program,
by Percentage of Time Assigned to Doctoral Program

Program	Percentage of Time to Doctoral Program				
	0%	1% - 24%	25% - 49%	50% and Over	Total Number of Faculty
TOTAL:					
Number	812	265	120	93	1,290
Percent	62.9%	20.5%	9.3%	7.2%	100.0%
ADELPHI UNIVERSITY	19	9	4	2	34
ARIZONA STATE UNIV	20	0	4	0	24
BARRY UNIVERSITY	11	3	7	2	23
BOSTON COLLEGE	10	13	5	1	29
BRYN MAWR COLLEGE	13	7	3	0	23
CASE WESTERN RESERVE	21	0	5	1	27
CATHOLIC UNIVERSITY	17	0	2	2	21
CLARK ATLANTA UNIV	10	0	0	2	12
COLUMBIA UNIVERSITY	22	7	2	3	34
FLORIDA STATE UNIV	12	5	1	3	21
HOWARD UNIVERSITY	6	8	5	2	21
HUNTER COLLEGE	32	3	1	3	39
LOYOLA UNIVERSITY	18	11	1	0	30
MICHIGAN STATE UNIV	12	2	1	1	16
NEW YORK UNIVERSITY	23	14	1	5	43
OHIO STATE UNIV	34	8	1	2	45
RUTGERS UNIVERSITY	30	7	1	2	40
SIMMONS COLLEGE	13	4	3	1	21
SMITH COLLEGE	8	2	0	3	13
ST LOUIS UNIVERSITY	26	1	0	0	27
SUNY/ALBANY	9	9	4	3	25
TULANE UNIVERSITY	8	6	3	2	19
U OF CALIFORNIA/BERK	13	2	3	12	30
U OF CHICAGO	20	8	3	3	34
U OF DENVER	17	7	1	0	25
U OF GEORGIA	27	0	2	1	30
U OF ILLINOIS/CHI	20	10	4	1	35
U OF ILLINOIS/URB	15	5	4	0	24
U OF KANSAS	22	6	1	1	30
U OF MARYLAND	30	7	2	2	41
U OF MICHIGAN	0	30	8	7	45
U OF MINNESOTA/MINN	4	5	5	2	16
U OF PENNSYLVANIA	7	6	1	6	20
U OF PITTSBURGH	23	5	2	5	35
U OF SOUTH CAROLINA	13	0	7	1	21
U OF SOUTHERN CAL	26	0	6	0	32
U OF TENNESSEE	26	1	1	3	31
U OF TEXAS/ARLINGTON	38	3	0	2	43
U OF TEXAS/AUSTIN	34	0	6	0	40
U OF UTAH	12	6	2	3	23
U OF WASHINGTON	24	10	2	0	36
VIRGINIA COMMON	35	5	2	1	43
WASHINGTON UNIV	4	19	1	1	25
YESHIVA UNIVERSITY	28	11	3	2	44

TABLE 301

Full-time Doctoral Students Enrolled on 11/1/91, by Ethnicity

Program	Total	African American	Asian American	Chicano/ Mex American	Native American	Puerto Rican	White	Other Minority	Foreign
TOTAL:									
Number	1,133	137	34	22	13	25	780	16	106
Percent	100.0%	12.1%	3.0%	1.9%	1.1%	2.2%	68.8%	1.4%	9.4%
ADELPHI UNIVERSITY	76	4	0	0	0	3	66	1	2
ARIZONA STATE UNIV	12	0	1	1	0	0	6	0	4
BARRY UNIVERSITY	28	5	0	0	0	0	19	0	4
BOSTON COLLEGE	1	0	0	0	0	1	0	0	0
BOSTON UNIVERSITY	1	0	1	0	0	0	0	0	0
BRYN MAWR COLLEGE	22	4	1	0	0	0	15	0	2
CASE WESTERN RESERVE	6	0	0	1	0	0	4	0	1
CATHOLIC UNIVERSITY	8	0	0	0	0	0	7	0	1
CLARK ATLANTA UNIV	22	0	0	0	0	0	21	0	1
COLUMBIA UNIVERSITY	32	5	7	1	0	2	17	0	0
FLORIDA STATE UNIV	34	2	1	1	1	1	22	0	6
FORDHAM UNIVERSITY	*	*	*	*	*	*	*	*	*
HOWARD UNIVERSITY	10	8	0	0	0	0	1	0	1
HUNTER COLLEGE	88	12	1	0	0	7	66	1	1
LOYOLA UNIVERSITY	25	4	2	1	0	0	18	0	0
MICHIGAN STATE UNIV	11	1	1	1	0	0	8	0	0
NEW YORK UNIVERSITY	44	1	0	0	0	2	37	2	2
OHIO STATE UNIV	39	12	0	0	0	1	17	3	6
RUTGERS UNIVERSITY	11	0	0	0	0	2	8	0	1
SIMMONS COLLEGE	0	0	0	0	0	0	0	0	0
SMITH COLLEGE	25	0	0	0	1	1	19	1	3
ST LOUIS UNIVERSITY	0	0	0	0	0	0	0	0	0
SUNY/ALBANY	12	2	0	1	0	0	8	0	1
TULANE UNIVERSITY	3	0	0	0	0	0	2	1	0
U OF ALABAMA	12	0	0	0	0	0	11	0	1
U OF CALIFORNIA/BERK	27	0	2	1	0	0	18	1	5
U OF CALIFORNIA/LA	30	4	4	4	1	0	14	0	3
U OF CHICAGO	14	2	2	0	0	0	8	0	2
U OF DENVER	12	1	0	0	1	0	10	0	0
U OF GEORGIA	14	1	0	0	0	0	11	0	2
U OF ILLINOIS/CHI	13	1	0	0	0	1	10	0	1
U OF ILLINOIS/URB	14	1	0	0	0	0	8	0	5
U OF KANSAS	18	0	0	0	0	0	16	1	1
U OF MARYLAND	51	7	0	2	0	1	38	1	2
U OF MICHIGAN	65	19	4	3	3	2	30	0	4
U OF MINNESOTA/MINN	18	0	0	0	1	0	12	0	5
U OF PENNSYLVANIA	5	0	0	0	0	0	2	0	3
U OF PITTSBURGH	15	5	0	0	0	0	6	0	4
U OF SOUTH CAROLINA	26	5	1	0	0	0	20	0	0
U OF SOUTHERN CAL	9	2	0	1	0	0	5	0	1
U OF TENNESSEE	24	3	0	0	0	0	16	0	5
U OF TEXAS/ARLINGTON	22	1	0	1	0	0	19	0	1
U OF TEXAS/AUSTIN	22	3	1	1	0	0	15	0	2
U OF UTAH	25	1	0	2	0	0	20	0	2
U OF WASHINGTON	26	3	3	0	2	0	14	4	0
U OF WISCONSIN/MAD	52	2	0	0	3	0	35	0	12
VIRGINIA COMMON	18	4	1	0	0	0	12	0	1
WASHINGTON UNIV	24	1	0	0	0	0	15	0	8
YESHIVA UNIVERSITY	67	11	1	0	0	1	54	0	0

* Missing data

94

TABLE 302**

Full-time Doctoral Students Enrolled on 11/1/91, by Age and Gender

Program	Total	Total		25 & under		26 - 30		31 - 40		41 & over	
		Men	Women	Men	Women	Men	Women	Men	Women	Men	Women
TOTAL:											
Number	1,133	376	757	10	30	39	74	155	279	142	310
Percent	100.0%	33.2%	66.8%	0.9%	2.6%	3.4%	6.5%	13.7%	24.6%	12.5%	27.4%
ADELPHI UNIVERSITY	76	27	49	*	*	*	*	*	*	*	*
ARIZONA STATE UNIV	12	2	10	0	2	1	0	0	4	1	4
BARRY UNIVERSITY	28	11	17	0	0	1	1	2	5	8	11
BOSTON COLLEGE	1	0	1	0	0	0	0	0	1	0	0
BOSTON UNIVERSITY	1	0	1	0	0	0	0	0	1	0	0
BRYN MAWR COLLEGE	22	7	15	0	0	0	2	4	7	3	6
CASE WESTERN RESERVE	6	1	5	0	0	1	1	0	1	0	3
CATHOLIC UNIVERSITY	8	2	6	0	0	0	0	1	5	1	1
CLARK ATLANTA UNIV	22	7	15	0	0	0	2	5	7	2	6
COLUMBIA UNIVERSITY	32	9	23	0	1	1	5	8	12	0	5
FLORIDA STATE UNIV	34	20	14	2	0	8	2	6	7	4	5
FORDHAM UNIVERSITY	*	*	*	*	*	*	*	*	*	*	*
HOWARD UNIVERSITY	10	3	7	0	0	0	0	2	4	1	3
HUNTER COLLEGE	88	28	60	0	0	0	2	7	23	21	35
LOYOLA UNIVERSITY	25	10	15	0	0	1	0	2	1	7	14
MICHIGAN STATE UNIV	11	4	7	0	0	1	1	3	3	0	3
NEW YORK UNIVERSITY	44	6	38	0	1	0	5	4	21	2	11
OHIO STATE UNIV	39	17	22	0	2	0	4	11	3	6	13
RUTGERS UNIVERSITY	11	1	10	0	0	0	3	1	2	0	5
SIMMONS COLLEGE	0	0	0	0	0	0	0	0	0	0	0
SMITH COLLEGE	25	10	15	0	0	0	3	4	4	6	8
ST LOUIS UNIVERSITY	0	0	0	0	0	0	0	0	0	0	0
SUNY/ALBANY	12	5	7	0	0	2	1	3	2	0	4
TULANE UNIVERSITY	3	0	3	0	1	0	0	0	1	0	1
U OF ALABAMA	12	3	9	0	0	0	2	2	4	1	3
U OF CALIFORNIA/BERK	27	6	21	1	0	2	3	3	10	0	8
U OF CALIFORNIA/LA	30	13	17	0	2	2	2	8	9	3	4
U OF CHICAGO	14	3	11	0	2	0	1	3	4	0	4
U OF DENVER	12	3	9	0	0	0	1	1	1	2	7
U OF GEORGIA	14	6	8	0	0	1	2	1	4	4	2
U OF ILLINOIS/CHI	13	5	8	0	0	2	0	0	1	3	7
U OF ILLINOIS/URB	14	8	6	1	1	3	2	2	2	2	1
U OF KANSAS	18	4	14	0	0	0	2	2	9	2	3
U OF MARYLAND	51	20	31	0	1	1	3	12	11	7	16
U OF MICHIGAN	65	21	44	5	12	4	6	8	14	4	12
U OF MINNESOTA/MINN	18	3	15	*	*	*	*	*	*	*	*
U OF PENNSYLVANIA	5	1	4	0	0	1	2	0	1	0	1
U OF PITTSBURGH	15	6	9	0	1	1	0	5	4	0	4
U OF SOUTH CAROLINA	26	8	18	0	0	0	0	2	8	6	10
U OF SOUTHERN CAL	9	5	4	0	0	0	0	3	1	2	3
U OF TENNESSEE	24	9	15	0	0	1	2	5	5	3	8
U OF TEXAS/ARLINGTON	22	6	16	0	0	0	1	3	3	3	12
U OF TEXAS/AUSTIN	22	10	12	0	0	1	1	5	8	4	3
U OF UTAH	25	8	17	0	0	0	0	1	10	7	7
U OF WASHINGTON	26	7	19	0	0	2	2	3	12	2	5
U OF WISCONSIN/MAD	52	19	33	1	2	2	5	9	17	7	9
VIRGINIA COMMON	18	6	12	0	0	0	0	4	5	2	7
WASHINGTON UNIV	24	3	21	0	2	0	3	3	11	0	5
YESHIVA UNIVERSITY	67	23	44	0	0	0	2	7	11	16	31

* Missing data

** Totals between columns may not correspond because of variation in item-specific reponse rates

TABLE 303

Applications for Admission to Doctoral Degree Programs During 1991, by Action Taken

Program	Applications			Registration		Enrollment			
	Total Received	Considered for Admission	Accepted	Accepted but not Registered	Accepted and Registered	Accepted in Prior Years	Total Newly Enrolled in 1991	Withdrawals by 11/1/91	Act Enrollment of New Students
TOTAL:	1,209	1,113	605	196	409	12	421	11	410
ADELPHI UNIVERSITY	26	23	18	2	16	0	16	4	12
ARIZONA STATE UNIV	18	16	11	5	6	0	6	0	6
BARRY UNIVERSITY	25	21	14	5	9	0	9	0	9
BOSTON COLLEGE	16	14	9	3	6	0	6	0	6
BOSTON UNIVERSITY	12	11	7	3	4	0	4	0	4
BRYN MAWR COLLEGE	18	13	4	1	3	0	3	0	3
CASE WESTERN RESERVE	51	48	14	0	14	0	14	1	13
CATHOLIC UNIVERSITY	22	18	17	9	8	0	8	0	8
CLARK ATLANTA UNIV	19	15	6	0	6	0	6	0	6
COLUMBIA UNIVERSITY	36	36	20	14	6	2	8	0	8
FLORIDA STATE UNIV	25	15	12	3	9	0	9	0	9
FORDHAM UNIVERSITY	18	18	14	2	12	0	12	0	12
HOWARD UNIVERSITY	12	12	9	4	5	0	5	0	5
HUNTER COLLEGE	*	*	*	*	*	*	*	*	*
LOYOLA UNIVERSITY	11	11	5	0	5	0	5	0	5
MICHIGAN STATE UNIV	8	7	4	0	4	0	4	0	4
NEW YORK UNIVERSITY	65	65	51	5	46	0	46	2	44
OHIO STATE UNIV	43	38	20	7	13	0	13	0	13
RUTGERS UNIVERSITY	30	30	17	8	9	1	10	0	10
SIMMONS COLLEGE	14	14	6	1	5	0	5	0	5
SMITH COLLEGE	25	23	13	1	12	0	12	0	12
ST LOUIS UNIVERSITY	0	0	0	0	0	0	0	0	0
SUNY/ALBANY	32	32	14	6	8	0	8	0	8
TULANE UNIVERSITY	16	14	10	3	7	0	7	0	7
U OF ALABAMA	14	12	7	3	4	2	6	0	6
U OF CALIFORNIA/BERK	32	31	12	8	4	1	5	0	5
U OF CALIFORNIA/LA	39	39	13	2	11	0	11	0	11
U OF CHICAGO	40	28	10	4	6	0	6	0	6
U OF DENVER	24	24	19	7	12	0	12	0	12
U OF GEORGIA	22	20	9	5	4	2	6	0	6
U OF ILLINOIS/CHI	25	25	14	5	9	0	9	0	9
U OF ILLINOIS/URB	13	12	8	2	6	0	6	0	6
U OF KANSAS	16	16	12	3	9	0	9	0	9
U OF MARYLAND	29	29	24	16	8	2	10	0	10
U OF MICHIGAN	89	88	24	9	15	0	15	0	15
U OF MINNESOTA/MINN	19	12	7	1	6	0	6	0	6
U OF PENNSYLVANIA	55	55	19	6	13	1	14	3	11
U OF PITTSBURGH	40	40	18	5	13	0	13	0	13
U OF SOUTH CAROLINA	24	24	12	3	9	0	9	0	9
U OF SOUTHERN CAL	13	12	8	3	5	0	5	0	5
U OF TENNESSEE	21	18	11	7	4	0	4	0	4
U OF TEXAS/ARLINGTON	21	21	14	2	12	0	12	0	12
U OF TEXAS/AUSTIN	34	34	14	1	13	0	13	1	12
U OF UTAH	17	11	10	6	4	0	4	0	4
U OF WASHINGTON	*	*	*	*	*	*	*	*	*
U OF WISCONSIN/MAD	19	18	11	3	8	1	9	0	9
VIRGINIA COMMON	10	8	7	1	6	0	6	0	6
WASHINGTON UNIV	21	17	7	3	4	0	4	0	4
YESHIVA UNIVERSITY	30	25	20	9	11	0	11	0	11

* Missing data

96

TABLE 304

Full-time Doctoral Students Receiving Financial Aid and Number of Grants Awarded, by Source of Funds

Program	Total Full-time Students	Public Funds — Federal Government: Child Welfare	Office of Aging	NIAAA	NIDA	NIMH	VA	FCWSP	Other	State or Local Gov't	Veterans' Benefits	Voluntary Funds: Social Welfare Agencies	Foundations or Other	School or University	Foreign Gov't	Formal Loan Programs	Work Study	Research or Graduate Assists	Other	Total From All Sources
TOTAL:	1,133	4	3	3	1	28	2	7	14	2	21	6	27	375	13	65	1	242	13	827
ADELPHI UNIVERSITY	76	0	0	0	0	0	0	0	0	0	0	0	0	0	0	0	0	6	0	6
ARIZONA STATE UNIV	12	0	0	0	0	0	0	0	0	0	0	0	0	10	0	0	0	0	0	10
BARRY UNIVERSITY	28	0	0	0	0	0	0	0	0	0	0	0	0	12	0	0	0	0	1	13
BOSTON COLLEGE	1	0	0	0	0	0	0	0	0	0	0	1	0	1	0	0	0	0	0	2
BOSTON UNIVERSITY	1	0	0	0	0	0	0	0	0	0	0	0	0	1	0	0	0	0	0	1
BRYN MAWR COLLEGE	22	0	0	0	0	0	0	0	0	0	2	0	3	7	0	1	0	1	0	14
CASE WESTERN RESERV	6	0	0	0	0	0	0	0	0	0	0	0	0	6	0	0	0	1	0	7
CATHOLIC UNIVERSITY	8	0	0	0	0	0	0	0	0	0	0	0	0	7	1	0	0	0	0	8
CLARK ATLANTA UNIV	22	0	0	0	0	0	0	0	0	0	0	0	0	18	0	0	0	0	0	18
COLUMBIA UNIVERSITY	32	0	0	0	0	6	0	0	0	0	0	0	3	3	0	6	0	4	0	22
FLORIDA STATE UNIV	34	2	0	0	0	1	0	0	0	0	0	0	0	2	1	0	0	17	2	25
FORDHAM UNIVERSITY	*	*	*	*	*	*	*	*	*	*	*	*	*	*	*	*	*	*	*	*
HOWARD UNIVERSITY	10	0	0	0	0	0	0	0	0	0	0	0	0	2	1	2	0	1	0	6
HUNTER COLLEGE	88	0	0	0	0	1	0	0	0	0	0	0	1	11	0	0	1	0	0	14
LOYOLA UNIVERSITY	25	0	0	0	0	0	0	0	0	0	0	0	0	4	0	0	0	0	0	4
MICHIGAN STATE UNIV	11	0	0	0	0	0	0	0	1	0	0	0	0	3	0	0	0	4	0	8
NEW YORK UNIVERSITY	44	0	0	0	0	0	0	0	0	0	0	0	0	32	0	18	*	0	*	50
OHIO STATE UNIV	39	0	0	0	0	0	0	0	0	0	0	0	2	22	0	0	0	0	1	25
RUTGERS UNIVERSITY	11	0	0	1	0	0	0	0	1	0	1	0	3	5	0	0	0	0	0	11
SIMMONS COLLEGE	0	0	0	0	0	0	0	0	0	0	0	0	0	0	0	0	0	0	0	0
SMITH COLLEGE	25	0	0	0	0	0	0	0	0	0	0	0	0	1	0	0	0	0	0	1
ST LOUIS UNIVERSITY	0	0	0	0	0	0	0	0	0	0	0	0	0	0	2	0	0	0	0	2
SUNY/ALBANY	12	0	0	0	0	0	1	0	0	0	0	0	0	2	0	0	0	10	0	13
TULANE UNIVERSITY	3	0	0	0	0	0	0	0	0	0	0	0	0	1	0	1	0	0	0	2
U OF ALABAMA	12	0	0	0	0	0	0	0	0	0	0	0	0	2	0	0	0	7	0	9
U OF CALIFORNIA/BERK	27	0	0	1	0	3	1	2	0	0	0	0	1	7	1	10	0	15	0	41
U OF CALIFORNIA/LA	30	0	0	0	0	0	0	0	0	0	0	0	0	21	0	5	0	6	0	32
U OF CHICAGO	14	0	0	0	0	3	0	0	0	0	0	0	0	11	0	*	0	0	0	14
U OF DENVER	12	0	0	0	0	0	0	0	5	0	3	2	0	10	0	11	0	0	3	34
U OF GEORGIA	14	0	0	0	0	0	0	0	0	0	0	0	0	1	1	0	0	11	0	13
U OF ILLINOIS/CHI	13	0	0	0	0	0	0	0	1	0	0	0	0	1	0	0	0	10	0	12
U OF ILLINOIS/URB	14	0	0	0	0	0	0	0	1	0	1	1	1	10	2	0	0	0	1	17
U OF KANSAS	18	0	0	0	0	0	0	0	0	0	0	0	0	0	0	0	0	23	2	25
U OF MARYLAND	51	0	0	0	0	0	0	0	0	0	0	0	2	12	0	0	0	7	0	22
U OF MICHIGAN	65	0	0	0	0	0	0	0	0	0	9	0	0	35	0	0	0	25	0	69
U OF MINNESOTA/MINN	18	0	0	0	0	0	0	0	1	0	0	0	0	3	0	0	0	10	0	14
U OF PENNSYLVANIA	5	0	0	0	0	0	0	0	0	0	0	1	1	23	2	0	0	14	0	41
U OF PITTSBURGH	15	0	2	0	0	0	0	0	0	0	0	0	0	0	0	0	0	13	0	15
U OF SOUTH CAROLINA	26	0	0	0	0	0	0	0	2	0	0	0	0	2	0	0	0	8	0	12
U OF SOUTHERN CAL	9	0	0	0	0	1	0	0	2	0	0	1	1	13	1	5	0	0	1	25

TABLE 304 (Continued)

Full-time Doctoral Students Receiving Financial Aid and Number of Grants Awarded, by Source of Funds

Program	Total Full-time Students	Public Funds										Voluntary Funds		School or University	Foreign Gov't	Formal Loan Programs	Work Study	Research or Graduate Assists	Other	Total From All Sources
		Federal Government								State or Local Gov't	Veterans' Benefits	Social Welfare Agencies	Founda-tions or Other							
		Child Welfare	Office of Aging	NIAAA	NIDA	NIMH	VA	FCWSP	Other											
U OF TENNESSEE	24	0	0	0	0	6	0	0	0	0	0	0	0	2	0	0	0	5	0	13
U OF TEXAS/ARLINGTON	22	0	0	0	0	0	0	0	0	0	0	0	1	0	0	0	0	3	0	4
U OF TEXAS/AUSTIN	22	0	0	0	0	0	0	0	0	2	0	0	0	9	0	0	0	3	5	19
U OF UTAH	25	0	0	0	0	0	0	0	0	0	0	0	0	10	0	0	0	0	0	10
U OF WASHINGTON	26	0	0	0	0	0	0	2	1	0	0	0	0	0	0	6	0	0	0	9
U OF WISCONSIN/MAD	52	0	0	0	0	0	0	0	0	0	0	0	0	13	0	0	0	19	0	32
VIRGINIA COMMON	18	0	0	0	0	0	0	0	1	0	0	0	2	6	0	0	0	4	0	13
WASHINGTON UNIV	24	0	1	1	0	4	0	3	0	0	4	0	0	19	1	0	0	14	0	47
YESHIVA UNIVERSITY	67	0	0	0	0	0	0	0	0	0	0	1	6	15	0	0	0	1	0	23

* Missing data

TABLE 305

Unduplicated Count of Full-time Doctoral Degree Students Receiving Financial Aid From All Sources, and Number of Grants Awarded

Program	Total Full-time Students	Students Receiving Grants	Total Number of Grants Awarded
TOTAL:	1,133	245	827
ADELPHI UNIVERSITY	76	5	6
ARIZONA STATE UNIV	12	2	10
BARRY UNIVERSITY	28	5	13
BOSTON COLLEGE	1	0	2
BOSTON UNIVERSITY	1	1	1
BRYN MAWR COLLEGE	22	6	14
CASE WESTERN RESERVE	6	9	7
CATHOLIC UNIVERSITY	8	5	8
CLARK ATLANTA UNIV	22	4	18
COLUMBIA UNIVERSITY	32	16	22
FLORIDA STATE UNIV	34	6	25
FORDHAM UNIVERSITY	*	8	*
HOWARD UNIVERSITY	10	4	6
HUNTER COLLEGE	88	6	14
LOYOLA UNIVERSITY	25	1	4
MICHIGAN STATE UNIV	11	1	8
NEW YORK UNIVERSITY	44	8	50
OHIO STATE UNIV	39	6	25
RUTGERS UNIVERSITY	11	11	11
SIMMONS COLLEGE	0	5	0
SMITH COLLEGE	25	6	1
ST LOUIS UNIVERSITY	0	4	2
SUNY/ALBANY	12	3	13
TULANE UNIVERSITY	3	5	2
U OF ALABAMA	12	4	9
U OF CALIFORNIA/BERK	27	13	41
U OF CALIFORNIA/LA	30	5	32
U OF CHICAGO	14	7	14
U OF DENVER	12	1	34
U OF GEORGIA	14	0	13
U OF ILLINOIS/CHI	13	4	12
U OF ILLINOIS/URB	14	5	17
U OF KANSAS	18	4	25
U OF MARYLAND	51	11	22
U OF MICHIGAN	65	7	69
U OF MINNESOTA/MINN	18	6	14
U OF PENNSYLVANIA	5	7	41
U OF PITTSBURGH	15	6	15
U OF SOUTH CAROLINA	26	2	12
U OF SOUTHERN CAL	9	1	25
U OF TENNESSEE	24	2	13
U OF TEXAS/ARLINGTON	22	5	4
U OF TEXAS/AUSTIN	22	4	19
U OF UTAH	25	7	10
U OF WASHINGTON	26	7	9
U OF WISCONSIN/MAD	52	2	32
VIRGINIA COMMON	18	0	13
WASHINGTON UNIV	24	5	47
YESHIVA UNIVERSITY	67	3	23

* Missing data

99

TABLE 400

Full-time Masters and Doctoral Students Enrolled in Social Work Programs, 1982 through 1991

Program	1982	1983	1984	1985	1986	1987	1988	1989	1990	1991	% Change 1990-91
TOTAL:	17,853	16,890	17,057	16,742	17,019	17,935	15,711	16,633	20,303	20,369	0.3%
ADELPHI UNIVERSITY	536	532	481	508	444	395	495	336	388	491	26.5%
ARIZONA STATE UNIV	146	134	136	128	146	169	172	171	158	186	17.7%
AURORA UNIVERSITY	---	---	---	---	---	---	67	62	22	61	177.3%
BARRY UNIVERSITY	140	94	131	151	132	142	147	197	205	232	13.2%
BOSTON COLLEGE	214	189	202	240	241	245	*	238	254	297	16.9%
BOSTON UNIVERSITY	313	256	254	254	203	243	265	283	269	291	8.2%
BRIGHAM YOUNG UNIV	---	---	41	40	41	42	42	43	46	45	-2.2%
BRYN MAWR COLLEGE	154	128	143	150	140	159	173	176	204	209	2.5%
CAL STATE UNIV/FRES	106	106	100	74	59	105	93	68	70	90	28.6%
CAL STATE UNIV/LB	---	---	---	---	---	---	95	99	88	82	-6.8%
CAL STATE UNIV/SAC	248	201	223	209	240	231	226	288	249	222	-10.8%
CASE WESTERN RESERVE	181	182	134	125	116	115	369	376	353	352	-0.3%
CATHOLIC UNIVERSITY	150	140	128	127	136	9	139	134	136	164	20.6%
CLARK ATLANTA UNIV	96	81	63	52	66	61	77	53	81	83	2.5%
COLORADO STATE UNIV	---	---	---	---	---	---	39	44	50	47	-6.0%
COLUMBIA UNIVERSITY	458	420	486	*	554	482	530	*	535	649	21.3%
DELAWARE STATE COLL	---	---	---	---	---	---	---	---	46	*	*
EAST CAROLINA UNIV	---	---	---	---	31	29	46	50	70	68	-2.9%
EASTERN WASHINGTON	90	78	101	77	74	74	78	77	83	79	-4.8%
FLORIDA INTERNATL	---	---	*	*	*	*	57	41	*	107	*
FLORIDA STATE UNIV	134	141	155	134	147	162	166	197	213	240	12.7%
FORDHAM UNIVERSITY	499	514	442	445	501	531	445	515	541	616	13.9%
GEORGE WILLIAMS	101	63	65	50	---	---	---	---	---	---	---
GRAMBLING STATE	---	---	---	---	---	---	---	---	86	*	*
GRAND VALLEY STATE	---	---	---	30	46	48	*	73	79	106	34.2%
HOWARD UNIVERSITY	142	138	119	99	95	116	131	119	113	121	7.1%
HUNTER COLLEGE	486	476	494	466	470	501	518	490	492	560	13.8%
INDIANA UNIVERSITY	154	143	139	157	162	170	178	182	194	263	35.6%
LOUISIANA STATE UNIV	131	168	183	150	*	168	136	131	148	165	11.5%
LOYOLA UNIVERSITY	91	94	91	122	117	131	148	171	207	243	17.4%
MARYWOOD COLLEGE	43	66	64	77	113	140	118	156	163	157	-3.7%
MICHIGAN STATE UNIV	131	135	161	165	142	132	141	126	135	150	11.1%
NEW MEXICO HIGHLANDS	38	55	37	46	*	69	*	51	75	101	34.7%
NEW YORK UNIVERSITY	411	385	413	423	389	399	463	458	456	549	20.4%
NORFOLK STATE UNIV	92	86	84	86	104	87	101	92	112	129	15.2%
OHIO STATE UNIV	206	211	214	213	212	244	223	246	209	260	24.4%
OUR LADY OF THE LAKE	109	127	114	104	97	106	107	106	147	151	2.7%
PORTLAND STATE UNIV	125	127	142	145	219	144	143	148	142	152	7.0%
RHODE ISLAND COLLEGE	73	77	79	82	90	73	80	77	104	114	9.6%
RUTGERS UNIVERSITY	439	364	326	314	317	289	*	306	320	330	3.1%
SALEM STATE COLL	---	---	---	---	---	---	---	---	---	*	*
SAN DIEGO STATE	228	195	*	204	225	216	175	131	188	190	1.1%
SAN FRANCISCO STATE	143	163	152	140	142	150	137	108	108	113	4.6%
SAN JOSE STATE	69	73	71	73	97	101	94	116	*	122	*
SIMMONS COLLEGE	167	190	202	208	192	167	*	170	197	201	2.0%
SMITH COLLEGE	204	188	176	178	192	201	203	217	246	256	4.1%
SOUTHERN BAPTIST	---	---	---	---	*	104	102	119	119	105	-11.8%
SOUTHERN CONNECTICUT	---	---	---	---	*	62	111	92	77	104	35.1%
SOUTHERN ILL/CARB	---	---	---	---	---	---	---	13	31	38	22.6%
SOUTHERN UNIVERSITY	---	---	---	---	*	52	65	*	73	*	*
ST LOUIS UNIVERSITY	74	59	68	64	79	70	64	78	77	98	27.3%
SUNY/ALBANY	247	201	177	152	207	*	200	203	228	261	14.5%
SUNY/BUFFALO	133	111	122	153	163	156	157	147	182	172	-5.5%
SUNY/STONY BROOK	224	219	250	222	243	239	259	271	281	287	2.1%
SYRACUSE UNIVERSITY	129	143	131	123	*	125	134	139	126	148	17.5%
TEMPLE UNIVERSITY	129	143	118	131	*	145	148	142	134	139	3.7%
TULANE UNIVERSITY	111	88	115	114	132	145	167	192	211	219	3.8%
U OF ALABAMA	101	98	109	95	103	106	107	119	173	226	30.6%
U OF ARKANSAS	45	38	57	39	*	52	45	60	97	82	-15.5%
U OF CALIFORNIA/BERK	236	201	209	200	210	252	241	227	192	218	13.5%

TABLE 400 (Continued)

Full-time Masters and Doctoral Students Enrolled in Social Work Programs, 1982 through 1991

Program	1982	1983	1984	1985	1986	1987	1988	1989	1990	1991	% Change 1990-91
U OF CALIFORNIA/LA	163	171	176	155	165	174	171	170	153	178	16.3%
U OF CHICAGO	216	171	153	212	222	164	168	207	214	203	-5.1%
U OF CINCINNATI	39	47	71	72	95	86	76	70	72	97	34.7%
U OF CONNECTICUT	479	533	548	589	472	314	230	176	174	193	10.9%
U OF DENVER	172	210	211	206	213	178	203	241	276	279	1.1%
U OF GEORGIA	231	146	138	137	156	200	219	214	178	194	9.0%
U OF HAWAII	168	166	155	165	109	112	99	139	107	138	29.0%
U OF HOUSTON	107	123	94	77	94	127	148	132	165	156	-5.5%
U OF ILLINOIS/CHI	307	348	341	354	331	336	344	310	330	393	19.1%
U OF ILLINOIS/URB	181	164	175	169	160	160	152	140	181	208	14.9%
U OF IOWA	136	145	152	138	138	123	98	92	82	111	35.4%
U OF KANSAS	222	253	234	230	251	253	265	253	259	292	12.7%
U OF KENTUCKY	74	67	93	129	*	211	*	*	267	312	16.9%
U OF LOUISVILLE	104	*	82	74	198	136	*	*	*	142	*
U OF MAINE	---	---	---	---	---	---	---	---	---	22	*
U OF MARYLAND	323	238	233	233	266	504	546	649	650	727	11.8%
U OF MICHIGAN	470	428	494	501	515	523	541	528	541	566	4.6%
U OF MINNESOTA/DUL	---	---	---	---	---	---	---	---	---	18	*
U OF MINNESOTA/MINN	115	111	132	129	*	125	100	116	126	154	22.2%
U OF MISSOURI	80	77	70	73	97	95	91	96	98	95	-3.1%
U OF NEBRASKA	80	85	94	83	88	99	95	114	89	97	9.0%
U OF NEW ENGLAND	---	---	---	---	---	---	---	---	---	47	*
U OF NORTH CAROLINA	120	127	147	148	149	157	125	140	125	151	20.8%
U OF OKLAHOMA	102	107	94	100	88	81	66	76	67	69	3.0%
U OF PENNSYLVANIA	174	118	144	107	103	113	126	155	156	198	26.9%
U OF PITTSBURGH	250	259	261	233	256	241	254	247	226	217	-4.0%
U OF PUERTO RICO	121	117	130	110	223	243	151	175	167	168	0.6%
U OF SOUTH CAROLINA	81	87	133	156	151	196	198	269	278	254	-8.6%
U OF SOUTH FLORIDA	---	---	---	---	42	44	36	49	57	54	-5.3%
U OF SOUTHERN CAL	247	238	245	234	222	244	*	296	271	282	4.1%
U OF SOUTHERN MISS	60	51	56	45	47	*	62	71	88	85	-3.4%
U OF TENNESSEE	209	183	190	208	221	250	238	241	235	228	-3.0%
U OF TEXAS/ARLINGTON	151	144	162	151	188	170	223	283	323	362	12.1%
U OF TEXAS/AUSTIN	136	153	125	119	109	103	96	152	150	173	15.3%
U OF UTAH	154	146	182	195	181	174	151	149	125	157	25.6%
U OF WASHINGTON	266	254	228	205	192	256	211	224	224	218	-2.7%
U OF WISCONSIN/MAD	271	208	197	196	179	196	196	*	178	185	3.9%
U OF WISCONSIN/MIL	143	126	126	143	121	141	152	158	149	183	22.8%
VIRGINIA COMMON	235	229	207	219	249	261	297	315	352	342	-2.8%
WASHINGTON UNIV	249	216	216	218	231	196	231	278	293	321	9.6%
WAYNE STATE UNIV	207	213	236	221	207	206	205	237	266	276	3.8%
WEST VIRGINIA UNIV	81	65	65	72	92	*	84	97	118	117	-0.8%
WESTERN MICHIGAN	127	97	99	104	100	103	113	106	88	108	22.7%
YESHIVA UNIVERSITY	343	265	282	308	283	299	333	344	432	458	6.0%

* Missing data

TABLE 401 **

Students Enrolled on 11/1/91, by Type of Enrollment

Program	Total	Total Masters and Doctoral	Full-time			Part-time			Other Students Taking Graduate Courses		
			Total	Masters	Doctoral	Total	Masters	Doctoral	Total Other	Undergrad as Part of Undergrad/ Grad Continuum	Not Working Toward Social Work Degree
TOTAL:	35,449	31,530	20,421	19,288	1,133	11,109	10,131	978	3,919	194	3,725
ADELPHI UNIVERSITY	871	660	491	415	76	169	169	0	211	81	130
ARIZONA STATE UNIV	378	323	186	174	12	137	124	13	55	0	55
AURORA UNIVERSITY	206	181	61	61	0	120	120	0	25	5	20
BARRY UNIVERSITY	474	466	232	204	28	234	207	27	8	0	8
BOSTON COLLEGE	514	473	297	296	1	176	134	42	41	4	37
BOSTON UNIVERSITY	628	616	291	290	1	325	308	17	12	0	12
BRIGHAM YOUNG UNIV	46	45	45	45	0	0	0	0	1	0	1
BRYN MAWR COLLEGE	288	279	209	187	22	70	35	35	9	0	9
CAL STATE UNIV/FRES	184	184	90	90	0	94	94	0	0	0	0
CAL STATE UNIV/LB	357	353	82	82	0	271	271	0	4	0	4
CAL STATE UNIV/SAC	437	427	222	222	0	205	205	0	10	0	10
CASE WESTERN RESERVE	464	460	352	346	6	108	41	67	4	0	4
CATHOLIC UNIVERSITY	373	359	164	156	8	195	156	39	14	0	14
CLARK ATLANTA UNIV	92	92	83	61	22	9	7	2	0	0	0
COLORADO STATE UNIV	73	51	47	47	0	4	4	0	22	0	22
COLUMBIA UNIVERSITY	925	823	649	617	32	174	168	6	102	0	102
EAST CAROLINA UNIV	118	117	68	68	0	49	49	0	1	0	1
EASTERN WASHINGTON	113	113	79	79	0	34	34	0	0	0	*
FLORIDA INTERNATL	341	184	107	107	0	77	77	0	157	0	157
FLORIDA STATE UNIV	459	459	240	206	34	219	209	10	0	0	*
FORDHAM UNIVERSITY	1,068	983	616	616	*	367	367	*	85	0	85
GRAMBLING STATE	0	0	0	*	0	0	0	0	0	0	0
GRAND VALLEY STATE	233	188	106	106	0	82	82	0	45	0	45
HOWARD UNIVERSITY	207	207	121	111	10	86	54	32	0	0	0
HUNTER COLLEGE	958	772	560	472	88	212	212	0	186	0	186
INDIANA UNIVERSITY	315	315	263	263	0	52	52	0	0	0	0
LOUISIANA STATE UNIV	218	218	165	165	0	53	53	0	0	0	0
LOYOLA UNIVERSITY	655	491	243	218	25	248	248	0	164	0	164
MARYWOOD COLLEGE	242	242	157	157	0	85	85	0	0	0	0
MICHIGAN STATE UNIV	198	186	150	139	11	36	32	4	12	0	12
NEW MEXICO HIGHLANDS	148	148	101	101	0	47	47	0	0	0	0
NEW YORK UNIVERSITY	1,016	824	549	505	44	275	104	171	192	0	192
NORFOLK STATE UNIV	255	180	129	129	0	51	51	0	75	0	75
OHIO STATE UNIV	444	432	260	221	39	172	169	3	12	0	12
OUR LADY OF THE LAKE	244	243	151	151	0	92	92	0	1	0	1
PORTLAND STATE UNIV	306	275	152	152	0	123	123	0	31	0	31
RHODE ISLAND COLLEGE	276	178	114	114	0	64	64	0	98	0	98
RUTGERS UNIVERSITY	1,224	878	330	319	11	548	483	65	346	36	310
SAN DIEGO STATE	321	321	190	190	0	131	131	0	0	0	0
SAN FRANCISCO STATE	275	218	113	113	0	105	105	0	57	0	57
SAN JOSE STATE	250	247	122	122	0	125	125	0	3	0	3
SIMMONS COLLEGE	309	309	201	201	0	108	73	35	0	0	0
SMITH COLLEGE	256	256	256	231	25	0	0	0	0	0	0
SOUTHERN BAPTIST	118	105	105	105	0	0	0	0	13	0	13
SOUTHERN CONNECTICUT	179	154	104	104	0	50	50	0	25	0	25
SOUTHERN ILL/CARB	56	52	38	38	0	14	14	0	4	0	4
SOUTHERN UNIVERSITY	3	0	0	*	0	0	*	0	3	0	3
ST LOUIS UNIVERSITY	215	210	98	98	0	112	108	4	5	0	5
SUNY/ALBANY	471	396	261	249	12	135	91	44	75	0	75
SUNY/BUFFALO	321	244	172	172	0	72	72	0	77	0	77

TABLE 401 (Continued)

Students Enrolled on 11/1/91, by Type of Enrollment

Program	Total	Total Masters and Doctoral	Full-time			Part-time			Other Students Taking Graduate Courses		
									Total Other	Undergrad as Part of Undergrad/ Grad Continuum	Not Working Toward Social Work Degree
			Total	Masters	Doctoral	Total	Masters	Doctoral			
SUNY/STONY BROOK	388	323	287	287	0	36	36	0	65	0	65
SYRACUSE UNIVERSITY	366	351	148	148	0	203	203	0	15	0	15
TEMPLE UNIVERSITY	400	392	139	139	0	253	253	0	8	0	8
TULANE UNIVERSITY	297	297	219	216	3	78	41	37	0	0	0
U OF ALABAMA	240	240	226	214	12	14	5	9	0	0	0
U OF ARKANSAS	181	181	82	82	0	99	99	0	0	0	0
U OF CALIFORNIA/BERK	218	218	218	191	27	0	0	0	0	0	0
U OF CALIFORNIA/LA	178	178	178	148	30	0	0	0	0	0	0
U OF CHICAGO	326	312	203	189	14	109	76	33	14	0	14
U OF CINCINNATI	144	144	97	97	0	47	47	0	0	0	0
U OF CONNECTICUT	755	346	193	193	0	153	153	0	409	0	409
U OF DENVER	326	319	279	267	12	40	33	7	7	0	7
U OF GEORGIA	256	255	194	180	14	61	61	0	1	0	1
U OF HAWAII	284	245	138	138	0	107	107	0	39	0	39
U OF HOUSTON	334	331	156	156	0	175	175	0	3	0	3
U OF ILLINOIS/CHI	622	622	393	380	13	229	200	29	0	0	0
U OF ILLINOIS/URB	300	298	208	194	14	90	80	10	2	0	2
U OF IOWA	353	261	111	111	0	150	150	0	92	45	47
U OF KANSAS	424	399	292	274	18	107	87	20	25	0	25
U OF KENTUCKY	358	312	312	312	0	0	0	0	46	0	46
U OF LOUISVILLE	203	197	142	142	0	55	55	0	6	0	6
U OF MAINE	61	56	22	22	0	34	34	0	5	0	5
U OF MARYLAND	978	975	727	676	51	248	236	12	3	0	3
U OF MICHIGAN	737	617	566	501	65	51	46	5	120	0	120
U OF MINNESOTA/DUL	42	35	18	18	0	17	17	0	7	0	7
U OF MINNESOTA/MINN	197	197	154	136	18	43	34	9	0	0	0
U OF MISSOURI	152	121	95	95	0	26	26	0	31	0	31
U OF NEBRASKA	193	187	97	97	0	90	90	0	6	0	6
U OF NEW ENGLAND	159	114	47	47	0	67	67	0	45	0	45
U OF NORTH CAROLINA	302	264	151	151	0	113	113	0	38	0	38
U OF OKLAHOMA	168	159	69	69	0	90	90	0	9	0	9
U OF PENNSYLVANIA	249	242	198	193	5	44	38	6	7	4	3
U OF PITTSBURGH	464	418	217	202	15	201	144	57	46	17	29
U OF PUERTO RICO	170	168	168	168	0	0	0	0	2	0	2
U OF SOUTH CAROLINA	420	379	254	228	26	125	125	0	41	0	41
U OF SOUTH FLORIDA	54	54	54	54	0	0	0	0	0	0	0
U OF SOUTHERN CAL	475	475	282	273	9	193	155	38	0	0	0
U OF SOUTHERN MISS	129	122	85	85	0	37	37	0	7	0	7
U OF TENNESSEE	397	364	228	204	24	136	133	3	33	0	33
U OF TEXAS/ARLINGTON	664	658	362	340	22	296	258	38	6	0	6
U OF TEXAS/AUSTIN	327	321	173	151	22	148	128	20	6	0	6
U OF UTAH	207	207	157	132	25	50	50	0	0	0	0
U OF WASHINGTON	316	305	218	192	26	87	81	6	11	0	11
U OF WISCONSIN/MAD	604	237	237	185	52	0	0	0	367	2	365
U OF WISCONSIN/MIL	378	318	183	183	0	135	135	0	60	0	60
VIRGINIA COMMON	704	689	342	324	18	347	329	18	15	0	15
WASHINGTON UNIV	431	431	321	297	24	110	110	0	0	0	0
WAYNE STATE UNIV	513	381	276	276	0	105	105	0	132	0	132
WEST VIRGINIA UNIV	150	145	117	117	0	28	28	0	5	0	5
WESTERN MICHIGAN	225	225	108	108	0	117	117	0	0	0	0
YESHIVA UNIVERSITY	508	508	458	391	67	50	45	5	0	0	0

* Missing data

** Totals between columns may not correspond because of variation in item-specific response rates

TABLE 402

Students Receiving Degrees During Academic Year 1990 - 1991, by Degree and Gender

Program	Masters Degree			Doctoral Degree		
	Total	Men	Women	Total	Men	Women
TOTAL:	10,969	1,948	9,021	243	78	165
ADELPHI UNIVERSITY	221	20	201	5	1	4
ARIZONA STATE UNIV	103	14	89	2	1	1
AURORA UNIVERSITY	49	5	44	0	0	0
BARRY UNIVERSITY	93	17	76	5	2	3
BOSTON COLLEGE	127	19	108	0	0	0
BOSTON UNIVERSITY	209	23	186	1	0	1
BRIGHAM YOUNG UNIV	22	10	12	0	0	0
BRYN MAWR COLLEGE	75	8	67	6	2	4
CAL STATE UNIV/FRES	54	10	44	0	0	0
CAL STATE UNIV/LB	123	37	86	0	0	0
CAL STATE UNIV/SAC	197	43	154	0	0	0
CASE WESTERN RESER	165	30	135	9	4	5
CATHOLIC UNIVERSITY	104	17	87	5	1	4
CLARK ATLANTA UNIV	71	12	59	4	1	3
COLORADO STATE UNIV	23	4	19	0	0	0
COLUMBIA UNIVERSITY	315	49	266	16	8	8
EAST CAROLINA UNIV	44	9	35	0	0	0
EASTERN WASHINGTON	41	13	28	0	0	0
FLORIDA INTERNATL	47	11	36	0	0	0
FLORIDA STATE UNIV	176	36	140	6	5	1
FORDHAM UNIVERSITY	238	35	203	8	0	8
GRAMBLING STATE	22	4	18	0	0	0
GRAND VALLEY STATE	58	10	48	0	0	0
HOWARD UNIVERSITY	61	11	50	4	1	3
HUNTER COLLEGE	259	61	198	6	1	5
INDIANA UNIVERSITY	143	26	117	0	0	0
LOUISIANA STATE UNIV	74	14	60	0	0	0
LOYOLA UNIVERSITY	126	21	105	1	0	1
MARYWOOD COLLEGE	95	18	77	0	0	0
MICHIGAN STATE UNIV	70	16	54	1	0	1
NEW MEXICO HIGHLAN	45	11	34	0	0	0
NEW YORK UNIVERSITY	243	35	208	8	2	6
NORFOLK STATE UNIV	57	10	47	0	0	0
OHIO STATE UNIV	126	14	112	6	3	3
OUR LADY OF THE LAKE	117	32	85	0	0	0
PORTLAND STATE UNIV	103	22	81	0	0	0
RHODE ISLAND COLLEG	47	5	42	0	0	0
RUTGERS UNIVERSITY	281	36	245	11	1	10
SAN DIEGO STATE	107	19	88	0	0	0
SAN FRANCISCO STATE	71	17	54	0	0	0
SAN JOSE STATE	90	17	73	0	0	0
SIMMONS COLLEGE	97	13	84	5	2	3
SMITH COLLEGE	114	12	102	6	2	4
SOUTHERN BAPTIST	47	15	32	0	0	0
SOUTHERN CONNECTIC	32	4	28	0	0	0
SOUTHERN ILL/CARB	27	2	25	0	0	0
SOUTHERN UNIVERSITY	44	10	34	0	0	0
ST LOUIS UNIVERSITY	40	7	33	4	1	3
SUNY/ALBANY	129	19	110	3	0	3
SUNY/BUFFALO	99	24	75	0	0	0
SUNY/STONY BROOK	132	27	105	0	0	0
SYRACUSE UNIVERSITY	125	23	102	0	0	0
TEMPLE UNIVERSITY	119	16	103	0	0	0
TULANE UNIVERSITY	112	19	93	5	1	4
U OF ALABAMA	79	14	65	4	1	3
U OF ARKANSAS	48	8	40	0	0	0
U OF CALIFORNIA/BERK	96	22	74	13	6	7
U OF CALIFORNIA/LA	72	15	57	5	5	0
U OF CHICAGO	108	20	88	7	2	5
U OF CINCINNATI	30	6	24	0	0	0
U OF CONNECTICUT	139	19	120	0	0	0
U OF DENVER	149	22	127	1	1	0
U OF GEORGIA	116	23	93	0	0	0
U OF HAWAII	59	10	49	0	0	0
U OF HOUSTON	105	23	82	0	0	0
U OF ILLINOIS/CHI	200	44	156	4	3	1
U OF ILLINOIS/URB	81	15	66	5	1	4
U OF IOWA	76	18	58	0	0	0
U OF KANSAS	150	32	118	4	1	3
U OF KENTUCKY	97	17	80	0	0	0
U OF LOUISVILLE	125	31	94	0	0	0
U OF MAINE	20	4	16	0	0	0
U OF MARYLAND	353	47	306	11	2	9
U OF MICHIGAN	278	57	221	7	1	6
U OF MINNESOTA/DUL	1	1	0	0	0	0
U OF MINNESOTA/MINN	65	9	56	6	3	3
U OF MISSOURI	62	11	51	0	0	0
U OF NEBRASKA	67	6	61	0	0	0
U OF NEW ENGLAND	33	4	29	0	0	0
U OF NORTH CAROLINA	100	16	84	0	0	0
U OF OKLAHOMA	45	11	34	0	0	0
U OF PENNSYLVANIA	77	7	70	7	2	5
U OF PITTSBURGH	130	38	92	6	2	4
U OF PUERTO RICO	168	25	143	0	0	0
U OF SOUTH CAROLINA	142	18	124	2	0	2
U OF SOUTH FLORIDA	32	8	24	0	0	0
U OF SOUTHERN CAL	135	12	123	1	0	1
U OF SOUTHERN MISS	47	5	42	0	0	0
U OF TENNESSEE	131	23	108	2	1	1
U OF TEXAS/ARLINGTO	186	34	152	5	1	4
U OF TEXAS/AUSTIN	107	18	89	4	1	3
U OF UTAH	69	26	43	7	4	3
U OF WASHINGTON	128	40	88	7	0	7
U OF WISCONSIN/MAD	122	17	105	0	0	0
U OF WISCONSIN/MIL	99	17	82	0	0	0
VIRGINIA COMMON	213	26	187	0	0	0
WASHINGTON UNIV	133	23	110	5	1	4
WAYNE STATE UNIV	188	25	163	0	0	0
WEST VIRGINIA UNIV	58	12	46	0	0	0
WESTERN MICHIGAN	80	16	64	0	0	0
YESHIVA UNIVERSITY	161	41	120	3	1	2

TABLE 403 **

Number of Full-time Non-Administrative Faculty Assigned 50 Percent or More Time to Social Work Program,
by Gender, Type of Appointment, and Academic Responsibility

Program	Total	Total Men	Total Women	Class Men	Class Women	Class and Field Men	Class and Field Women	Field Men	Field Women	Other Men	Other Women	Professor Men	Professor Women	Associate Professor Men	Associate Professor Women	Assistant Professor Men	Assistant Professor Women	Other Faculty Men	Other Faculty Women
TOTAL: Number	1,756	812	943	645	675	66	81	30	120	71	67	321	134	252	261	172	339	65	208
Percent	100.0%	46.2%	53.7%	36.7%	38.4%	3.8%	4.6%	1.7%	6.8%	4.0%	3.8%	18.3%	7.6%	14.4%	14.9%	9.8%	19.3%	3.7%	11.9%
ADELPHI UNIVERSITY	26	15	11	13	9	0	1	2	1	0	0	6	0	6	4	1	3	2	4
ARIZONA STATE UNIV	24	16	8	15	8	1	0	0	0	0	0	6	3	5	3	5	2	0	0
AURORA UNIVERSITY	1	0	1	0	1	0	0	0	0	0	0	0	0	0	0	0	1	0	0
BARRY UNIVERSITY	23	12	11	7	7	1	0	0	2	3	2	6	3	5	6	1	2	0	0
BOSTON COLLEGE	18	12	6	11	5	0	0	0	1	1	0	4	1	4	2	2	3	2	0
BRIGHAM YOUNG UNIV	7	4	3	4	3	0	0	0	0	0	0	3	0	1	1	0	2	0	0
BRYN MAWR COLLEGE	18	5	13	5	8	0	0	0	5	0	0	2	1	2	5	1	2	0	5
CAL STATE UNIV/FRES	12	8	4	7	3	1	0	0	1	0	0	6	1	2	0	0	1	0	2
CAL STATE UNIV/LB	16	6	10	5	8	1	0	0	2	0	0	4	3	1	3	0	1	1	3
CAL STATE UNIV/SAC	24	14	10	13	9	0	1	1	0	1	0	14	4	0	4	0	1	0	1
CASE WESTERN RESERVE	19	9	10	8	8	0	0	0	0	1	2	2	0	4	5	2	4	1	1
CATHOLIC UNIVERSITY	15	2	13	2	12	0	1	0	0	0	0	0	2	1	2	1	8	0	1
CLARK ATLANTA UNIV	7	2	5	2	5	0	0	0	0	0	0	0	0	1	2	0	2	0	1
COLL OF ST CATHERINE	5	1	4	1	1	0	1	0	2	0	0	0	1	0	0	1	3	0	0
COLORADO STATE UNIV	6	3	3	3	2	0	1	1	0	0	0	1	0	0	1	2	2	0	0
COLUMBIA UNIVERSITY	34	15	19	10	14	0	1	0	0	5	4	10	4	3	5	2	9	0	1
EAST CAROLINA UNIV	12	5	7	3	3	2	3	0	1	0	0	2	1	1	2	2	2	0	2
EASTERN WASHINGTON	18	8	10	5	5	2	1	1	4	0	0	4	2	2	2	1	3	1	3
FLORIDA INTERNATL	14	5	9	5	6	0	0	0	1	0	1	3	0	1	4	0	2	0	3
FLORIDA STATE UNIV	13	6	7	5	5	0	0	0	2	1	0	4	0	2	2	0	2	0	3
GALLAUDET UNIVERSITY	5	1	4	1	4	0	0	0	0	0	0	0	0	0	1	1	3	0	0
GRAMBLING STATE	6	2	4	2	1	0	0	0	2	0	0	1	0	0	0	1	4	0	0
GRAND VALLEY STATE	10	4	6	4	5	0	0	0	1	0	0	4	1	0	3	0	1	0	1
HOWARD UNIVERSITY	15	5	10	5	9	0	0	0	0	0	1	2	2	2	5	1	3	0	0
HUNTER COLLEGE	30	10	20	9	20	1	0	0	0	0	0	8	2	1	10	1	5	0	3
INDIANA UNIVERSITY	20	12	8	11	4	0	0	1	1	0	3	2	0	8	3	1	0	1	5
LOUISIANA STATE UNIV	21	13	8	10	7	1	0	0	1	2	0	5	0	6	4	2	2	0	2
LOYOLA UNIVERSITY	24	11	13	11	13	0	0	0	0	0	0	4	2	4	3	3	8	0	0
MARYWOOD COLLEGE	10	5	5	4	4	0	1	1	0	0	0	0	0	2	5	3	0	0	0
MICHIGAN STATE UNIV	13	7	6	7	6	0	0	0	0	0	0	1	0	4	1	2	5	0	0
NEW MEXICO HIGHLANDS	11	5	6	2	6	3	0	0	0	0	0	2	0	0	1	3	5	0	0
NEW MEXICO STATE	13	4	9	3	4	0	0	1	5	0	0	0	0	0	1	4	8	0	0
NEW YORK UNIVERSITY	29	6	23	4	15	0	1	0	4	2	3	2	3	2	6	1	11	1	3
NORFOLK STATE UNIV	20	8	12	8	10	0	0	0	0	0	1	2	1	2	4	4	5	0	2
OHIO STATE UNIV	39	17	22	17	19	0	0	0	0	0	3	4	2	8	3	3	6	2	11
OUR LADY OF THE LAKE	9	3	6	3	5	0	0	0	1	0	0	2	1	1	0	0	1	0	4
PORTLAND STATE UNIV	26	14	12	8	6	4	3	0	2	2	1	3	2	3	2	5	3	3	5
RHODE ISLAND COLLEGE	13	4	9	3	8	0	0	1	0	0	1	1	0	0	6	3	3	0	0
RUTGERS UNIVERSITY	35	16	19	13	18	1	0	0	1	2	0	9	5	6	7	1	3	0	4
SAN DIEGO STATE	24	15	9	11	4	2	3	0	0	2	2	5	2	2	2	4	1	4	4
SAN FRANCISCO STATE	17	9	8	2	5	5	2	1	0	1	1	9	4	0	1	0	2	0	2
SAN JOSE STATE	11	8	3	5	2	2	0	1	1	0	0	7	0	1	1	0	1	0	1
SIMMONS COLLEGE	19	1	18	1	11	0	0	0	7	0	0	0	3	0	7	1	8	0	0

TABLE 403 (Continued)

Number of Full-time Non-Administrative Faculty Assigned 50 Percent or More Time to Social Work Program, by Gender, Type of Appointment, and Academic Responsibility

Program	Total	Total Men	Total Women	Class Men	Class Women	Class and Field Men	Class and Field Women	Field Men	Field Women	Other Men	Other Women	Professor Men	Professor Women	Associate Professor Men	Associate Professor Women	Assistant Professor Men	Assistant Professor Women	Other Faculty Men	Other Faculty Women
SMITH COLLEGE	3	1	2	1	1	0	0	0	1	0	0	0	0	0	0	1	1	0	0
SOUTHERN BAPTIST	4	2	2	2	1	0	1	0	0	0	0	0	0	2	1	0	1	0	0
SOUTHERN CONNECTICUT	17	6	11	3	6	2	3	1	2	0	0	0	2	2	3	1	1	2	5
SOUTHERN ILL/CARB	7	4	3	3	3	1	0	0	0	0	0	0	0	0	0	3	1	1	2
SOUTHERN UNIVERSITY	15	7	8	2	4	3	2	2	2	0	0	0	0	4	0	2	6	1	1
ST LOUIS UNIVERSITY	22	10	12	9	12	1	0	0	0	0	0	4	1	1	1	2	3	2	8
SUNY/ALBANY	17	8	9	6	5	1	2	0	0	1	2	4	2	1	2	2	3	1	2
SUNY/BUFFALO	13	7	6	4	3	3	2	0	0	0	1	2	0	4	0	1	6	0	0
SUNY/STONY BROOK	20	11	9	9	6	0	0	1	3	1	0	2	1	5	1	4	4	0	4
SYRACUSE UNIVERSITY	15	7	8	7	7	0	1	0	0	0	0	5	2	1	2	0	3	0	1
TEMPLE UNIVERSITY	20	10	10	9	10	0	0	0	0	1	0	5	5	5	4	0	1	0	0
TULANE UNIVERSITY	14	7	7	6	5	0	2	0	0	1	0	3	0	3	4	1	1	0	2
U OF ARKANSAS	11	6	5	5	4	1	1	0	0	0	0	1	1	3	1	1	2	1	1
U OF CALIFORNIA/BERK	26	12	14	0	0	0	4	2	5	10	5	8	2	1	1	1	2	2	9
U OF CHICAGO	30	13	16	6	15	0	1	2	0	5	0	6	6	3	2	2	3	2	5
U OF CINCINNATI	8	5	3	5	3	0	0	0	0	0	0	2	0	3	1	0	2	0	2
U OF CONNECTICUT	22	9	13	8	9	1	0	0	2	0	2	6	3	0	6	2	2	1	2
U OF DENVER	19	8	11	7	11	0	0	1	0	0	0	2	1	0	5	5	4	1	1
U OF GEORGIA	22	12	10	12	9	0	0	0	1	0	0	4	2	5	2	3	3	0	3
U OF HAWAII	26	12	14	9	4	2	2	0	5	1	3	4	2	3	3	2	3	3	6
U OF ILLINOIS/CHI	31	16	15	13	12	2	0	1	3	0	0	6	1	3	5	4	5	3	4
U OF ILLINOIS/URB	19	11	8	10	8	0	0	1	0	0	0	2	0	1	2	5	6	3	0
U OF IOWA	13	4	9	1	4	2	1	1	1	0	3	1	1	1	1	1	2	1	5
U OF KANSAS	21	16	5	14	4	0	0	2	0	0	1	4	1	6	3	4	1	2	0
U OF LOUISVILLE	15	9	6	9	6	0	0	0	0	0	0	5	2	3	0	1	4	0	0
U OF MAINE	5	0	5	0	4	0	0	0	0	0	1	0	0	0	0	0	5	0	0
U OF MARYLAND	34	20	14	18	10	1	0	0	3	1	1	9	2	6	3	5	6	0	3
U OF MICHIGAN	41	24	17	16	8	1	4	0	0	7	5	15	4	4	6	5	7	0	0
U OF MINNESOTA/DUL	4	3	1	3	1	0	0	0	0	0	0	1	0	0	1	1	0	1	0
U OF MINNESOTA/MINN	11	6	5	6	3	0	1	0	0	0	1	2	2	2	2	2	0	0	1
U OF MISSOURI	7	5	2	5	2	0	0	0	0	0	0	0	0	4	2	1	0	0	0
U OF NEBRASKA	10	3	7	3	6	0	0	0	0	0	1	1	2	1	3	1	0	0	2
U OF NEVADA/LV	6	3	3	3	1	0	0	0	2	0	0	0	0	1	1	2	2	0	0
U OF NEVADA/RENO	5	1	4	1	4	0	0	0	0	0	0	0	0	0	3	0	3	0	0
U OF NEW ENGLAND	5	2	3	2	2	0	0	0	0	0	1	0	0	1	1	1	2	0	0
U OF NORTH DAKOTA	10	4	6	4	4	0	0	0	1	0	1	1	0	1	3	2	3	0	3
U OF OKLAHOMA	10	6	4	4	4	2	0	0	0	0	0	2	1	3	1	0	2	1	0
U OF PENNSYLVANIA	13	5	8	5	8	0	0	0	0	0	0	1	3	3	1	1	3	0	1
U OF PITTSBURGH	30	15	15	13	15	1	0	0	0	1	0	7	3	7	9	1	3	0	0
U OF PUERTO RICO	20	3	17	2	13	0	3	0	0	0	1	0	7	2	8	1	2	0	0
U OF SOUTH CAROLINA	18	11	7	11	6	0	0	0	0	0	1	3	0	7	2	1	4	0	1
U OF SOUTH FLORIDA	8	6	2	3	0	3	2	0	0	0	0	1	0	3	0	2	2	0	0
U OF SOUTHERN CAL	28	6	22	5	13	0	2	0	6	1	1	1	1	5	6	0	7	0	8
U OF SOUTHERN MISS	4	3	1	3	1	0	0	0	0	0	0	2	0	0	1	1	1	0	0
U OF ST THOMAS	5	0	5	0	3	0	0	0	2	0	0	0	0	0	2	0	2	0	1
U OF TENNESSEE	22	13	9	12	8	1	1	0	0	0	0	5	3	5	3	3	3	0	0

TABLE 403 (Continued)

Number of Full-time Non-Administrative Faculty Assigned 50 Percent or More Time to Social Work Program, by Gender, Type of Appointment, and Academic Responsibility

Program	Total	Total		Major Responsibility								Academic Rank							
		Total Men	Total Women	Class		Class and Field		Field		Other		Professor		Associate Professor		Assistant Professor		Other Faculty	
				Men	Women	Men	Women	Men	Women	Men	Women	Men	Women	Men	Women	Men	Women	Men	Women
U OF TEXAS/ARLINGTON	33	16	17	15	17	0	0	0	0	1	0	5	2	3	5	3	5	5	5
U OF TEXAS/AUSTIN	29	9	20	6	8	0	0	2	10	1	2	5	1	0	0	1	2	3	17
U OF UTAH	15	6	9	3	7	0	0	0	0	3	2	2	1	1	3	3	5	0	0
U OF VERMONT	8	4	4	3	2	0	0	0	0	1	2	0	0	3	0	1	3	0	1
U OF WASHINGTON	31	17	14	11	8	1	3	1	3	4	0	5	2	9	1	2	9	1	2
U OF WISCONSIN/MAD	24	9	15	3	7	4	7	0	1	2	0	2	4	1	0	3	4	3	7
VIRGINIA COMMON	38	12	26	6	11	1	2	1	11	4	2	7	1	3	5	2	11	0	9
WASHINGTON UNIV	21	11	10	11	10	0	0	0	0	0	2	1	1	7	2	2	6	1	1
WAYNE STATE UNIV	33	15	18	13	9	2	1	0	3	0	5	2	0	8	6	1	4	4	8
WEST VIRGINIA UNIV	8	4	4	2	4	0	0	1	0	1	0	2	0	0	0	0	4	2	0
WESTERN MICHIGAN	15	10	5	9	3	0	0	0	0	1	2	5	1	3	3	2	1	0	0
WIDENER UNIVERSITY	4	1	3	1	3	0	0	0	0	0	0	0	0	0	0	1	3	0	0
YESHIVA UNIVERSITY	39	18	21	15	10	2	8	1	3	0	0	8	1	5	4	5	15	0	1

** Totals may not correspond between columns because of variation in item-specific response rates

TABLE 404

Ethnic Characteristics of Full-time and Part-time Graduate Faculty

Program	At Least 50 Percent in Social Work Program								Less Than 50 Percent in Social Work Program							
	Total	African American	Asian American	Chic/Mex American	Native American	Puerto Rican	White	Other	Total	African American	Asian American	Chic/Mex American	Native American	Puerto Rican	White	Other
TOTAL: Number	2,233	329	73	66	17	45	1,675	28	1,137	124	16	14	9	11	954	8
Percent	100.0%	14.7%	3.3%	3.0%	0.8%	2.0%	75.0%	1.3%	100.0%	10.9%	1.4%	1.2%	0.8%	1.0%	83.9%	0.7%
ADELPHI UNIVERSITY	34	3	0	0	0	1	30	0	64	1	0	0	1	0	62	0
ARIZONA STATE UNIV	24	0	2	6	1	0	15	0	0	0	0	0	0	0	0	0
AURORA UNIVERSITY	2	0	0	0	0	0	2	0	18	1	0	0	0	1	15	0
BARRY UNIVERSITY	23	4	1	0	0	0	16	2	1	1	0	0	0	0	0	0
BOSTON COLLEGE	29	4	2	0	0	0	23	0	47	6	0	0	0	2	38	1
BRIGHAM YOUNG UNIV	10	0	1	0	0	0	9	0	10	0	1	1	0	0	8	0
BRYN MAWR COLLEGE	23	5	0	0	0	0	18	0	14	2	0	0	0	0	11	1
CAL STATE UNIV/FRES	14	2	1	1	0	0	10	0	3	0	0	1	0	0	1	0
CAL STATE UNIV/LB	22	3	3	1	1	0	14	0	8	2	0	0	0	0	6	0
CAL STATE UNIV/SAC	28	4	2	2	2	0	18	0	14	1	1	0	2	0	10	0
CASE WESTERN RESERVE	27	4	0	0	0	0	23	0	0	0	0	0	0	0	0	0
CATHOLIC UNIVERSITY	21	4	1	0	0	0	16	0	20	5	0	0	0	0	15	0
CLARK ATLANTA UNIV	12	12	0	0	0	0	0	0	9	9	0	0	0	0	0	0
COLL OF ST CATH **	11	0	0	0	0	0	11	0	14	0	0	0	0	0	13	0
COLORADO STATE UNIV	10	0	0	1	0	0	9	0	0	0	0	0	0	0	0	0
COLUMBIA UNIVERSITY	34	5	1	0	1	0	26	1	0	0	0	0	0	0	0	0
EAST CAROLINA UNIV	16	4	0	0	0	0	12	0	2	0	0	0	0	0	2	0
EASTERN WASHINGTON	18	0	0	1	1	0	16	0	0	0	0	0	0	0	0	0
FLORIDA INTERNATL	18	0	0	0	0	0	14	4	15	2	0	0	0	0	11	2
FLORIDA STATE UNIV	21	3	0	0	0	0	18	0	17	2	2	0	0	0	13	0
GALLAUDET UNIVERSITY	8	2	0	0	0	0	6	0	1	0	0	0	0	0	1	0
GRAMBLING STATE	13	4	3	0	0	0	6	0	0	0	0	0	0	0	0	0
GRAND VALLEY STATE	14	3	1	1	0	0	8	1	8	2	0	0	1	0	3	2
HOWARD UNIVERSITY	21	17	0	0	0	0	2	2	5	3	0	0	0	0	2	0
HUNTER COLLEGE	39	3	1	0	0	4	31	0	6	2	0	0	0	0	4	0
INDIANA UNIVERSITY	28	5	2	0	0	0	20	1	27	1	0	0	0	0	26	1
LOUISIANA STATE UNIV	23	3	2	0	0	0	18	0	0	0	0	0	0	0	0	0
LOYOLA UNIVERSITY	30	4	1	0	0	0	25	0	16	1	0	0	0	0	15	0
MARYWOOD COLLEGE	15	1	0	1	0	0	13	0	12	0	0	0	0	0	12	0
MICHIGAN STATE UNIV	16	2	1	0	0	0	13	0	1	0	0	0	0	0	1	0
NEW MEXICO HIGHLANDS	14	0	0	6	0	0	8	0	4	0	0	2	0	0	2	0
NEW MEXICO STATE	16	0	0	4	1	0	11	0	0	0	1	0	1	0	0	0
NEW YORK UNIVERSITY	43	3	0	1	0	2	37	0	49	4	0	0	0	0	45	0
NORFOLK STATE UNIV	25	18	2	0	0	0	5	0	0	0	0	0	0	0	0	0
OHIO STATE UNIV	45	14	0	0	0	1	29	1	7	0	1	0	0	0	7	0
OUR LADY OF THE LAKE	14	1	0	5	0	1	7	0	10	0	0	2	0	0	8	0
PORTLAND STATE UNIV	30	3	0	0	1	0	26	0	15	0	1	0	1	0	13	0
RHODE ISLAND COLLEGE	17	2	0	0	0	0	15	0	12	0	0	0	0	0	12	0
RUTGERS UNIVERSITY	40	8	0	1	0	1	30	0	76	8	0	0	0	0	68	0
SAN DIEGO STATE	33	3	2	3	0	0	25	0	10	1	1	1	0	0	7	0
SAN FRANCISCO STATE	20	4	3	0	0	1	11	1	9	2	0	0	0	1	6	0
SAN JOSE STATE	19	1	2	8	0	1	6	1	18	1	0	4	0	0	13	0
SIMMONS COLLEGE	21	4	0	2	0	0	15	0	51	1	1	1	0	0	48	0

TABLE 404 (Continued)

Ethnic Characteristics of Full-time and Part-time Graduate Faculty

Program	At Least 50 Percent in Social Work Program								Less Than 50 Percent in Social Work Program							
	Total	African American	Asian American	Chic/Mex American	Native American	Puerto Rican	White	Other	Total	African American	Asian American	Chic/Mex American	Native American	Puerto Rican	White	Other
SMITH COLLEGE	13	2	0	0	0	0	11	0	1	1	0	0	0	0	0	0
SOUTHERN BAPTIST	6	1	0	1	0	0	4	0	3	1	0	0	0	0	2	0
SOUTHERN CONNECTICUT	21	2	1	0	0	0	18	0	3	1	0	0	0	0	2	0
SOUTHERN ILL/CARB	9	1	0	0	0	0	7	1	3	0	0	0	0	0	3	0
SOUTHERN UNIVERSITY	19	11	0	0	0	0	8	0	6	3	0	0	0	0	3	0
ST LOUIS UNIVERSITY	27	2	0	0	0	0	25	0	0	0	0	0	0	0	0	0
SUNY/ALBANY	25	1	0	1	0	0	23	0	1	0	0	0	0	0	1	0
SUNY/BUFFALO	19	3	1	0	0	0	15	0	21	4	0	0	0	0	17	0
SUNY/STONY BROOK	22	5	0	0	0	3	14	0	3	1	0	0	0	0	2	0
SYRACUSE UNIVERSITY	21	2	0	1	0	0	18	0	1	0	0	1	0	0	0	0
TEMPLE UNIVERSITY	25	7	0	0	0	1	16	1	1	0	0	0	0	1	1	0
TULANE UNIVERSITY	19	2	0	0	0	2	15	0	34	1	0	0	0	0	33	0
U OF ARKANSAS	14	1	0	1	0	0	11	1	0	0	0	0	0	0	0	0
U OF CALIFORNIA/BERK	30	4	1	3	0	0	22	1	21	2	2	0	0	0	17	0
U OF CHICAGO	34	3	0	2	0	0	29	0	27	0	0	1	0	0	26	0
U OF CINCINNATI	12	3	0	0	0	0	9	0	4	1	0	0	0	0	3	0
U OF CONNECTICUT	35	3	2	0	0	3	27	0	21	2	0	0	0	3	16	0
U OF DENVER	25	1	0	1	1	0	22	0	19	1	0	0	0	0	18	0
U OF GEORGIA	30	6	0	0	0	0	24	0	0	0	0	0	0	0	0	0
U OF HAWAII	26	0	12	0	0	0	13	1	6	0	1	0	0	0	5	0
U OF ILLINOIS/CHI	35	10	0	1	0	0	23	1	0	0	0	0	0	0	0	0
U OF ILLINOIS/URB	24	2	2	0	0	0	19	1	1	0	0	0	0	0	1	0
U OF IOWA	18	3	0	0	0	0	15	0	26	1	0	0	0	0	25	0
U OF KANSAS	30	6	0	0	0	0	24	0	14	1	0	0	0	0	13	0
U OF LOUISVILLE	18	1	1	0	0	0	16	0	5	2	0	0	0	0	3	0
U OF MAINE	8	0	0	0	0	0	8	0	4	0	0	0	0	0	4	0
U OF MARYLAND	41	6	1	0	1	0	32	1	4	2	0	0	0	0	2	1
U OF MICHIGAN	45	6	1	1	0	0	36	1	7	1	0	0	0	0	6	1
U OF MINNESOTA/DUL	6	0	0	0	2	0	4	0	0	0	0	0	0	0	0	0
U OF MINNESOTA/MINN	16	2	0	0	0	0	14	0	16	0	1	0	0	0	15	0
U OF MISSOURI	11	1	0	0	0	0	10	0	0	0	0	0	0	0	0	0
U OF NEBRASKA	13	1	2	1	0	0	9	0	11	1	0	0	0	0	10	0
U OF NEVADA/LV	10	3	1	0	0	0	6	0	0	0	0	0	0	0	0	0
U OF NEVADA/RENO	10	2	0	0	1	0	7	0	0	0	0	0	0	0	0	0
U OF NEW ENGLAND	6	1	0	0	0	0	5	0	4	0	0	0	0	0	4	0
U OF NORTH DAKOTA	12	0	1	0	0	0	11	0	0	0	0	0	0	0	0	0
U OF OKLAHOMA	14	2	1	1	0	0	10	0	9	0	0	0	1	0	8	0
U OF PENNSYLVANIA	20	4	0	0	0	0	15	1	19	4	0	0	0	1	14	0
U OF PITTSBURGH	35	9	2	0	0	1	23	0	7	1	0	0	0	0	6	0
U OF PUERTO RICO	20	0	0	0	0	20	0	0	0	0	0	0	0	0	0	0
U OF SOUTH CAROLINA	21	3	0	0	0	0	18	0	14	3	0	0	0	0	11	0
U OF SOUTH FLORIDA	10	1	1	0	0	0	8	0	10	0	0	0	0	0	10	0
U OF SOUTHERN CAL	32	2	1	2	0	1	26	0	29	2	2	0	0	0	25	0
U OF SOUTHERN MISS	7	0	0	0	0	0	7	0	7	0	0	0	0	0	7	0
U OF TENNESSEE	31	4	1	1	0	0	25	1	0	0	0	0	0	0	0	1
U OF TEXAS/ARLINGTON	43	4	2	1	0	1	35	0	1	0	0	1	0	0	0	0

TABLE 404 (Continued)

Ethnic Characteristics of Full-time and Part-time Graduate Faculty

Program	At Least 50 Percent in Social Work Program								Less Than 50 Percent in Social Work Program							
	Total	African American	Asian American	Chic/Mex American	Native American	Puerto Rican	White	Other	Total	African American	Asian American	Chic/Mex American	Native American	Puerto Rican	White	Other
U OF TEXAS/AUSTIN	40	3	0	3	1	0	33	0	2	0	0	0	0	0	2	0
U OF UTAH	23	0	0	0	1	1	21	0	2	0	0	0	0	0	2	0
U OF VERMONT	13	1	0	0	0	0	12	0	12	1	0	0	0	0	11	0
U OF WASHINGTON	36	3	3	1	1	0	27	1	34	3	1	0	1	1	28	0
U OF WISCONSIN/MAD	29	1	0	0	0	0	27	1	23	0	0	0	1	1	21	0
VIRGINIA COMMON	43	9	0	1	0	0	33	0	20	5	0	0	0	0	14	1
WASHINGTON UNIV	25	4	2	0	1	0	16	2	25	1	0	0	1	0	23	0
WAYNE STATE UNIV	33	9	0	0	0	0	24	0	31	14	1	0	0	0	16	0
WEST VIRGINIA UNIV	12	0	0	0	0	0	12	0	8	2	0	0	0	0	6	0
WESTERN MICHIGAN	19	2	0	0	0	0	17	0	14	2	0	0	0	0	11	1
WIDENER UNIVERSITY	7	1	0	0	0	0	6	0	0	0	0	0	0	0	0	0
YESHIVA UNIVERSITY	44	1	0	0	0	0	43	0	10	0	0	0	0	1	9	0

* Missing data

** Combined with University of St Thomas

110

APPENDIX B

Baccalaureate Social Work Degree Programs
Accredited by the Council on Social Work Education
1990-91

Alabama

Alabama A & M University
Social Work Program

Alabama State University
Social Work Program

Auburn University
Department of Sociology,
   Anthropology and Social Work

Oakwood College
Social Work Program

Talladega College
Social Work Program

Troy State University
Social Work Program

Tuskegee University
Department of Social Work

University of Alabama, Birmingham
Department of Social Work

University of Alabama, Tuscaloosa
School of Social Work

University of Montevallo
Social Work Program

University of North Alabama
Social Work Department

Alaska

University of Alaska, Anchorage
Social Work Program

University of Alaska, Fairbanks
Social Work Program

Arizona

Arizona State University
School of Social Work

Northern Arizona University
Social Work Program

Arkansas

Arkansas College
Social Work Program

Arkansas State University
Department of Sociology,
   Social Work and Geography

Harding University
Department of Behavioral Sciences

University of Arkansas, Fayetteville
Social Work Program

University of Arkansas, Pine Bluff
Department of Social and
   Behavioral Sciences

California

Azusa Pacific University
Department of Social Work

California State Polytechnic University
Department of Social Work

California State University, Chico
Department of Sociology
   and Social Work

California State University, Fresno
Department of Social Work Education

California State University, Long Beach
Department of Social Work

California State University, Los Angeles
Department of Sociology
   and Social Work

California State University, Sacramento
Division of Social Work

La Sierra University
Social Work Program

111

Pacific Union College
Social Work Program

San Diego State University
School of Social Work

San Francisco State University
Department of Social Work Education

San Jose State University
School of Social Work

Whittier College
Social Work Program

Colorado

Colorado State University
Department of Social Work

University of Southern Colorado
Social Work Program

Connecticut

Sacred Heart University
Department of Sociology, Social Work
  and Criminal Justice

Southern Connecticut State University
School of Social Work and Human Services

St. Joseph College
Social Work Program

Western Connecticut State University
Social Work Program

Delaware

Delaware State College
Department of Social Work

District of Columbia

Catholic University of America
National Catholic School of Social Service

Gallaudet University
Department of Social Work

Howard University
Social Work Program

University of the District of Columbia
Department of Social Work

Florida

Florida A & M University
Department of Social Work

Florida Atlantic University
Department of Social Work

Florida International University
Social Work Department

Florida State University
School of Social Work

St. Leo College
Social Work Program

University of Central Florida
Department of Social Work

University of South Florida
School of Social Work

University of West Florida
Department of Social Work

Georgia

Clark Atlanta University
School of Social Work

Georgia State University
Department of Social Work

Savannah State College
Social Work Program

University of Georgia
School of Social Work

Hawaii

Brigham Young University
Social Work Program

University of Hawaii
School of Social Work

Idaho

Boise State University
Department of Social Work

Idaho State University
Department of Sociology,
  Anthropology and Social Work

Northwest Nazarene College
Department of Social Work

Illinois

Augustana College
Department of Social Work

Aurora University
School of Social Work

College of St. Francis
Undergraduate Social Work Program

Illinois State University
Department of Sociology,
   Anthropology and Social Work

Loyola University Chicago
Undergraduate Social Work Department

Northeastern Illinois University
Department of Social Work

Southern Illinois University, Carbondale
School of Social Work

Southern Illinois University, Edwardsville
Department of Sociology and Social Work

University of Illinois, Chicago
Jane Addams College of Social Work

University of Illinois, Urbana-Champaign
School of Social Work

Indiana

Anderson University
Department of Sociology and Social Work

Ball State University
Department of Social Work

Goshen College
Social Work Education Program

Indiana University
School of Social Work

Indiana Wesleyan University
Social Work Program

Manchester College
Social Work Program

Purdue University
Department of Sociology and Anthropology

St. Francis College
Department of Social Work

Taylor University
Department of Social Work

University of Southern Indiana
Social Work Department

Valparaiso University
Department of Social Work

Iowa

Briar Cliff College
Social Work Program

Buena Vista College
Social Work Program

Clarke College
Tri-College Social Work Program
Sociology and Social Work Department

Dordt College
Social Work Program

Iowa State University
Social Work Program

Loras College
Tri-College Social Work Program

Luther College
Department of Sociology,
   Anthropology and Social Work

Mount Mercy College
Department of Social Work

Northwestern College
Social Work Program

Teikyo Marycrest College
Department of Social Work/Sociology

University of Dubuque
Tri-College Social Wk Program

University of Iowa
School of Social Work

University of Northern Iowa
Department of Social Work

Wartburg College
Department of Social Work

Kansas

Bethany College
Social Work Program

Bethel College
Social Work Department

Kansas State University
Department of Sociology,
 Anthropology and Social Work

Pittsburg State University
Social Work Program

Southwestern College in Kansas
Social Work Program

St. Mary of the Plains College
Social Work Program

Tabor College
Department of Social Work

University of Kansas
School of Social Welfare

Washburn University
Department of Social Work

Wichita State University
Social Work Program

Kentucky

Eastern Kentucky University
Social Work Program

Kentucky State University
Department of Social Work and Criminal Justice

Morehead State University
Department of Sociology,
 Social Work and Corrections

Murray State University
Department of Sociology,
 Anthropology and Social Work

Northern Kentucky University
Social Work Program

Spalding University
Department of Social Work

Thomas More College
Social Work Program

University of Kentucky
College of Social Work

Western Kentucky University
Social Work Program

Louisiana

Grambling State University
School of Social Work

Northeast Louisiana University
Social Work Program

Northwestern State University
Department of History, Social
 Sciences and Social Work

Southeastern Louisiana University
Social Work Program

Southern University and A & M College
Department of Social Work

Southern University in New Orleans
School of Social Work

Maine

University of Maine
Social Work Program

University of Southern Maine
Department of Social Welfare

Maryland

Bowie State University
Social Work Program

Coppin State College
Department of Social Sciences

Hood College
Department of Sociology and Social Work

Morgan State University
Department of Social Work

Salisbury State University
Department of Social Work

University of Maryland at Baltimore
School of Social Work

Western Maryland College
Social Work Program

Massachusetts

Anna Maria College
Social Work Program

Atlantic Union College
Social Work Program

Boston University-Metropolitan College
Social Work Program

Bridgewater State College
Department of Social Work

Eastern Nazarene College
Sociology-Social Work Dept

Elms College
Social Work Program

Gordon College
Social Work Program

Regis College
Social Work Program

Salem State College
School of Social Work

Western New England College
Social Work Program

Wheelock College
Social Work Program

Michigan

Eastern Michigan University
Department of Social Work

Ferris State University
Social Work Program

Grand Valley State University
School of Social Work

Madonna University
Baccalaureate Social Work Program

Marygrove College
Social Work Program

Michigan State University
School of Social Work

Northern Michigan University
Department of Sociology and Social Work

Saginaw Valley State University
Department of Social Work

University of Detroit Mercy
Department of Social Work

Wayne State University
School of Social Work

Western Michigan University
School of Social Work

Minnesota

Augsburg College
Department of Social Work

Bemidji State University
Social Work Program

Bethel College
Social Work Program

College of St. Benedict
Social Work Program

College of St. Catherine
Social Work Department

College of St. Scholastica
Social Work Program

Concordia College
Social Work Program

Mankato State University
Department of Social Work

Moorhead State University
Department of Social Work

St. Cloud State University
Social Work Department

St. Olaf College
Department of Social Work

University of St. Thomas
Social Work Department

Winona State University
Social Work Department

Mississippi

Delta State University
Social Work Program

Jackson State University
Department of Social Work

Mississippi Valley State University
Social Work Program

University of Mississippi
Social Work Program

Missouri

Avila College
Social Work Program

Central Missouri State University
Social Work Program

Missouri Western State College
Social Work Program

Southeast Missouri State University
Department of Social Work

Southwest Missouri State University
Department of Social Work

Saint Louis University
School of Social Service

University of Missouri, Columbia
School of Social Work

University of Missouri, St. Louis
Department of Social Work

William Woods College
Social Work Program

Montana

Carroll College
Department of Social Work

University of Montana
Department of Social Work

Nebraska

Dana College
Department of Social Work

Nebraska Wesleyan University
Social Work Program

Union College
Social Work Program

University of Nebraska, Kearney
Social Work Program

University of Nebraska, Omaha
School of Social Work

Nevada

University of Nevada, Las Vegas
School of Social Work

University of Nevada, Reno
School of Social Work

New Hampshire

University of New Hampshire
Department of Social Service

New Jersey

Kean College of New Jersey
Department of Sociology,
   Anthropology and Social Work

Monmouth College
Department of Sociology, Anthropology,
   Social Work and Criminal Justice

Ramapo College
Social Work Program

Rutgers University
School of Social Work

Rutgers University-Camden
School of Social Work

Rutgers University-Newark
Social Welfare/Social Work

Seton Hall University
Department of Social Work

Stockton State College
Social Work Program

Upsala College
Social Work Program

New Mexico

New Mexico Highlands University
Department of Social Work

New Mexico State University
Department of Social Work

New York

Adelphi University
School of Social Work

Buffalo State College
Department of Social Work

College of New Rochelle
Social Work Department

Concordia College
Social Work Program

Cornell University
Human Services Studies

D'Youville College
Social Work Program

Daemen College
Department of Social Work and Sociology

Dominican College of Blauvelt
Social Work Program

Herbert H. Lehman College
Department of Sociology and Social Work

Iona College
Social Work Program

Keuka College
Social Work Program

Marist College
Social Work Program

Marymount College
Social Work Program

Mercy College
Social Work Program

Molloy College
Sociology, Anthropology,
   and Social Work Department

Nazareth College of Rochester
Department of Social Work

New York University
School of Social Work

Niagara University
Social Work Program

Roberts Wesleyan College
Social Work Department

Rochester Institute of Technology
Social Work Department

Siena College
Department of Social Work

Skidmore College
Social Work Program

State University College, Brockport
Department of Social Work

State University of New York, Albany
School of Social Welfare

State University of New York, Stony Brook
School of Social Welfare

Syracuse University
School of Social Work

York College
Social Work Program

North Carolina

Appalachian State University
Social Work Program

Bennett College
Social Work Program

East Carolina University
School of Social Work

Livingstone College
Social Work Program

Mars Hill College
Social Work Program

Meredith College
Department of Sociology and Social Work

North Carolina A & T State University
Department of Sociology and Social Work

North Carolina State University
Department of Sociology,
   Anthropology and Social Work

Pembroke State University
Social Work Program

University of North Carolina
Department of Social Work

Warren Wilson College
Social Work Program

Western Carolina University
Department of Social Work

North Dakota

Minot State University
Social Work Program

University of Mary
Social Work Program

University of North Dakota
Department of Social Work

Ohio

Ashland University
Social Work Program

Bluffton College
Social Work Program

Bowling Green State University
Department of Social Work

Capital University
Department of Social Work

Cleveland State University
Department of Social Work

Defiance College
Social Work Program

Malone College
Social Work Program

Ohio State University
College of Social Work

Ohio University
Department of Social Work

University of Akron
School of Social Work

University of Cincinnati
School of Social Work

University of Dayton
Social Work Program

University of Toledo
Social Work Program

Wright State University
Department of Social Work

Xavier University
Department of Social Work

Oklahoma

East Central Oklahoma University
Social Work Program

Oral Roberts University
Social Work Program

University of Oklahoma
School of Social Work

Pennsylvania

Albright College
Social Work Program

Bloomsburg University
Department of Sociology and Social Welfare

California University of Pennsylvania
Social Work Department

Cedar Crest College
Department of Sociology-Social Work

College Misericordia
Division of Professional Studies

Eastern College
Social Work Department

Edinboro University
Department of Sociology/
    Anthropology/Social Work

Elizabethtown College
Department of Social Work

Gannon University
Social Work Program

Juniata College
Department of Sociology,
    Anthropology and Social Work

La Salle College
Department of Sociology, Social Work
    and Criminal Justice

Lock Haven University of Pennsylvania
Department of Sociology,
  Anthropology and Social Work

Mansfield University
Social Work Program

Marywood College
BSW Program
Department of Social Sciences

Mercyhurst College
Department of Sociology/Social Work

Messiah College
Social Work Program

Millersville University
Department of Social Work

Pennsylvania State University
Social Work Program

Philadelphia College of Bible
Department of Social Work

Shippensburg University
Social Work Department

Slippery Rock University
Social Work Program

St. Francis College
Social Work Program

Temple University
School of Social Administration

University of Pittsburgh
School of Social Work

West Chester University
Department of Social Work

Widener University
Center for Social Work Education

Puerto Rico

Catholic University of Puerto Rico
Social Work Department

Inter American University
Social Work Program

University of Puerto Rico, Humacao
Social Sciences Department

University of Puerto Rico, Rio Piedras
Social Welfare Program

University of the Sacred Heart
School of Social Work

Rhode Island

Providence College
Department of Social Work

Rhode Island College
School of Social Work

Salve Regina College
Department of Social Work

South Carolina

Benedict College
Social Work Department

Columbia College
Social Work Program

Winthrop College
Department of Social Work

South Dakota

Augustana College
Joint Social Work Program
Department of Sociology,
  Social Work & Minority Studies

Sioux Falls College
Joint Social Work Program
Social Science Area

University of South Dakota
Social Work Program

Tennessee

Austin Peay State University
Social Work Program

East Tennessee State University
Department of Social Work

Freed-Hardeman University
Social Work Program

Memphis State University
Division of Social Work

Middle Tennessee State University
Social Work Program

Tennessee State University
Social Work Program

University of Tennessee, Chattanooga
Social Work Program

University of Tennessee, Knoxville
College of Social Work

University of Tennessee, Martin
Social Work Program

Texas

Abilene Christian University
Sociology/Social Work
  and Gerontology Department

Baylor University
Division of Social Work

East Texas State University
Social Work Program

Hardin-Simmons University
Social Work Program

Lamar University
Department of Sociology,
  Social Work and Criminology

Lubbock Christian University
Social Work Department

Our Lady of the Lake University
Worden School of Social Service

Paul Quinn College
Social Work Program

Prairie View A & M University
Department of Social Work and Sociology

Southwest Texas State University
Walter Richter Institute of Social Work

St. Edward's University
Social Work Program

Stephen F. Austin State University
Social Work Program

Tarleton State University
Department of Social Sciences

Texas Christian University
Undergraduate Social Work Program

Texas Southern University
Social Work Program

Texas Tech University
Social Work Program

Texas Woman's University
Department of Sociology and Social Work

University of North Texas
Department of Sociology and Social Work

University of Texas, Arlington
School of Social Work

University of Texas, Austin
School of Social Work

University of Texas, Pan American
Department of Social Work

West Texas State University
Undergraduate Social Work Program

Utah

Brigham Young University
School of Social Work

Utah State University
Social Work Program

Weber State University
Department of Social Work and Gerontology

Vermont

Castleton State College
Social Work Program

Trinity College
Social Work Program

University of Vermont
Department of Social Work

Virginia

Christopher Newport College
Social Work Program

Eastern Mennonite College
Department of Sociology and Social Work

Ferrum College
Social Work Program

George Mason University
Social Work Program

Hampton University
Social Work Program

James Madison University
Department of Social Work

Longwood College
Department of Social Work

Norfolk State University
School of Social Work

Radford University
Department of Social Work

Virginia Commonwealth University
School of Social Work

Virginia Intermont College
Department of Social Work

Virginia State University
Social Work Program

Virginia Union University
Department of Social Work

Washington

Eastern Washington University
Inland Empire School of Social Work
  and Human Services

Pacific Lutheran University
Department of Social Work

University of Washington
School of Social Work

Walla Walla College
Department of Sociology and Social Work

West Virginia

Alderson-Broaddus College
Social Work Program

Bethany College
Department of Sociology and Social Work

Concord College
Social Work Department

Marshall University
Social Work Department

Shepherd College
Social Work Program

West Virginia State College
Social Work Department

West Virginia University
School of Social Work

West Virginia Wesleyan College
Social Work Program

Wisconsin

Carroll College
Social Work Program

Carthage College
Social Work Program

Marian College of Fond du Lac
Social Work Program

Marquette University
Undergraduate Social Work Program

Mount Mary College
Social Work Program

University of Wisconsin, Eau Claire
Department of Social Work

University of Wisconsin, Green Bay
Social Work Program

University of Wisconsin, La Crosse
Department of Social Work

University of Wisconsin, Madison
School of Social Work

University of Wisconsin, Milwaukee
School of Social Welfare

University of Wisconsin, Oshkosh
Department of Social Work

University of Wisconsin, Superior
Social Work Program

University of Wisconsin, Whitewater
Social Work Department

Wyoming

University of Wyoming
Department of Social Work

Alabama

Jacksonville State University
Department of Sociology and Social Work

California

Humboldt State University
Social Work Program

Connecticut

Central Connecticut State University
Social Work Program

Illinois

Governors State University
Social Work Program

Indiana

St. Mary's College
Social Work Program

Louisiana

Louisiana College
Department of Sociology and Social Work

Maryland

Frostburg State University
Department of Sociology and Social Work

Michigan

Andrews University
Social Work Program

Calvin College
Department of Sociology and Social Work

Spring Arbor College
Social Work Program

Mississippi

University of Southern Mississippi
School of Social Work

Missouri

Columbia College
Social Work Program

Nebraska

Chadron State College
Social Work Program

Creighton University
Department of Social Work

North Carolina

Campbell University
Social Work Program

New Jersey

Georgian Court College
Social Work Program

Ohio

Lourdes College
Social Work Program

University of Rio Grande
Social Work Program

Youngstown State University
Undergraduate Social Work Program

Oklahoma

Northeastern State University
Social Work Department

Pennsylvania

Kutztown University
Social Welfare Program

South Carolina

South Carolina State College
Social Work Program

Tennessee

David Lipscomb University
Department of Sociology and Social Work

Texas

Midwestern State University
Social Work Program

Wisconsin

University of Wisconsin, River Falls
Social Work Program

APPENDIX C

Graduate Social Work Degree Programs
Accredited by the Council on Social Work Education
1990-91

Alabama

University of Alabama
School of Social Work

Arizona

Arizona State University
School of Social Work

Arkansas

University of Arkansas
Department of Social Work

California

California State University, Fresno
Department of Social Work Education

California State University, Long Beach
Department of Social Work

California State University, Sacramento
Division of Social Work

San Diego State University
School of Social Work

San Francisco State University
Department of Social Work Education

San Jose State University
School of Social Work

University of California, Berkeley
School of Social Welfare

University of California, Los Angeles
School of Social Welfare

University of Southern California
School of Social Work

Colorado

Colorado State University
Department of Social Work

University of Denver
Graduate School of Social Work

Connecticut

Southern Connecticut State University
School of Social Work and Human Services

University of Connecticut
School of Social Work

Delaware

Delaware State College
Department of Social Work

District of Columbia

Catholic University of America
National Catholic School of Social Service

Howard University
School of Social Work

Florida

Barry University
School of Social Work

Florida International University
Social Work Department

Florida State University
School of Social Work

University of South Florida
School of Social Work

Georgia

Clark Atlanta University
School of Social Work

University of Georgia
School of Social Work

Hawaii

University of Hawaii
School of Social Work

Illinois

Aurora University
School of Social Work

Loyola University of Chicago
School of Social Work

Southern Illinois University
School of Social Work

University of Chicago
School of Social Service Administration

University of Illinois, Chicago
Jane Addams College of Social Work

University of Illinois, Urbana-Champaign
School of Social Work

Indiana

Indiana University
School of Social Work

Iowa

University of Iowa
School of Social Work

Kansas

University of Kansas
School of Social Welfare

Kentucky

Southern Baptist Theological Seminary
Carver School of Church Social Work

University of Kentucky
College of Social Work

University of Louisville
Kent School of Social Work

Louisiana

Grambling State University
School of Social Work

Louisiana State University
School of Social Work

Southern University in New Orleans
School of Social Work

Tulane University
School of Social Work

Maine

University of Maine
Department of Social Work

University of New England
School of Social Work

Maryland

University of Maryland at Baltimore
School of Social Work

Massachusetts

Boston College
Graduate School of Social Work

Boston University
School of Social Work

Salem State College
School of Social Work

Simmons College
School of Social Work

Smith College
School for Social Work

Michigan

Grand Valley State University
School of Social Work

Michigan State University
School of Social Work

University of Michigan
School of Social Work

Wayne State University
School of Social Work

Western Michigan University
School of Social Work

Minnesota

University of Minnesota, Duluth
Department of Social Work

University of Minnesota, Minneapolis
School of Social Work

Mississippi

University of Southern Mississippi
School of Social Work

Missouri

Saint Louis University
School of Social Service

University of Missouri, Columbia
School of Social Work

Washington University
George Warren Brown School of Social Work

Nebraska

University of Nebraska, Omaha
School of Social Work

North Carolina

East Carolina University
School of Social Work

University of North Carolina
School of Social Work

New Jersey

Rutgers University
School of Social Work

New Mexico

New Mexico Highlands University
Department of Social Work

New York

Adelphi University
School of Social Work

Columbia University
School of Social Work

Fordham University
Graduate School of Social Service

Hunter College
School of Social Work

New York University
School of Social Work

State University of New York, Albany
School of Social Welfare

State University of New York, Buffalo
School of Social Work

State University of New York, Stony Brook
School of Social Welfare

Syracuse University
School of Social Work

Yeshiva University
Wurzweiler School of Social Work

Ohio

Case Western Reserve University
Mandel School of Applied Social Sciences

Ohio State University
College of Social Work

University of Cincinnati
School of Social Work

Oklahoma

University of Oklahoma
School of Social Work

Oregon

Portland State University
Graduate School of Social Work

Pennsylvania

Bryn Mawr College
Graduate School of Social Work
 and Social Research

Marywood College
School of Social Work

Temple University
School of Social Administration

University of Pennsylvania
School of Social Work

University of Pittsburgh
School of Social Work

Puerto Rico

University of Puerto Rico
Beatriz Lassalle
 Graduate School of Social Work

Rhode Island

Rhode Island College
School of Social Work

South Carolina

University of South Carolina
College of Social Work

Tennessee

University of Tennessee
College of Social Work

Texas

Our Lady of the Lake University
Worden School of Social Service

University of Houston
Graduate School of Social Work

University of Texas, Arlington
School of Social Work

University of Texas, Austin
School of Social Work

Utah

Brigham Young University
School of Social Work

University of Utah
Graduate School of Social Work

Virginia

Norfolk State University
School of Social Work

Virginia Commonwealth University
School of Social Work

Washington

Eastern Washington University
Inland Empire School of Social Work
 and Human Services

University of Washington
School of Social Work

Wisconsin

University of Wisconsin, Madison
School of Social Work

University of Wisconsin, Milwaukee
School of Social Welfare

West Virginia

West Virginia University
School of Social Work

Graduate Programs in Candidacy for Accreditation 1990-91

California

California State University, San Bernardino
Department of Social Work

District of Columbia

Gallaudet University
Department of Social Work

Massachusetts

Springfield College
Social Work Program
School of Human Services

Minnesota

Augsburg College
Department of Social Work

College of St. Catherine
University of St. Thomas
Social Work Department

Nevada

University of Nevada, Las Vegas
School of Social Work

University of Nevada, Reno
School of Social Work

New Mexico

New Mexico State University
Department of Social Work

North Dakota

University of North Dakota
Department of Social Work

Pennsylvania

Widener University
Center for Social Work Education

Vermont

University of Vermont
Department of Social Work

Washington

Walla Walla College
Graduate Program in Social Work